From Vocational to Higher Education

SRHE and Open University Press Imprint
General Editor: Heather Eggins

Current titles include:

Catherine Bargh *et al.*: *University Leadership*
Ronald Barnett: *Beyond all Reason*
Ronald Barnett: *Higher Education: A Critical Business*
Ronald Barnett: *Realizing the University in an age of supercomplexity*
Ronald Barnett and Kelly Coate: *Engaging the Curriculum in Higher Education*
Tony Becher and Paul R. Trowler: *Academic Tribes and Territories (2nd edn)*
John Biggs: *Teaching for Quality Learning at University (2nd edn)*
Richard Blackwell and Paul Blackmore (eds): *Towards Strategic Staff Development in Higher Education*
David Boud *et al.* (eds): *Using Experience for Learning*
David Boud and Nicky Solomon (eds): *Work-based Learning*
Tom Bourner *et al.* (eds): *New Directions in Professional Higher Education*
Anne Brockbank and Ian McGill: *Facilitating Reflective Learning in Higher Education*
Stephen D. Brookfield and Stephen Preskill: *Discussion as a Way of Teaching*
Ann Brooks and Alison Mackinnon (eds): *Gender and the Restructured University*
Sally Brown and Angela Glasner (eds): *Assessment Matters in Higher Education*
Burton R.Clark: *Sustaining Change in Universities*
James Cornford and Neil Pollock: *Putting the University Online*
John Cowan: *On Becoming an Innovative University Teacher*
Sara Delamont, Paul Atkinson and Odette Parry: *Supervising the Doctorate (2nd edn)*
Sara Delamont and Paul Atkinson: *Successful Research Careers*
Gerard Delanty: *Challenging Knowledge*
Chris Duke: *Managing the Learning University*
Heather Eggins (ed.): *Globalization and Reform in Higher Education*
Heather Eggins and Ranald Macdonald (eds): *The Scholarship of Academic Development*
Gillian Evans: *Academics and the Real World*
Merle Jacob and Tomas Hellström (eds): *The Future of Knowledge Production in the Academy*
Peter Knight: *Being a Teacher in Higher Education*
Peter Knight and Paul Trowler: *Departmental Leadership in Higher Education*
Peter Knight and Mantz Yorke: *Assessment, Learning and Employability*
Ray Land: *Educational Development*
John Lea *et al.*: *Working in Post-Compulsory Education*
Mary Lea and Barry Stierer (eds): *Student Writing in Higher Education*
Dina Lewis and Barbara Allan: *Virtual Learning Communities*
Ian McNay (ed.): *Beyond Mass Higher Education*
Elaine Martin: *Changing Academic Work*
Louise Morley: *Quality and Power in Higher Education*
Lynne Pearce: *How to Examine a Thesis*
Moira Peelo and Terry Wareham (eds): *Failing Students in Higher Education*
Craig Prichard: *Making Managers in Universities and Colleges*
Stephen Rowland: *The Enquiring University Teacher*
Maggi Savin-Baden: *Problem-based Learning in Higher Education*
Maggi Savin-Baden: *Facilitating Problem-based Learning*
Maggi Savin-Baden and Kay Wilkie: *Challenging Research in Problem-based Learning*
David Scott *et al.*: *Professional Doctorates*
Peter Scott: *The Meanings of Mass Higher Education*
Michael L. Shattock: *Managing Successful Universities*
Maria Slowey and David Watson: *Higher Education and the Lifecourse*
Colin Symes and John McIntyre (eds): *Working Knowledge*
Richard Taylor, Jean Barr and Tom Steele: *For a Radical Higher Education*
Malcolm Tight: *Researching Higher Education*
Penny Tinkler and Carolyn Jackson: *The Doctoral Examination Process*
Susan Toohey: *Designing Courses for Higher Education*
Melanie Walker (ed.): *Reconstructing Professionalism in University Teaching*
Melanie Walker and Jon Nixon (eds): *Reclaiming Universities from a Runaway World*
Diana Woodward and Karen Ross: *Managing Equal Opportunities in Higher Education*
Mantz Yorke and Bernard Longden: *Retention and Student Success in Higher Education*

From Vocational to Higher Education

An International Perspective

Gavin Moodie

Open University Press
McGraw-Hill Education
McGraw-Hill House
Shoppenhangers Road
Maidenhead
Berkshire
England
SL6 2QL

email: enquiries@openup.co.uk
world wide web: www.openup.co.uk

and Two Penn Plaza, New York, NY 10121–2289, USA

First published 2008

A catalogue record of this book is available from the British Library

ISBN-13: 978-0-33-522715-0 (pb) 978-0-335-22716-7 (hb)
ISBN-10: 0-33-522715-5 (pb) 0-33-522716-3 (hb)

Library of Congress Cataloging-in-Publication Data
CIP data applied for

Typeset by RefineCatch Limited, Bungay, Suffolk
Printed in the UK by Bell and Bain Ltd., Glasgow

The **McGraw·Hill** Companies

To Leesa

Contents

List of tables

List of boxes

Acknowledgements

I thank my doctoral supervisor Emeritus Professor Grant Harman of the University of New England's Center for Higher Education Management and Policy for his encouragement, support, mentorship, wise counsel and for challenging me to attempt a better study than I thought myself capable of. The late Martin Trow was very generous with his time and probing comments for a new and unknown researcher and, as a thesis examiner, Professor Jeroen Huisman, Director of the International Centre for Higher Education Management at the University of Bath's School of Management, provided most helpful and supportive advice on developing the book proposal and valuable comments on draft chapters. My employer, Griffith University in Brisbane and the Gold Coast, Australia, gave me flexibility in my allocation of time and access to office facilities, computer equipment, the Internet and, most importantly, to its library; through them I was able to gain access to other Australian university libraries and electronic resources from around the world, which I found invaluable.

I thank James Ashburner of the Australian Bureau of Statistics for constructing and providing tables from the survey of education and work; Khin Thin Aye of the Department of Education, Science and Training's University Statistics Unit for providing tables from universities' enrolment submissions; Lorraine Edmunds, also of the Australian Bureau of Statistics, for constructing tables from the survey of education, training and information technology and for checking my interpretation of the survey of education and work tables; Jim Jacobs of the Colorado Commission on Higher Education for providing a data file from his research group on transfers between Colorado 2-year and 4-year higher education institutions; Dr Andrew R. Giles-Peters, then of the Australian National Training Authority, for his expert comments on an earlier version of Chapter 9, which saved it from serious mistakes and for his contribution of data from internal reports that, unfortunately, have not been published; Dr Tom Karmel, Managing Director of the National Centre for Vocational Education Research for his helpful comments and suggestions for further work; and I am most grateful to David

Scott of the New Zealand ministry of education for commenting on an earlier draft of Chapter 9 and for providing the tables on New Zealand reported therein.

Gavin Moodie
Brisbane, Australia
January 2008

1

Introduction

1.1 Why read this book?

This book seeks to increase our understanding of how vocational and higher education are structured as tertiary education systems in developed countries and possibilities for alternative structures. The study uses the method of comparative education to yield these insights and the book develops an analytical framework for international educational comparisons in Chapter 2. As is elaborated later in this introduction, the study found two broad tendencies or patterns for structuring tertiary education and the book seeks to explain why countries adopt one or the other of the patterns.

In the Anglo-US pattern of vocational and higher education institutions having relatively general and overlapping roles, there is a range of practices in structuring higher education. Some jurisdictions such as California formally divide their higher education institutions into segments with markedly different roles and funding levels. Other jurisdictions distinguish between their higher education institutions, but less markedly or less formally. At the other end of the continuum, some jurisdictions such as Australia and Scotland have formally unified systems of higher education. The book considers the merits of these arrangements and, in particular, considers whether formally segmenting an elite sector of higher education makes highly selective institutions less accessible to students transferring from vocational education. The book finds that it does not and seeks to explain why this is so.

A final aim is to systematize the options available to governments for structuring vocational and higher education and this is done in Chapter 9. These several aims of the book are aspects of one overall question that the book seeks to answer: Why have sectors?

1.2 Why have sectors?

Most countries divide tertiary education – further education that follows secondary education – into two sectors. The more prominent sector is higher education, which comprises programmes that typically require a minimum of 3 years' full-time study after the final year of secondary schooling, are theoretically based and either provide access to high-status occupations or prepare students for research in basic disciplines. While many countries have higher education institutions that are not universities, the sector is dominated by universities that are similar throughout the western world, the oldest of which trace a continuous history back to the Middle Ages.

The less prominent sector of tertiary education is called in this book vocational education: it is the upper levels of further education colleges in the UK and it is offered by 2-year colleges in the USA, community colleges in Canada and the USA, *Berufsakademien* (vocational academies) and *Fachschulen* (trade and technical schools) in Germany, *instituts universitaires de technologie* (university institutes of technology) and *sections de technicien supérieur* (higher technical education units) in France, *hogescholen* (higher vocational colleges) in the Netherlands, vocational education and training providers in Australia and polytechnics in New Zealand. Vocational education comprises programmes that typically require no longer than 2 years' equivalent full-time study, are practical and either provide access to middle-status occupations or prepare students for higher education. There is considerable variation between countries in vocational education's structure and orientation and, as we have seen, there is considerable variation in their nomenclature. While organized vocational education probably predates higher education, few if any vocational education institutes can trace a continuous history beyond the Industrial Revolution.

As is elaborated in Chapter 8, some countries have established tertiary education institutes that include both vocational and higher education. The USA has over 400 'concurrent use campuses' that offer both vocational and higher education programs. In the 1970s two of the then 11 *alte Bundesländer* (old states of West Germany) established *Gesamthochschulen* (comprehensive universities), which incorporated in one institution the programmes of universities, technical universities, *pädagogische Hochschulen* (teacher training colleges), *Fachhochschulen* (then polytechnics) and *Kunsthochschulen* (art colleges). Five dual-sector universities emerged in Australia in the 1990s and a few emerged somewhat later in the UK. Since 2002 South Africa has merged universities and technikons, the former vocational education institutes, to form 14 universities of technology. *Gesamthochschulen* have not been successful – of the six established only one remains. As promising as some of the other developments may be, they are exceptions to tertiary education systems that overwhelmingly comprise institutions that offer exclusively either vocational or higher education.

This would be surprising were it not so familiar that it has become embedded in our thinking and practice. On their surface, vocational and higher education seem to share important characteristics: they both offer advanced education beyond the compulsory years of schooling, they prepare students for skilled occupations and they also prepare students for advanced study. Vocational education tends to be more practical and have a more vocational orientation than higher education. But, arguably, university engineering programmes have a similar amount of practical work as vocational education engineering programmes and university accounting programmes are as vocational as vocational education accounting programmes. Nonetheless, the distinctions between vocational and higher education remain as bright as ever.

1.2.1 To reflect fundamental differences between types of education

Many people argue that vocational and higher education should be separated because they are fundamentally different, that there is a characteristic or group of characteristics that distinguishes vocational from higher or general education. Such a characteristic would also be the basis for a common definition of 'vocational education', which is desirable to avoid the misunderstandings that may arise from different countries' name and arrangements for the sector. The various distinguishing features and definitions proposed for 'vocational education' and its cognates and their distinction from general education are examined critically in Chapter 3.

1.2.2 To accommodate mass higher education

Vocational education became increasingly important from the second half of the twentieth century in accommodating mass higher education. Countries have tended to adopt one of two courses to accommodate an expansion of higher education from enrolling a small elite, typically around 5 per cent of the group that provides most higher education students, to providing higher education for more than 15 per cent of the relevant age group (Trow 1974: 63). Some countries such as France have achieved mass higher education by expanding their university systems to accommodate most of the additional students. Governments have not felt that they are able to continue funding massively expanded university systems at the same rate per student that they funded much smaller proportions of university students. So countries that have massively expanded their university systems have reduced their university funding rates, leading to a deterioration of ratios of staff to students, less time and fewer resources for academic staff to conduct research and a general deterioration in university facilities and resources.

As is discussed in Chapter 7, other countries such as the USA, Canada and, to some extent, the UK have accommodated massively expanded higher education students in vocational education institutions that were established or expanded to fill this new role. Vocational education institutions are not funded for research and so are cheaper than universities. In addition, almost all governments fund undergraduate teaching in universities at a higher rate than undergraduate teaching in the vocational institutes that specialize in the role. In this approach, governments often make access to lower level and lower cost tiers reasonably broad and limit the funding needed for higher level and higher cost tiers by limiting access to them. So many governments have accommodated the massive expansion of higher education in vocational education institutes to preserve the admission selectivity and higher funding rates – the elite position – of at least some universities, typically those that were well established and thus were elite before the massification of higher education.

1.3 How sharply to differentiate vocational from higher education?

There are two broad patterns or tendencies in structuring tertiary education. Some countries meet the different needs of different students, employers and of society generally by structuring sectors and institutions to serve specific needs, most commonly to establish vocational institutes to specialize in developing skills for employment and higher education institutions to provide general education and education for the high-status, high-paying occupations. This tendency, which is most associated with Germany and other countries of northern continental Europe, sharply differentiates and separates vocational education from higher education in organization, curriculum and student groups. In these systems, students enter a vocational or academic education track towards the upper level of secondary education and proceed along that track to a vocational or higher education tertiary institution and thence to an occupation specific to their vocational or higher education track. These systems are therefore often known as 'tracked' systems.

Another tendency has been to seek to accommodate more diverse needs by giving institutions and sectors broader, more general roles. Institutions are structured into sectors that have different emphases and orientations, but this is within a generalist framework. Students in the generalist systems may defer their choice between vocational and academic routes later than in the tracked systems, often until after compulsory schooling. Even after embarking on a vocational or academic route students in the generalist systems often can transfer readily between routes without a big loss of progress. This is the pattern in many Anglophone countries – Canada, New Zealand, the UK and the USA. In these countries the vocational and higher education sectors and institutions merge and overlap considerably. As Furth (1992: 1217) argued, both strategies accommodate diversity, but in structurally different ways.

1.4 Relation to economic arrangements

These patterns in tertiary education provision coincide with two patterns for structuring economies and their relationship with tertiary education, described by Hall and Soskice (2001) as the contrast between coordinated market economies and liberal market economies. Northern continental Europe tends to have market economies which are coordinated by their social partners: governments at national and regional levels, business and labour. Vocational and higher education students might be placed on quite separate post-compulsory education tracks, but the coordinated market economy matches graduates and job vacancies for most. These systems have a sufficiently stable labour market to encourage enterprises and employees to invest heavily in vocationally specific skills.

The market economies of the Anglophone countries are rather more fluid, relying more on the market to sort and match graduates and employment. In liberal market economies, formal vocational education concentrates more on general skills because companies are loath to invest in apprenticeships that impart skills valuable throughout an industry since they have no guarantee that other firms will not poach their apprentices without investing in training themselves. Liberal market economies also place more responsibility on students and workers to suit themselves to the needs of current and prospective employers. Workers facing short job tenures and fluid and unpredictable labour markets therefore prefer general vocational education since career success depends on acquiring the general skills that can be used in many different firms. Greater mobility between vocational and higher education give students more flexibility to match their education with employment opportunities as they arise.

Coordinated and liberal market economies are also likely to value qualifications differently. This may be illustrated by comparing the use value and exchange value (Marx 1990 [1867]: 126) of a qualification, or more precisely of the labour power of someone who holds a qualification. The use value of a commodity is its utility in satisfying a need or want of members of a society. This is different from a commodity's exchange value, which is the quantity of other commodities the commodity may be traded for. A commodity's price is the more or less accurate monetary expression of its exchange value. Employers in a coordinated market economy are reasonably closely involved in the production of qualifications. They therefore have a reasonably good idea of the use value of the labour power of someone who holds a qualification, subject to the natural variations in people's personality, aptitude and application. There is therefore likely to be a reasonably good alignment between a qualification's use value and exchange value in a coordinated market economy.

In contrast, employers in the liberal market economy are less involved in the production of qualifications. They are therefore less certain of the use value of the labour power of someone who holds a qualification. Employers in a liberal market economy will therefore tend to discount the wages they pay to a new employee with a qualification not only for the uncertainty in their personality, aptitude and application, but they will further discount the wages they pay to a new qualified employee for the uncertainty in the use value of their qualification. There is therefore likely in general to be a bigger gap between the exchange value and the use value of qualifications in a liberal market economy than in a coordinated market economy. In particular, employers in a liberal market economy are in general likely to under price qualifications, leading to both employees and employers under-investing in training.

1.5   Education's positional value

Hirsch (1976) pointed out that some products and services have positional value. Consider a diamond. It has special characteristics that give it objective value such as extreme hardness, clarity and lustre. But these characteristics are no more special or objectively valuable than other characteristics of other precious and semi-precious stones. Yet diamonds are much more valuable than other stones. This value is a result of their scarcity. Diamonds have a positional value – they are a *positional good* – because their possession indicates a high position in the social hierarchy. Similarly, highly sought real estate, the 'best' table in the 'best' restaurant and membership of exclusive clubs are positional goods that are valued far more highly than their objective characteristics warrant because they indicate high social standing.

Education, likewise, is a positional good. Possession of a university qualification indicates an academic achievement that makes the graduate a more valuable employee. But when university education was accessible only to the social elite possession of a university qualification also indicated membership of the elite: it therefore also had considerable positional value. With the mass expansion of higher education following World War II possession of a university degree no longer signals such exclusivity. However, some institutions remain accessible mostly only to members of the social elite. These institutions, normally the oldest, and almost always the universities well established before the mass expansion of higher education, have greater positional value than other, normally younger institutions. Examples of these institutions are the Ivy League in the USA, Oxbridge in the UK and the 'sandstones' in Australia. So, as access to higher education expands, the desire for social differentiation is increasingly sought not just in the fact of graduating from a university, but in the choice of institution, programme and higher degree studies (James 2007: 10). The expansion of participation therefore leads to overtly tiered systems, whatever their official designation by government.

1.6 How many sectors?

Some countries and some US states not only separate vocational and higher education, but also formally segment higher education into sectors. Thus, prominently, California divides its public universities into two sectors, or segments as it calls them. The more selective and higher funded sector is the University of California, which has a formal research role, offers doctorates in a wide range of disciplines and is restricted to admitting the top 12.5 per cent of high school graduates. The other sector is the California State University, which does not have a formal research role (although research is conducted in the university), does not offer doctorates in its own right and is restricted to admitting the top 33.3 per cent of high school graduates. In some other jurisdictions, there is no formal segmentation of universities but the older, more research-intensive and more selective institutions have formed themselves into a group. In the UK, an informal self-selected body of 20 research-led institutions formed itself into the Russell Group in 1994. In the same year in Australia the eight universities with the biggest research expenditure formed itself into the Group of Eight.

In the light of the formal and informal structuring of tertiary education in several jurisdictions, in Chapter 7, I posit four tiers, segments or sectors of tertiary education. At the top is world research universities. These are the universities listed in Shanghai Jiao Tong University's academic ranking of world universities. These institutions are at least 50 years old, but most are much older and some are as much as 500 years old. They are very research intensive, which is supported by considerable research funding from government and often from philanthropists, business and alumni. They compete internationally for staff, students and research funding.

The second tier or sector is selecting universities and colleges. These institutions offer at least bachelor degrees but probably also masters and doctorates. Most conduct research and some have areas of international research strength. However, their research strengths are not sufficient to win them a place in the Shanghai Jiao Tong University's academic rank. These institutions nonetheless have very high standing at least in their region if not nationally and internationally and thus enjoy strong demand for their programmes. The third sector of recruiting universities and colleges comprises institutions that may be similar in many ways to selecting universities and colleges but they don't have the national or perhaps even the regional standing of their selecting counterparts, probably because they are distinctly younger. The fourth tier is of vocational institutes, which enrol 75 per cent or more of their load in vocational education programmes such as vocational associate's degree in the USA and higher national certificate and diplomas and diplomas of higher education in the UK.

The distinguishing characteristic of world research universities is their research strength, the distinguishing characteristic of selecting universities is their strong student demand, the distinguishing characteristic of recruiting

universities is their lower student demand and the distinguishing characteristic of vocational institutes is their predominance of vocational programmes.
Yet there is one general characteristic that underlies the whole classification:
positional value. The sectors or tiers are organized in order of their positional value from world research universities, which have the highest positional value, in descending order to vocational institutes, which generally
have the lowest positional value in tertiary education, although they still have
markedly more positional value than secondary education.

1.7   Salience of student transfer

Performance in the highly differentiated and tracked systems of tertiary
education is optimized when there is a good match of students, sectors and
society's needs. In these systems, large numbers of students transferring
between vocational and higher education indicate a failure of the system to
place students on the appropriate track initially. In contrast, high rates of
student transfer in the generalist systems may indicate that they are working
well in providing students with the flexibility to change routes as their interests and perception of labour force demand change.

For countries that preserve elite universities by providing mass access to
vocational education institutions, ready transfer from vocational to the top
tier of higher education is essential to maintain equality of opportunity and
social mobility. While students who do not gain direct access to the top tier of
higher education are streamed out of the level of education that is best
resourced and gives the best access to jobs with high salaries and status, this is
often justified by noting that students may transfer from the mass and lower
funded tiers to the top elite tier of higher education. Clark (1983: 51)
observed that the lower tier is both a screen and a route to access the upper
tier. Kerr (1994: 92) insisted that 'for the sake of equality of opportunity
in a segmented system, it is essential that highly successful students, with
appropriate academic backgrounds, be able to move from one segment to a
segment or segments at a higher level, as we provided in the Californian
master plan and increasingly also elsewhere'. Ready student transfer is
also often said to give students who leave school early or who do not per-
form well in secondary education a 'second chance' to prepare for or
start higher education in an institution that provides more student learning
support. High upward student transfer thus indicates the success of these
systems.

Student transfer from vocational to higher education also demonstrates
an important aspect of segmenting higher education into tiers. By comparing upward student transfer into different tiers of formally and strongly
segmented university systems, into less strongly segmented university systems and into formally unified university systems, we may examine the effect
of segmentation on upward student mobility. The results are shown in
Chapter 9, but, in summary, the study found that upward transfer to the

highly selective and highly segmented University of California system was at about the same rate as upward transfer to the highly selective and moderately segmented universities in Colorado and Texas. But upward transfer rates to the highly selective universities in the segmented US states were at least twice the rate of upward transfer to the highly selective universities in the formally unified university systems of Scotland and Australia.

This suggests that the rates of upward student transfer are affected less by the formal segmentation of systems into sectors than by informal differences between institutions and groups of institutions. Transfer student admission rates are probably influenced by several factors, but I hypothesize is that the strength of transfer policies and practices is more important than official structural designations. Many US states, including the ones in this study, have legislated strong transfer provisions. In contrast, no Australian government has a policy on student transfer beyond a general statement of encouragement. While the Scottish government seems more concerned with supporting student transfer than Australian governments, this concern is relatively recent and has not yet moved much beyond commissioning the studies cited in Chapter 9.

1.8 Qualifications frameworks and the European area

Within Europe, each country's tertiary education is increasingly subject to international forces. Two specifically educational factors are considered in Chapters 5 and 6. There is a fast developing international trend to establish qualifications frameworks to represent the relations between types of qualification. A qualifications framework is one way of depicting the relations between vocational and higher education and they are often promoted as ways of facilitating students' transfer between sectors. Chapter 5 describes the most prominent qualifications frameworks and discusses their future.

The Bologna declaration to establish the European area of higher education has important implications not only for its 46 signatories – which are much wider than the 27 countries of the European Union – but also for many other countries that have close educational interactions with the European area of higher education and look to it to inform their own higher education practices. The more recent Copenhagen declaration on enhanced European cooperation in vocational education and training to some extent complements the Bologna declaration and is growing in importance. These developments and their implications for the future of vocational and higher education are considered in Chapter 6.

1.9 Comparative education

As will be evident from the foregoing, this study seeks to understand vocational and higher education by comparing them with each other and by
comparing vocational and higher education in different countries. Comparing education and indeed other systems can be difficult to do at all, let alone
in a way that allows one to draw useful lessons for one's own area of interest.
This study compares systems that are as similar as possible except in their
structuring of tertiary education sectors. This eliminates all the characteristics that the systems share as possible explanations for different transfer
rates and examines the remaining differences between the systems for factors that might cause their different rates. The method used in the study, its
limitations and alternatives are considered in Chapter 2.

1.10 Conclusion

The study notes that while sectors were initially segmented by orientation
(vocational or general education) and student intake (selective or open
entry), it is now common to distinguish sectors by research role. The study
finds that student transfer is complex and non-linear. So while the segmentation of a higher education system into sectors does not necessarily inhibit the
transfer of vocational education students, special measures are necessary to
promote the transfer of students across sectoral boundaries.

The differences in transfer student admission rates between different types
of higher education institution suggest that Skilbeck and colleagues (1998:
104) are right in arguing that structures are not as important as the relationships between the organizations that form them. Nonetheless, as Geiger
(1992: 1031) points out, while structures do not determine outcomes, different structures require different mechanisms to achieve similar outcomes.
The findings of the study are used to consider six options for structuring the
relations between vocational and higher education: segregation, duplication,
integration, systematizing a cross-sectoral enrolments, establishing an intermediate sector and 'wise and masterly inactivity'.

2

Comparing education

This chapter addresses one of the main issues in education: how to make sensible comparisons between different systems and how to adapt lessons from one system to implement them in another without eroding either the strengths of the host system or the value of the imported lessons.

2.1 Nature of comparative education

Comparative education is most commonly understood to be the comparison of one country's education system with another's. Thus, one might compare vocational education in England with vocational education in Germany or higher education in both Canada and the USA. While that was the first and remains the most common form of comparative education, there are other useful forms of comparative education. One is the comparison of jurisdictions within a country. Thus surveys of the US states are common and 'home international' comparisons of education in England, Scotland, Wales and Northern Ireland are becoming increasingly popular. Although not always characterized as 'comparative education', the comparison of different education systems within one jurisdiction is also a reasonably common form of comparative education. Thus, one might compare vocational with higher education in Quebec.

'System' in this context is normally understood to be a group of several institutions participating in a common enterprise, often within a policy established by government. But an institution can also be understood as a system of several constituents engaged in a common enterprise guided by an institutional policy that has its own culture, internal economy and social relations. So a comparison of European universities' progress with implementing the Bologna declaration is an example of comparative education. There is no reason, in principle at least, why the smallest unit of comparison should be the institution since analogous reasoning would lead one to characterize as comparative education a comparison of faculties within a university or a comparison of departments within a faculty. But because most such studies examine academic disciplines and individual scholars more closely than studies of state systems, they are not usually considered comparative education.

The aim of the comparative study shapes the type of study undertaken and the tools chosen, as we shall see later in this chapter. There are at least four possible aims of comparative education. One of the most important aims was posed as a question in the most famous statement in the history of comparative education by one of the founders of the modern field, Sir Michael Sadler (1964): 'How far can we learn anything of practical value from the study of foreign systems of education?' Thus, for Sadler, the aim of comparative education was to inform and improve one's educational practice. A comparison with other systems may generate new ideas and it may reveal tacit assumptions in one's own practices. This has in turn led to the development of three aspects to learning from other systems, which Cowen (2006: 561) notes are transfer, translation and transformation. *Transfer* is the movement of an educational idea or practice to a different place. *Translation* is the reshaping of educational institutions or the reinterpretation of educational ideas that routinely occurs when they are transferred to a different context. *Transformations* are the changes to the host environment caused by incorporating foreign ideas and practices.

A second possible aim of comparative education is to test alternative approaches to common problems by conducting a sort of artificial experiment. So one might test whether introducing a common curriculum would improve students' transfer from vocational to higher education by examining whether a common curriculum has improved student transfer in states that are otherwise similar to the subject state. A third aim of comparative education is to improve our understanding of a system by studying its development and by noting which of its characteristics are common to most other systems and which are idiosyncratic. Comparisons can begin to separate the effects of specific circumstances from the general effects of a policy. A fourth aim of comparative education is to contribute to the theory of education by testing generalizations in more than one system.

These comparisons and the inferences commonly drawn from them quickly encounter methodological problems. How can one be sure that a comparative study is comparing like with like or at least that salient distinguishing features have been identified and accounted for? If we observe that university graduation rates in the UK are much higher than rates in France, Germany and the USA, can we conclude that, for example, student selection for UK universities is better at identifying students likely to succeed than the other countries' methods? Should one conclude that student selection 'causes' different graduation rates or is only a more modest claim permissible? The rest of this chapter seeks to address these issues by considering comparative education from first principles.

2.2 'Comparative education' as a term of art

To say that the tertiary education sectors are more deeply divided in Australia than those in Colorado and England is to make a comparative statement in undoubtedly two and, arguably, three senses. First, any general statement implies a comparison. Thus, the simpler proposition 'The water is deep', clearly embeds a comparison disclosed by its grammatical form as a comparative adjective.

Consider, second, the statement 'The book is red'. Again, 'red' could be understood as the absolute form of the adjective whose comparative and superlative forms are redder and reddest. But the statement, 'The book is red', could also be understood to mean that it is not blue, green or any other colour in the spectrum. Turning now from adjectives to nouns, consider a scientific instrument that identifies a specimen by comparing the specimen with all the types in its database. If the instrument finds a match it identifies its specimen as the matched type. One epistemology says that all propositions are comparative in this sense. On this theory, the statement, 'The object is a book', means that the object is not a ball or a computer or any other object and that this is determined by comparing the object with all object types until a match is found. So 'The object is a book' is really an elliptical way of saying that 'The object matches the ideal type of the book' or on another ontology, 'The object has enough resemblances with the class of books to be considered a member of that class'. This theory therefore posits that all statements of this type are taxonomies and that all classifications are made by comparison.

These understandings of comparisons go beyond the purposes of this study, which are served by a third, narrower sense of comparative education. While simple comparisons of observations may be a common mental operation, a systematic comparison of the relations between objects in one system with the relations between corresponding objects in another system becomes a social science. Comparative education is that type of social science that makes comparison of educational systems the main purpose of the study rather than the incidental outcome of a study mainly conducted for another purpose.

2.3 Functional analysis

If we wanted to improve France's primary education, we might start by comparing it with primary education in other European countries by constructing a table with countries along one axis and along the other axis the characteristics of the systems that might be considered relevant to their performance: how they are administered, their pedagogy and demographic information about their staff and students. This is precisely what was proposed by Marc-Antoine Jullien (de Paris) (1775–1836), who is widely understood to be the founder of the discipline of comparative education. Jullien proposed to collect data by questionnaire, a tool now ubiquitous, and to arrange the collected facts and observations in 'analytical tables so that they can be correlated and compared with a view to deducing therefrom firm principles and specific rules' (Jullien 1817: 324–5). Jullien modelled his method of comparative education on comparative anatomy in which Georges de Cuvier had achieved important results at the turn of the nineteenth century and which also was the model for the comparative study of language, religion, government and jurisprudence such as Montesquieu's *Esprits des Lois* [The spirit of laws] (Schriewer 2006: 303). Cuvier's method was to deduce from his study of similarities and differences objects' functions and structural patterns or underlying laws of organization.

Thus, if we were to find that all primary education systems included in the study had some idea of progression from one level of learning to another we might infer that staged learning is a core attribute of all primary education, perhaps relating this to Piaget's theory of child cognitive development. If we found further that some primary education systems streamed pupils by ability within level while others did not stream pupils, we may conclude that streaming is contingent and we might further investigate whether streaming is related to other characteristics and perhaps even to the systems' performance.

2.4 History as well as geography

It is possible to compare not only different places at the same time, but also the same place at different times; that is, comparative education may be an historical as well as a geographic study. Thus one of the modern lights of the discipline Nicholas Hans (1964: 94) defined comparative education as the study of historical evolution and many argue that a system is best understood by examining its antecedents. Comparing education in different periods can be illuminating. The next chapter compares different uses of the terms 'vocational education' and 'technical education' at different times to demonstrate their different meanings and, elsewhere in the book, we note different educational arrangements at previous times to argue that the present arrangement is contingent, its entrenchment notwithstanding.

But historical comparison is not often the core comparative method to inform policy for two, rather prosaic, reasons. First, there are methodological problems with comparing educational arrangements at different times. Changed arrangements are almost always accompanied by changed data collection and reporting arrangements and often by changes to the bodies responsible for collecting system data. Those responsible for implementing such changes are preoccupied with things other than the interests of future policy analysts and so rarely ensure that data are comparable between eras.

But even were the continuity of data preserved or if they could be reconstructed, problems would remain with comparing educational arrangements between eras. The binary divide in Australian higher education was dismantled to achieve 'a new era of growth and opportunity' in higher education (Dawkins 1988) or to change from an elite to a mass system of higher education as would be said now. The premise of such a change is that the demands and needs of students in previous eras are not comparable with current or emerging needs. That a previous arrangement adequately met the needs of a previous era says little about its capacity to meet the different needs of the present.

2.5 Experiment by analogy

It is necessary to understand society to improve it and the foundations for a scientific understanding society were laid by Auguste Comte (1798–1857), who coined the term sociology. Comte held that knowledge can come only from the positive affirmation of theories by observation and thus founded the philosophy of positivism. Comte posited three forms of observation:

> The means of exploration are three: direct observation, observation by experiment, and observation by comparison. In the first case, we look at the phenomenon before our eyes; in the second, we see how it is modified by artificial circumstances to which we have subjected it; and in the third, we contemplate a series of analogous cases, in which the phenomenon is more and more simplified.
>
> (Comte 1975 [1830–42]: 132)

One of Comte's frequent correspondents was John Stuart Mill (1806–73). Mill was the first to elaborate systematically the comparative sociological method in *A System of Logic*, first published in 1843. Mill's method is used to explain a social phenomenon, say, student attrition. Mill starts with two methods for identifying the causes of the phenomenon from circumstances that precede it. One method is to compare systems in which there are high rates of student attrition and see what they have in common. Mill calls this method the *method of agreement*. His method of difference is to compare systems that have high attrition rates with systems that have low attrition rates to see what differences between them may cause their different student attrition rates. These two methods may also be used to identify the consequences of a phenomenon, the circumstances that follow the phenomenon which are 'really connected by an invariable law' (Mill 1925 [1843], chapter VIII, section 1: 253). This method was also propounded by Émile Durkheim (1858–1917) in *The Rules of Sociological Method*, first published in 1895 (Durkheim 1938 [1895]: 125).

Mill's methods of agreement succeeds inasmuch as it is able to eliminate factors that do not affect the phenomenon being considered. Przeworski and Teune's (1970) most similar systems design also uses such a process of elimination. Continuing our example of student attrition, the aim in the most similar systems design is to compare systems that are as similar as possible except in their student attrition. One eliminates all the factors that the systems share as possible causes for the different attrition rates and examines the remaining differences between the systems for factors that might cause their different rates. The obverse of the most similar systems design is Przeworski and Teune's most different systems design. In the most different systems design, one compare systems that are as different as possible except in having similar student attrition rates. Thus while the most similar systems design compares similar systems with different attrition rates and eliminates as possible causes the factors that systems have in common, the most different systems design compares different systems with similar attrition rates and eliminates as possible causes the differences between the systems, leaving the characteristics that they share as possible causes of their similar rates.

Przeworski and Teune (1970: 34) identify what is at least a limitation of the most similar systems design and the method of agreement, but which may be considered a flaw. Even very similar systems have several differences that are plausible causes of the phenomenon of interest and the method has no way of identifying which of the differences is the cause. One possible solution of this difficulty is to study systems that are so simple that only one variable is plausibly the cause of the phenomenon of interest. Thus economists build models that are simple enough to be described mathematically. But while mathematics may adequately describe the model, it is less clear that the simplified model adequately describes society. This approach, therefore, sacrifices the explanatory power of the model for the explanatory power of mathematics.

A second problem with the method of agreement and also with the method of difference is that they cannot identify multiple causation, which Mill called *plural causation* (Ragin 1987). Student attrition may be the outcome of either poorly prepared students or of poor teaching. There may be instances where student attrition has resulted only from poorly prepared students and other instances when it results only from poor teaching. The methods of agreement and difference would lead one to conclude incorrectly that neither caused student attrition.

2.6 The problem of induction

A more fundamental difficulty with both Mill's methods of agreement and difference and Przeworski and Teune's most (dis)similar systems designs is their inability to deal with the problem of induction, first elaborated strongly by David Hume (1711–76). The problem of induction is the fallacious belief that the constant conjunction of events establishes a causal relationship between them or, more generally, that one may infer universal statements from individual observations (Hume 1964 [1738], book 1, part III, section XII: 139). One may correctly observe that a cock crows every day before the sun rises, but one would be wrong to infer that the cock causes the sun to rise. Even the fact that every swan seen by a European before 1770 was white would not have justified the general statement that all swans are white.

Likewise, we may observe that almost all students who drop out of tertiary study used the library very little if at all before they dropped out and, conversely, we may observe that students who continue their studies are very likely to use the library. But are we thereby justified in concluding that library use causes student retention or that the lack of library use causes student attrition?

The early comparative educationalist Kandel (1933: xix) sought to escape the problem of induction by referring to the 'intangible, impalpable spiritual and cultural forces' that act on educational systems and Sadler (1964 [1900]: 309) referred to the 'spiritual force' that he claimed supports educational systems and accounts for their efficacy. Gilbert Ryle (1975: 15–16) used the expression 'the dogma of the Ghost in the Machine' to refer 'with deliberate abusiveness' to the Cartesian dualism of the physical body animated by the spiritual mind, but the expression also seems apt to refer to Kandel and Sadler's attempts to escape the problem of induction. For, while, as we shall see later, it is appropriate to refer to the causes of social phenomena, these have to be derived from a mechanism; it is not appropriate to posit some additional spiritual entity.

A possible solution to the problem of induction is to avoid it by declining to claim causation, at least for the methods described so far. This minimalist position is acceptable and, indeed, is commonly held. But it is inconsistent with popular understanding and usage which routinely ascribes causation when Hume's conditions for making causal inferences are not met. It is, of course, possible that the popular understanding is badly deluded, but it would be preferable if popular and rigorous understandings were better aligned. Another possible solution is the theory of falsification propounded by Karl Popper (1902–94). Popper (1972 [1934]: 40) argued that all general statements are hypotheses that remain conjectural but possibly true until falsified. So the statement, 'All swans are white', is a conjecture that no amount of sightings of white swans can prove, but a single sighting of a black swan disproves. According to Popper all generalizations including scientific propositions or laws are hypotheses which are yet to be disproved. Popper's understanding of science is not accepted by critical realists who have another way of handling the problem of induction, to which we now turn.

2.7 Critical realism

Critical realism is the philosophy that originated in the early twentieth century that holds that our knowledge is of an independent physical world but that this knowledge is mediated by mental processes of perception and cognition. More recently, the term is associated with the philosophy of science of Roy Bhaskar. Bhaskar (1998 [1979]: 9) argues that positivists such as Hume, Mill and Popper misunderstand the nature of the scientific method. While some constant conjunctions occur naturally, overwhelmingly natural phenomena do not occur with that regularity: most constant conjunctions are produced by humans. We, nevertheless, routinely apply scientific knowledge in open systems – outside closed or controlled experimental conditions – where there is no constant conjunction of events and where formal proofs are impossible. It therefore follows, writes Bhaskar (1998 [1979]: 10–11) that deduction from the constant conjunction of events can be neither necessary nor sufficient for a natural scientific explanation.

For Bhaskar, the scientific method starts with identifying a phenomenon that may not be an event but a state of affairs. So a scientist may start with the observation that the sky is blue. The scientist then builds an explanation for the phenomenon, possibly using analogy or metaphor. The scientist then tests the explanation, often in a closed system or carefully controlled experiment. If it is verified the explanation is itself a phenomenon demanding explanation. So science is an iterative process of developing explanations of phenomena that are then, in turn, explained, leading to higher and higher levels of explanation. While positivists see science as induction or deduction from conjunctions of events, Bhaskar sees science as the development and testing of causal laws or explanations of the mechanism of phenomena.

The social scientific method can proceed in much the same way. The social scientist identifies a phenomenon to be investigated such as a social structure. The social scientist then builds an explanation for the phenomenon, again possibly using analogy or metaphor. The social scientist tests the explanation, one step of which is eliminating alternative possible explanations (Bhaskar (1998 [1979]: 129). However, unlike natural scientists, social scientists cannot test their explanations decisively in carefully controlled experiments. For unlike natural scientists, social scientists cannot construct controlled experiments in systems that are closed to external influences and in which constant conjunctions may be constructed and tested. This is because social systems are open and can never be artificially closed. Therefore, unlike scientific theories, social theories cannot be predictive and must be exclusively explanatory. But social theories can still be tested empirically, although not necessarily quantitatively. While many theories in the natural sciences may be tested directly, other mechanisms such as magnetism and gravitation are observed only by their effects. In that they are similar to social mechanisms that exist only by virtue of their effects and which thus may be tested only by observing their effects.

Societies are both reproduced and transformed by individuals so they change over time. The law like statements of the social sciences are therefore typically restricted to a period of time. Social activities are both interdependent and interconnected. But social sciences laws typically apply to only one relatively autonomous part of the social structure that is nonetheless connected to other parts of society. Both limitations result in laws that typically designate tendencies (Bhaskar 1998 [1979]: 54), such as education systems tend to reflect the inequities of the economies and societies that support them. This method reflects the multiplicity and plurality of causes of any event.

Because social systems are open they have no beginning and end, either in time or space. This makes delimitating the objects of study an acute issue for the social sciences. Most of the phenomena studied by social scientists have already been identified by their participants and social scientists may base their definition of social phenomena on participants' usage. But meanings must be precise if they are to have any explanatory value so the social sciences attempt to define phenomena before rather than after finding successful causal hypotheses as in the natural sciences. Nonetheless, in both the social and natural sciences causal hypotheses can be justified only empirically, that is, by the revealed explanatory hypotheses that can be deduced from them (Bhaskar 1998 [1979]: 46, 49–50).

2.8 Developing a comparative method

There are several possible comparative methods available, each suitable for a range of possible studies. Choosing between the methods suitable for a particular study largely depends on personal taste provided we keep within the technical limits of the method. I chose for this study the method developed by one of the early US comparative educationalists, George Z. F. Bereday (1920–83). Bereday's (1964) *Comparative Method in Education* has seven steps:

1. select a topic, issue or problem;
2. collect and collate from relevant countries educational data relevant to the topic;
3. interpret the data, applying such disciplines as are relevant to an understanding of it in its social context;
4. juxtapose the interpreted data in to reveal possible bases for comparison;
5. develop hypotheses;
6. test hypotheses by comparative analysis of the interpreted data;
7. draw conclusions.

For the purposes of this study some of Bereday's steps may be collapsed. For the reasons given by Bhaskar just discussed, it is also necessary to define precisely the parts of tertiary education being studied, in particular, it is necessary to define vocational education precisely since as we shall see it has had a most slippery meaning. This study therefore follows four steps, adopting a mostly orthodox method for comparative studies. The first step is to state the issue to be investigated. The second step is to ensure that like is being compared with like. Third, the study classifies the phenomena observed and, in the fourth step, it generalizes from the data.

2.8.1 First step: state an issue

Stating the issue is an obvious first step and has already been followed in this study. Thus the introduction says that the study investigates why most systems of tertiary education are divided into sectors and the effect of segmenting higher education into different levels. In brief, why have sectors? But Bereday's method is linear. Having stated an issue, Bereday proceeds to the other steps, returning to the issue only to draw conclusions. Another founder of the discipline, Edmund King (1914–2002) describes a more iterative approach. King (1967: 58) starts by conceptualizing an appropriate theme of inquiry. This soon brings King to institutions and thence to institutionalize his study. He then observes that the same kind of institution or function might produce different results in different circumstances and thus are operationalized differently. King concludes that the three aspects of comparative inquiry – conceptual, institutional and operational – to some extent overlap and are interdependent. King's more iterative approach is followed in this study.

2.8.2 Second step: identify identity

An obvious requirement is to ensure that like is being compared with like. As will be elaborated in some detail in the next chapter, the problem of equivalence is particularly acute in the study of vocational education. Bliss and Garbett (1990) observe that the concept of technical education is not always and not necessarily interpreted in the same way in different systems. Indeed, they argue, in some ways it is necessary to challenge the very notion of technical education as a clearly definable sector:

> Problems of interpreting data, of learning lessons from abroad, are thus not simply technical, statistical ones, but take us to central definitional problems about what are to count as legitimate usages of terms such as 'education' and 'technical education'. The notion of 'education' has been much debated, but even the apparently more precise notion of 'technical education' is by no means transparent in meaning
> (Bliss and Garbett 1990: 190)

Rainbird (1996: 117) argues that terms such as 'skill', 'qualification' and 'apprenticeship' derive from distinctive historical traditions and do not necessarily have equivalents from one country to another. And as Clarke and Winch (2006) and Brockmann *et al.* (2007) demonstrate, outwardly similar terms have different understandings and meanings in Dutch, English and German societies and presumably in other cultures. For Rainbird, the problem of equivalence is a problem of understanding the conceptual language of different social and intellectual traditions. I argue later that terminological ambiguity not only causes problems of equivalence in comparative studies, but is also a special problem of identity for vocational education.

Goedegebuure and van Vught (1994: 11–12) restate the problem, but helpfully propose an admittedly partial solution. This is to reduce the risk of mistranslating concepts by comparing countries that are similar. This study seeks a balance between similarity and difference in selecting jurisdictions to compare, but leans heavily towards the similarity proposed by Goedegebuure and van Vught to minimize the problems with the incommensurability of concepts and data.

2.8.3 Third step: classify

The third step followed in the study is to classify the phenomena observed. Anderson (1961: 7) says that three sorts of correlation are used to compare educational systems in depth, for both qualitative and quantitative data. The first step is to identify patterns of relationship among various aspects of educational systems. The second step is to develop a typology of educational systems, which is a way of summarising vast quantities of data that have already received a preliminary ordering in the first step. Anderson's third step is to display the relationships between various educational characteristics and associated sociological, economic or other non-educational features.

The classification of data is also an analytical tool, a way of building a simplified but explanatory model of reality. This raises the issue referred to earlier, of the tension between the explanatory power of models and the loss of accuracy that they necessarily entail. According to Koehl (1977) comparative education is still developing its analogue of the life science's taxonomy and chemistry's periodic table. Koehl (1977: 177) says that

> some of the crucial theoretical problems facing contemporary comparative education, particularly those of classification, terminology, and morphology, were confronted by the practitioners of these early sciences and have analogies if not exact parallels in the taxonomic manuals of chemistry, geology, and biology of the not too distant past.

That is, comparative education still hasn't caught up with Georges de Cuvier's nineteenth-century comparative anatomy noted earlier.

2.8.4 Fourth step: generalize

Finally, generalization is an obvious goal of comparative studies. Kandel's (1933) method suggests a sequence: description leading successively to explanation, to comparative analysis and, finally, to the identification of patterns, trends or principles of education. This is entirely consistent with Bhaskar's description of social science which he says develops laws that typically designate tendencies.

2.8.5 Several tools will be used

We have seen in Bhaskar's work that while the social sciences present empirically verifiable laws or explanations of social mechanisms, they are necessarily limited. Societies are open systems: it is not possible to conduct experiments on societies in closed, controlled conditions. Any social phenomenon or event thus has a multiplicity and plurality of causes. Societies also change over time and so any investigation is likely to be bound by its time. For these reasons, it is highly unlikely that a single tool will be adequate for all studies of comparative education. The following list of possible tools in comparative education is taken from Paulston's (2000: 359) typology:

- *Narrative:* chronicles and stories of educational customs and practices; histories of educational ideas.
- *Statistics:* methods for the numerical representation and measurement of educational data and practices.
- *Science:* positive models for representing educational functions and systems.
- *Analysis:* causal explanations of social and economic relations and outcomes.
- *Ethnography:* thick descriptions of cultural processes and world making.
- *Rhetoric:* translations and deconstructions of literary texts and discursive practice.
- *Spatial representation:* metaphorical mappings of diverse ways of seeing and nets of relationships.
- *Pictorial representation:* visual displays and image making.

This discussion has distinguished between comparative education's method and the tool(s) used to implement a method. It has sought to construct a single method – at least for the purposes of this study – but has foreshadowed the use of multiple tools. Those who define a discipline by its method and reduce method to a tool of observation or analysis conclude that comparative education is a pluralist undertaking.

3

Defining 'vocational education'

The previous chapter on comparing education systems demonstrated the importance of comparing like with like and identifying key national differences despite inconsistencies in terminology. This is particularly important in vocational education, where differences in practice are disguised by similarities in terminology and similarities in practice are confounded by inconsistencies in terminology. This chapter overcomes these difficulties by propounding a common understanding of 'vocational education' and ways of handling national variations.

3.1 Identify identity

The second step in the comparative method outlined in Chapter 2 is to establish the equivalence or, more precisely, the comparability of the entities being compared. This is a particular problem in comparing tertiary education systems because one of the key parts or functions of tertiary education, which for convenience will be called 'vocational education', is beset by definitional problems. The chapter opens by finding that while UNESCO's international standard classification of education is very useful for collecting international statistics, it does not represent institutional types well in many jurisdictions and so is not suitable for this study. Most of the chapter therefore seeks a better definition of 'vocational education' and proposes a general compound definition. The chapter concludes by discussing the German concept of *Beruf*, which is much broader than the closest English term 'vocation' and suggests, first, that care must be exercised in translating concepts between languages. Second, *Berufsbildung* or vocational education suggests a broader and longer term concept than is common in English-speaking jurisdictions.

3.2 International standard classification of education

The most widely accepted classification of education is the international standard classification of education (ISCED) developed by the United Nations Educational Scientific and Cultural Organisation (UNESCO) in the early 1970s to facilitate comparisons of education statistics and indicators within and between countries. It was originally endorsed at the General Conference of UNESCO in 1978 and the current version (ISCED-97) was formally adopted in November 1997.

ISCED-97 classifies formal education into seven levels:

0   pre-primary education;
1   primary education or first stage of basic education;
2   lower secondary or second stage of basic education;
3   (upper) secondary education;
4   post secondary non-tertiary education;
5   first stage of tertiary education;
6   second stage of tertiary education.

ISCED-97 divides programmes by orientation:

- general education develops a deeper understanding of a subject
- pre-vocational education mainly introduces students to the world of work and to prepare them for entry into vocational or technical education programme
- vocational or technical education mainly develops students' practical skills, know-how and understanding necessary for employment in a particular occupation (UNESCO 1997: paras 57–9).

UNESCO describes ISCED level 4, postsecondary non-tertiary education programmes, as often not significantly more advanced than programmes at ISCED level 3, but which broaden the knowledge of students who have already completed a programme at level 3. Typical examples are programmes designed to prepare students for studies at level 5 who, although having completed ISCED level 3, did not follow a curriculum that would allow entry to level 5, i.e. pre-degree foundation programmes or short vocational programmes. UNESCO distinguishes between 4A programmes that prepare for entry to ISCED level 5 and 4B programmes that do not give access to level 5 but are primarily designed for direct labour market entry. Thus level 4 programmes are in orientation general education, pre-vocational or pre-technical education, or vocational or technical education.

UNESCO (1997) describes ISCED level 5, first stage of tertiary education, simply as programmes that have an educational content more advanced than those offered at levels 3 and 4. Entry to level 5 programmes normally requires the successful completion of ISCED level 3A or 3B or a similar qualification at ISCED level 4A.

UNESCO introduces a subdivision of tertiary education in ISCED-97. This distinction is based on two elements: theoretical/practical and profession/trade:

> 84. The first dimension to be considered is the distinction between the programmes which are theoretically based/research preparatory (history, philosophy, mathematics, etc.) or giving access to professions with high skills requirements (e.g. medicine, dentistry, architecture, etc.), and those programmes which are practical/technical/ occupationally specific. To facilitate the presentation, the first type will be called 5A, the second, 5B.
>
> (UNESCO 1997: para. 84)

UNESCO says that because the organizational structure of tertiary education programmes varies greatly across countries no single criterion can be used to define boundaries between ISCED 5A and ISCED 5B. However, in general, ISCED level 5A programmes have a minimum cumulative theoretical duration at tertiary level of 3 years' full-time equivalent, although typically they are of 4 or more years (UNESCO 1997: para. 87). Tertiary type B programmes are of shorter duration, a minimum of 2 years' full-time equivalent duration but generally they are of 2 or 3 years (UNESCO 1997: 90). These expected durations apply less to Europe since the adoption of the Bologna process which has reduced many 5A qualifications to 3 years' duration.

For many purposes it is useful to adopt the classification of education programmes in ISCED-97 and, in particular, to identify vocational education as 5B or tertiary type B programmes and higher education as 5A or tertiary type A programmes. However, this does not map directly to institutional types. For example, the 2-year academic associate degree, which is a major offering of 2-year or community colleges in the USA, are not classified as 5B programmes in ISCED since they are considered 'intermediate degrees'. A substantial part of many the UK's further education colleges' provision is level 3, (upper) secondary education, level 4, postsecondary non-tertiary education and tertiary type A as well as B. Much of the provision of vocational education institutions in Australia is classified as level 4, postsecondary non-tertiary education and a small amount of higher education provision is classified as tertiary type B.

Neither, as well shall see later, is UNESCO's theoretical/practical nor the profession/trade distinction adequate to found a definition of 'vocational education' and distinguish it consistently from other forms of education. It is therefore worth exploring whether there may be an analytically sound definition of 'vocational education'.

3.3   Defining 'vocational education' and its cognates[1]

The inconsistencies and difficulties in defining vocational education have concerned many authors. 'Vocational education' is not only used inconsistently from place to place at the same time, but inconsistently in the same place at different times. The problem is longstanding. Over a century ago T. H. Huxley (1877) lamented that 'it passes the wit of man, so far as I know, to give a legal definition of technical education'. In 1937 Bennett (1937: 275) observed that 'technical education' has been applied to general science subjects, to trade teaching, to higher instruction in science and engineering and to commercial and management studies and two decades later Henninger (1959: 115) reported that his 'survey has shown a tremendous spread and considerable carelessness or capriciousness in the use of the term "technical institute" by various schools and related groups'.

As will be explored in some detail later in this chapter, vocational education is often contrasted with general education, but this does not assist comparisons since ' "vocational" and "general" education . . . can mean different things in different countries, depending on the traditions that have formed in the education system' (Lachenmann 1988: 26). Indeed, Skilbeck and colleagues (1994: 3) argue that inconsistent use affects not only 'vocational education' but also its cognates 'education', 'vocational', 'training', 'skill', 'competence', 'working life' and so on.

3.3.1 Establishing equivalence

Raivola (1985: 367–8) posited three ways of establishing equivalence: correlative equivalence, functional equivalence and genetic equivalence. These are considered in turn.

3.3.1.1 Correlative equivalence
One of the key markers of vocational education in many countries including Australia has been apprenticeships and this is useful in identifying correlative equivalence of vocational education in the countries that have apprenticeships. Apprenticeship systems rely on a set of interlocking institutional supports such as coordination of employment relations and training to ensure consistency in training content and standards, statutory regulation of employment and training of apprentices, regulation of training and employment wages of apprentices and often state financial support for training and overall supervision of the system. But as will be observed in the review of Canada

---

[1] An earlier and much briefer version of this chapter was published as Moodie, G. (2002) Identifying vocational education and training. *Journal of Vocational Education and Training*, 54(2): 251–67. I thank one of the journal's anonymous reviewers for their generous suggestions to improve the paper.

and the USA, these countries' institutional supports for apprenticeships are weak and therefore there are almost no apprenticeships in the USA and they are few and patchy in Canada. Is there, therefore, no 'vocational education' in the USA? That seems unlikely, particularly since even though education is constitutionally a state responsibility in the USA as it is in Australia, the US federal government has fostered vocational education since the Smith-Hughes Act of 1917, which allocated federal funds for vocational education in high schools.

Other possible markers of vocational education are education for a specific occupation, the use of workshops and other technical facilities in teaching and on the job training. Yet, as we shall see later, these characteristics are either not common to what is commonly understood to be vocational education or they are also shared with other types of education such as for the professions that are not commonly understood to be vocational education. This study finds that there is no simple correlative equivalence of vocational education in any of the jurisdictions it examines: their equivalence, and the basis for comparisons, will have to be founded on a more complex understanding.

3.3.1.2 Functional equivalence

Comparing tertiary education systems is fruitful because their different functions are served differently in different systems. Thus the functions served by apprenticeships in Australia and the UK are served differently in Canada. Apprenticeships do not exist in all Canadian provinces and are fragmentary in their coverage of occupations in the provinces where they do exist. In the absence of strong institutional supports for an occupational labour market, employers satisfy their need for skilled labour by establishing their own internal labour markets. So new employees enter the lower levels of the organization, where they may be given an opportunity to move up to more highly skilled jobs.

Educational functions are not even necessarily served by an education sector. Hall and Soskice (2001: 30) argue that in liberal market economies companies are loath to invest in skills that are valuable through out their industry since they have no guarantee that other firms will not poach their apprentices without investing in training themselves. Therefore in these economies formal vocational education concentrates on general education, while companies conduct substantial additional in-house training that is specific to their enterprise and thus less portable to other companies. In contrast, coordinated market economies have a sufficiently stable labour market to encourage enterprises and employees to invest heavily in apprenticeships that impart skills that are specific to a vocation but not to an enterprise.

This substitution of functions is likely to be particularly prevalent at the intersection of sectors such as in applied education. So while establishing functional equivalence is often instructive, it is not sufficiently consistent between different types of economy to found a definition of vocational education.

3.3.1.3 Genetic equivalence

This analysis starts with Raivola's third way of establishing equivalence, genetic equivalence, by which he means membership of the same conceptual class. The section analyses several attempts to define 'vocational education' and its cognates, classifying them into four types: epistemological, teleological, hierarchical and pragmatic. None of these attempts is found to be satisfactory so those types are used to pose a new compound description of 'vocational education' which the section argues is adequate to identify the 'family resemblance' (Wittgenstein 1968) of vocational education and its cognates.

3.3.2 Epistemological

The most fundamental foundation of vocational education's identity is as the development of a distinctive way of knowing; some writers make associated claims for vocational education and training's distinctive way of learning and some consider it a field of knowledge. These are considered in turn.

3.3.2.1 Ways of knowing

In *Nichomachean Ethics* Aristotle distinguished 'five ways in which the soul arrives at truth' – pure science (episteme), art or applied science (techne), prudence or practical wisdom (phronesis), intelligence or intuition (nous) and wisdom (sophia). Wisdom or theoretical wisdom is knowledge of first principles and therefore is the most precise and perfect form of knowledge. Art or applied science is essentially a trained ability of rationally producing or, in other translations, producing under the guidance of true reason. Similarly, in the *Metaphysics*, Aristotle says that theoretical kinds of knowledge are more of the nature of wisdom than the productive or practical kinds of knowledge because they deal with the first causes and the principles of things.

Durkheim (1977 [1938]) relates the medieval construction of the curriculum to a distinction between theory and practice:

> First of all there were three disciplines, grammar, rhetoric and dialectic, which formed what was called the 'trivium' . . . The quadrivium included geometry, arithmetic, astronomy and music.
>
> These two cycles were not only distinguished by the number disciplines which they included. There was also a profound difference in the nature of the disciplines which were taught within the two cycles. The trivium was intended to instruct the mind about the mind itself, that is to say the laws which it obeys when it thinks and when it expresses itself, and the rules it ought to follow in order to think and express itself correctly . . . The quadrivium, by contrast, consisted of a set of branches of learning related to things. Its role was to generate understanding of external realities and the laws which govern them, the laws of number,

the laws of space, the laws concerning the stars, and those which govern sounds.

(Durkheim 1977 [1938]: 47)

There are several variants and partial applications of such epistemological distinctions. One of the earliest descriptions of 'technical instruction' is as the training of the hand, which is contrasted with the education of the mind (Magnus 1888: 26). While no one would propose such a crude Cartesian dualism now, many descriptions of vocational education tacitly propound other mind/body distinctions such as the distinction between knowing and doing, theory and practice and between reason and experience.

Newman (1959 [1853]: 138) distinguished between liberal education which is general, and mechanical education, which is particular, a distinction adopted by others. Ashby (1974) proposes a similar distinction between *Bildung* (education) and *Ausbildung* (training) or between *allgemeine Bildung* (general education) and *berufliche Bildung* (vocational education/training) as Jochimsen (1978) prefers. Ashby (1974: 81) distinguished between a subject that leads to generalization and a technique that presumably is specific; and H. S. Williams argues that technical education is practical, in contrast to university education, which is, by implication, (more) theoretical (1963: 92) or academic. At other times Williams rests the distinctiveness of technical education on its applied nature in contrast to university education, which is by implication more 'pure' (1965: 71).

At its most general, this is a distinction between the abstract thought said to characterize general education and the concrete action thought to characterize vocational education. This is reflected in UNESCO's (1997) international standard classification of education, which distinguishes between general education, designed mainly to lead participants to a deeper understanding of a subject or group of subjects, and 'vocational or technical education', which is mainly designed to lead participants to acquire the practical skills, know-how and understanding necessary for employment in a particular occupation or trade or class of occupations or trades. The international standard subdivides tertiary education programmes into those that are primary theoretically oriented and those that are primarily practically oriented. In a recommendation on the integration of general and technical and vocational education UNESCO (1986: 334) maintained its definition of technical and vocational education as 'the acquisition of practical skills, attitudes, understanding and knowledge relating to occupations in various sectors of economic and social life'.

Associated with this dualism is the connotation if not definition of vocational education as being concerned with training to do repetitive tasks in contrast with higher level education, which is considered adaptive, generative and innovative. This in turn can be reduced to a distinction between skill and knowledge (Stevenson 1996).

Blunden (1995: 5) and Stevenson (1995) note the modern association of general education with conceptual understanding or declarative knowledge

and vocational education's association with demonstrated knowledge or pro-
cedural knowledge, which they trace to Ryle's (1975 [1949]: 28) distinction
between knowing that and knowing how, between propositional knowledge
and operational competence.

Shapin and Barnes (1976, cited in Skilbeck *et al.* 1994: 139) draw out this
distinction in three sets of dichotomies that have long persisted in educational discussions: 'the *sensual* and *concrete* character of the thought of the
lower orders against the *intellectual, verbal* and *abstract* qualities of the thinking of those above them'; 'the *simplicity* of the thought of the lower orders
and the *complexity* of that of their betters'; 'the *active use* of knowledge and
experience of the higher orders, contrasted with the *passive* and *automatic*
way in which the lower ranks were assumed to react to experience' (original
emphasis).

Some contemporary vocational education reformers found its epistemological distinctiveness in being based on competence. One arm of the definition of vocational and technical education in the US federal education
code is that it should 'include competency-based applied learning that con-
tributes to the academic knowledge, higher-order reasoning and problem-
solving skills, work attitudes, general employability skills, technical skills, and
occupation-specific skills, of an individual' (Legal Information Institute
2002). Similar claims have been made for vocational education in Australia,
South Africa, the UK and elsewhere.

While different epistemologies may be accepted, these do not map to any
familiar educational domain or sector such as vocational education or
higher education. Scientific experimental technique and the surgeon's skill
are clearly 'technical' as Huxley (1895) himself argued, but these have been
part of higher education at least since the early nineteenth century. Conversely, vocational education is clearly concerned with general theoretical
knowledge in accounting, electronics and information technology, to give
just three examples. Stevenson argues further that the theoretical knowledge
of the high-status occupations – the professions – is routinized by experienced
practitioners, thus collapsing the distinction between the types of knowledge
ascribed to vocational education and higher education:

> The differentiation between theoretical and practical knowledge is also
> based on the view that one set of occupations denoted professions (e.g.
> medicine, engineering, law and architecture) draws essentially on theory
> in pursuit of practice; while another set of occupations denoted vocations
> (e.g. the trades and office work) draws essentially upon highly routinised
> procedural knowledge in practice. This knowledge is often put down in
> such terms as personal, direct, experiential, tacit or implicit knowledge,
> to denote that it is 'unsophisticated' and 'trapped' in practice. However,
> there is now considerable research evidence that, with experience,
> so-called professionals also draw upon highly routinised procedural
> knowledge ('scripts') attached to templates for frequently encountered
> case types [references omitted]. That is, professionals transform their

theoretical knowledge into ('encapsulated') knowledge of proto-typical instances, and skills (scripts) for dealing with these instances. Clients or problems are seen in terms of types rather than underlying theoretical principles. Indeed the more experienced the professional, the more likely that contact will be lost with the initial discipline-based theoretical ideas taught to novices in the profession. Thus, the professional/vocational differentiation appears to have more to do with class considerations than with any essential differences in expert practice.

(Stevenson 2003)

3.3.2.2 Ways and place of learning

Many writers found vocational education's distinctiveness not only on ways of knowing but on ways of learning. This resonates with vocational education's historical identification with apprenticeships, where the learning–teaching method is said to be by observation, imitation and personal correction, rather than by application of general propositions delivered in classrooms and textbooks. This, in turn, is related to a distinction between general education's verbal or propositional knowledge and vocational education's non verbal or tacit knowledge (Stevenson 1998a: 134). There has also been some attempt to found vocational education's distinctiveness on the place of learning, at work or on the job.

While some vocational education may currently place more emphasis on a particular style or place of learning–teaching, this is surely highly contingent and is, in any case, only weakly distinctive of vocational education. The physician's art of diagnosis and the lawyer's skill of advocacy are learned on the job at least partly by imitation and, indeed, some research doctoral programmes seem to have similarities with apprenticeships.

3.3.2.3 As a field of knowledge

Some describe vocational education not so much as a way of knowing as a broad field of knowledge comparable to social sciences, physical sciences and the humanities. Summerfield and Evans (1990: 5) observe that in the early stages of the UK technical and vocational education initiative in the late 1970s and early 1980s technical and vocational education was understood to imply a specific curriculum content – 'technical' subjects such as information technology, electronics and 'craft, design and technology' and 'vocational' ones, including business education, food technology, community care and horticulture. But these fields are clearly not distinctive of vocational education since they are shared with higher education. They are therefore not sufficient to found vocational education's identity.

3.3.3 Teleological

Many thinkers found vocational education's identity on the purpose it serves; three types are identified here.

3.3.3.1 *Training for an extrinsic purpose compared with cultivation for intrinsic worth*

In the *Metaphysics*, Aristotle distinguishes philosophy, the knowledge of first principles and causes, which 'alone of the sciences is free since it alone is pursued for its own sake' from other activities which are pursued for extrinsic reasons. In *The Politics*, Aristotle contrasted the training for extrinsic purposes suitable for artisans, slaves and women with the cultivation of the arts for their intrinsic worth appropriate for leisured, free men. Newman (1959 [1853]: discourse v) expressed Aristotle's distinction as one between liberal or gentleman's knowledge and education and servile or mercantile education. Dewey (1916: 250–1, 260) observes that this association of liberal, intellectual education with the leisured class and practical education in preparation for useful labour with the servile class lead to 'probably the most deep seated antithesis which has shown itself in educational history' between culture and utility and to 'preparation for useful work [to] be looked down upon with contempt as an unworthy thing'. It informed the philosophy of civic humanism, which Cunningham and Hartley (2001: 2) note was espoused by those like the Earl of Shaftesbury, writing in the early 1700s, who revived a classical distinction between 'liberal' arts, which were free in the sense of civic freedom, and 'mechanical', 'useful' or even 'servile' artisanship. Cunningham and Hartley (2001: 2) argue that Shaftesbury's aristocratic schema was firmly based on the idea that 'trade' – commercial activity including creative work – was 'servile' or even 'slavish', as in 'slavish imitation'. Hyland (1999: 32–3) argues that the system of vocational education established in the UK in the early twentieth century 'was completely dominated by class interests and divisions, and could not escape the power relationships and educational connotations linked to such divisions'.

The distinction between training for an extrinsic purpose and cultivation for intrinsic worth also informs some modern conceptions of vocational education. Thus, Williams (1970) argued that the 'inner logic' of university and advanced education provides a 'functional differentiation' between them, between university education's intrinsic value and vocational education's instrumental value. Feinberg (1983) claims that the aim of vocational education is to transmit exploitable knowledge to participate in the market, whereas general education is to create a democratic society. Mitter (1988) recounts the establishment of secondary schools during the time when child labour laws were imperfectly enforced to draw a distinction between education as a preparation for work and education as a protection from work. Stevenson (1997: 6–7) notes differences in the valuing of knowledge, which, interestingly, he constructs more completely than the normal dualism: academic valuing of the production of new knowledge, general education's valuing of the development of the whole person for life, vocational education's valuing of competences for work and some parts of adult education's valuing of critical thinking leading to empowerment.

As Dewey pointed out (1916: 346), Aristotle's distinction between training for an extrinsic purpose and education for intrinsic worth is a special application of a more general distinction between means and ends. While this distinction between training and education has an attractive neatness, it is not an adequate characterization of vocational education. For in vocational education as much as in higher education there is a continuum between studies taught and learned for instrumental purposes and those pursued for intrinsic interest. Furthermore, in both sectors a study that may be of mainly intrinsic interest to some scholars has more instrumental value to others: studies are not one or the other for all scholars. Nonetheless, the distinction between means and ends has spawned cognate characterizations of vocational education.

3.3.3.2 Training for work, education for life

Huxley (1895: 405, 437) defined technical education as the teaching of handicrafts or trades. The US federal government adopted this understanding of vocational education as education for work. Palmer (1990: 22) notes that the US federal Vocational Education Act and its subsequent amendments, along with community college enabling legislation in many states, tie community college occupational studies to labour force development for jobs that require more than the high school diploma but less than the baccalaureate. From the US federal government's first direct funding of vocational education pursuant to the Smith-Hughes Act of 1917, vocational education was defined as education 'less than college grade' 'to fit for useful employment'. A similar definition was used in the George-Dean Act of 1936 and the George-Barden Act of 1946. The Vocational Education Act of 1963 retained the vocational purpose in the definition of vocational education but redefined the level to be 'semi-skilled or skilled' and excluded training for employment 'generally considered professional or as requiring a baccalaureate or higher degree'.

This view is current. Skilbeck and colleagues (1994: 3) wrote recently that ' "vocational" refers to those educational functions and processes which purport to prepare and equip individuals and groups for working life whether or not in the form of paid employment' and a similar definition had been proposed by several others. But training for work includes much of higher education, as Ashby observes:

> Notice that this distinction cuts across some familiar boundaries. It puts into the same category the education provided by the faculty of medicine at Cambridge and by the department of catering at Colchester Technical College; and it puts into the same category Oxford Greats and Workers' Education Association courses on archaeology.
>
> (Ashby 1974: 135)

Notwithstanding ahistorical claims that universities' modern vocationalism is a betrayal of their supposed essentially non-utilitarian virtues, from their foundation in the Middle Ages universities were largely vocational schools training for the church, medicine and the law (Cobban 1975: 165). The classical European model of the four faculties – philosophy,

theology, medicine and law – was an entirely vocational institution, producing graduates for teaching, the church, medical practice and state
administration (Tribe 2004: 607). Universities of the Italian Renaissance, or
Rinascimento as it was known in Italy its country of origin, were renowned for
their teaching of law and medicine, which typically comprised at least three-
quarters of the university (Grendler 2002). Universities have expanded the
occupations for which they train until the present time, as Dearing (1997)
observed.

So simple vocationalism is not sufficient to found technical education's
distinctiveness. Some writers, like the US federal legislature, seek to escape
this difficulty by restricting vocational education to 'below college grade'
explicitly or implicitly or with more consistency and frankness restrict
vocational education to the middle and lower occupational levels. This is
considered later.

3.3.3.3 Training for work directed by others, education for self-directed work

Aristotle's distinction is also a distinction between training for slaves and
artisans whose work is directed by others and education for free or self-
directing men. This has been characterized as a distinction between training
for paid employment and education for gentlemen of leisure but such a
distinction would not be seriously entertained in modern times.

More common has been a distinction between vocational education for
paid employment and higher education for the professions. This might have
had some value when there were fewer occupations claiming the status of
profession and most professionals practised on their own account. But even
then it had some uncomfortable anomalies. Insurance underwriting is a
venerable and highly skilled occupation in which brokers have long practised on their own account – we recall Shakespeare's Shylock and the
'names' of Lloyds of London – but insurance was very much 'trade' rather
than a profession. And most of the practitioners of the profession whose
training led to the formation of many venerable universities north of the
Alps – the clergy – were and remain employees of large bureaucracies, not
independent practitioners.

These days most lawyers, engineers and many doctors are employees and
so can not claim the autonomy of independent practice. Neither can they
claim special status from their exercise of independent judgement – carpenters, personal care attendants and bus drivers, for example, all exercise
considerable independent judgement in their work. But, arguably, the practitioners of the higher status occupations have more independence in the
direction of their work than lower status workers. This distinction, then,
collapses into a distinction of occupational level, which has informed many
accounts of the distinctive character of vocational education.

3.3.4 *Hierarchical*

Three types of hierarchical classification are identified: occupational level, educational level and cognitive level. They are considered in turn.

3.3.4.1 *Occupational level*

Plato expounds the view in *The Republic* that each person has different aptitudes that should be developed for the job to which they are best suited. Jobs in turn are commonly classified by level and vocational education is also commonly defined by derivation from the occupational level of its graduates. This has also been related to class. Educational institutions import the prestige from the range of occupations for which they normally prepare. Burton Clark (1960: 169) suggested that this in turn determined the relative esteem or status of vocational education institutions. Institutions that prepare students for high-status occupations enjoy high status by transference, whereas vocational education institutions prepare students for lower status vocations and thus are ascribed less esteem.

Williams (1961: 101) provided one of the most finely graded classifications of occupations in which to place vocational education:

6. post-professional;
5. professional;
4. technician (research design);
3. technician (production maintenance);
2. post-trade;
1. trade.

The category of 'technician' was considered problematic. Nonetheless, the British national vocational qualifications institutionalized an alignment of educational and occupational levels. Thus the national council for vocational qualifications established five levels of qualification:

5. professional level;
4. higher technician and management;
3. advanced craft or technician;
2. basic craft or intermediate level;
1. workers closely supervised.

The French classification of qualifications also sought to institutionalize an alignment of education and occupation in six levels:

Levels I and II: staff occupying positions usually requiring a level of training/ education equal or superior to the 'licence' (degree) obtained in engineering schools (ISCED 5 and higher).

Level III: staff occupying positions usually requiring the *brevet de technicien supérieur* (BTS – higher technician diploma) or a diploma from the *instituts universitaires de technologie*

	(IUTs) or at the end of the first cycle of higher education (ISCED 4).
Level IV:	staff occupying supervisory staff positions or possessing a level of qualification equivalent to a general, technical or vocational *baccalauréat* (ISCED 3).
Level V:	personnel occupying positions usually requiring a training level equivalent to the *brevets d'études professionnelles* (BEP – vocational studies certificate) or the certificate of vocational aptitude (CAP) (ISCED 2).
Level Va:	staff occupying positions requiring a short training of 1 year maximum, usually leading to the *certificat d'éducation professionnelle* (certificate of vocational education) or any other certification of the same nature.
Level VI:	personnel occupying positions requiring no training beyond the end of compulsory education.

Australia sought to link rates of pay to composite educational–occupational levels in the restructuring of industrial awards from the late 1980s (Carmichael 1992), leading to the reductive compartmentalization of knowledge and hierarchies noted by Stevenson (1992). Stevenson posited six different skill levels, from the routine proceduralized tasks to management responsibility over others and eight occupational levels, from operative to senior professional. This potentially generates 48 skill–occupational types and levels, although Stevenson observes that not all of the categories are used in practice.

However, no sooner had this alignment been established than it became outmoded by changes in the economy and therefore in the construction of work. Burgess (1986: 123) notes that the existing classification of occupations as craftsworker, technician, technologist and engineer already seems inappropriate in the light of the changes wrought by the new technology. So while occupational level or class may be part of a reasonably accurate descriptive definition of vocational education, such a definition would be contingent on the ascription of level or status in a particular society at a particular time. It also assumes that the current understanding of class is applicable to both contemporary and emerging economic developments.

3.3.4.2 Educational level

An obvious definition of vocational education is by educational level. Quebec neatly places its *collèges d'enseignement général et professionnel* (general and vocational colleges) as stage three in a comprehensive four-tiered total system of primary, secondary, college and university, since it is not possible to proceed from school to university without first completing the CEGEP's *diplôme d'études collégiales* (diploma of collegial studies). However, this neatness is unusual.

At least until 1993 programmes that led to skilled worker level in social work, commerce, agriculture and forestry in Austria were offered in secondary schools to students from the age of 15 and even now not all these programmes have been transferred to *Fachhochschulen* (tertiary vocational education institutions) and nurse training is still offered at secondary level in Germany. While vocational education had been transferred to tertiary education institutions earlier in most countries, there was nonetheless frequent equivocation, particularly in the early years, over whether vocational education is truly tertiary education. This led the sector's heads to try to define a level of occupational education that would differentiate such preparation for employment from secondary occupational programmes and from those of special postsecondary schools. Many vocational programmes assume an educational level of 10 years of formal schooling, which suggests that at least many vocational courses are secondary in level. Thus Medsker (1960: 54–5) argues that not all occupational training in 2-year colleges is at a semi-professional level. In his view it takes on the characteristics of trade training such as is frequently offered by high schools.

This leads some to argue that vocational education should be defined by students' achievement on their exit rather on their entry to the sector but this is hardly satisfactory. Venables took a longer view, arguing (1978: 15) that the then 'present overlap between secondary schools and technical colleges is likely to be a transient problem and there are sound psychological considerations for making the attainment of adult citizenship at 18 in an unambiguous educational way, that is by eligibility for entry to tertiary institutions'. This view seems to have been supported by experience. While the traditional locus of vocational education in the USA has been high schools, secondary vocational enrolments declined substantially since the second half of the twentieth century. The institutions that educate and train people for employment have grown in number and complexity over the past 30 years. Increasingly vocational education takes place in postsecondary institutions including community colleges, technical institutes and area vocational schools.

Even if vocational education's lower boundary is now secure, its reach at the upper level is contested. One history of vocational education is the development of upper levels of technical education, which are progressively transferred to upwardly mobile institutions and sectors, a history which is shared at least by the UK, Australia and New Zealand. Thus Pratt (1970: 33) noted in Britain the continuing shifting of responsibility for lower level programs as colleges aspired to higher status and therefore concentrated on higher level programmes.

In Australia, in the period of the implementation of the Martin report from 1964 the technical education sector lost many of its technology programmes, initially to the universities and later to the colleges of advanced education and institutes of technology. Following adoption of the Kangan report in Australia in the mid-1970s there was a contest between the technical and further education sector and the advanced education sector over associate diploma-level qualifications which advanced education won. Currently the Australian qualifications framework has an overlap between vocational education and training and higher education in responsibility for diplomas, and for advanced diplomas, which at least some technical and further education commentators fear will result in higher education again taking over their more popular upper level programmes.

Medsker and Tillery (1971: 60) noted attempts by leaders of US community colleges to establish a distinctive place between secondary and other postsecondary schools but this has generally failed. In most US states community colleges have two roles: vocational education, which is shared with a plethora of other secondary and postsecondary institutions; and offering the first 2 years of baccalaureates, which is shared with 4-year colleges and universities. This dual role places community colleges at an ambiguous level in US education.

Even community colleges' transfer role in providing the first 2 years of baccalaureates is problematic. It is clearly higher education in level. But direct admission to a 4-year college or university is generally available only to students who complete their high school diploma with a grade point average in about the top third or for those who gain a comparable score in one of the national scholastic aptitude tests. Community colleges have open entry and thus admit students who do not meet the entry standards of selective colleges and universities, as well as students who meet these requirements but who prefer to take at least the first 2 years of their baccalaureate locally. So even this role is confounded for community colleges: they tend to be perceived to be of a lower level of higher education – that is, of a lower standard – because of their open entry. So while vocational education may occupy a distinctive place among some educational sectors in some jurisdictions at some times, this is variable and contingent: it is different in different jurisdictions at any one time and changes within many jurisdictions over time.

3.3.4.3 Cognitive level

Engeström (1994) posited a hierarchy of learning: first-order learning (conditioning, imitation and rote learning); second-order learning (trial and error or learning by doing and problem solving or investigative learning); and third-order learning (questioning and transforming the context or community of practice). This is sometimes mapped to educational levels, with vocational education said to involve first- and second-order learning and higher education involving second- and third-order learning and the development of Schön's critically reflective practitioner.

UNESCO's (1997) international standard classification of education makes a related distinction between the programmes that give 'access to professions with high skills requirements (e.g. medicine, dentistry, architecture, etc.), and those programmes that are practical/ technical/ occupationally specific' and which, by implication, have low-skill requirements. But this section has already noted Stevenson's (2003) questioning of the distinction between levels of expert practice used to support the differentiation of professional from vocational occupations and therefore educational programmes.

3.3.5 Pragmatic

Having failed to find an analytical or principled definition of vocational education, many people resort to a pragmatic definition of vocational education, one that seeks to state actual practice. The first pragmatic definition of vocational education is residual, that which is left over from the specification of the other sectors.

3.3.5.1 Residual – not elsewhere included

In many jurisdictions, vocational education is the last sector to be established formally. It is therefore sometimes made up of the parts of post-compulsory education left over from previous structurings. Thus Cotgrove (1958: 194) observed:

> The role of technical colleges in the educational system can be seen to be a changing and unstable one. They have acted historically as a residual category – making up the educational deficiencies of the primary and secondary system, providing vocational training rejected by the universities, meeting the need for an intermediate level, and of those who, for a variety of reasons, wished to pursue a university course in a technical college.

Vocational education has also been described as 'not elsewhere included', 'non-university sector', education that is neither secondary nor higher education and as 'filling in the gaps or complementing the provisions of other sectors of education' (Batrouney 1985: 134). In the United Kingdom, 'the further education sector may be described as the "ragbag" into which are deposited courses not provided elsewhere' (*THES* 1973: 1). In the USA, part of the definition of vocational and technical education in the federal education code is that it prepares individual 'for careers (other than careers requiring a baccalaureate, master's, or doctoral degree)'.

In Australia, the Kangan committee established a mission for technical and further education from the mid-1970 to the mid-1990s, which is still influential in shaping the scope and values of the sector. But Kangan did not define an identity for the sector, as it itself acknowledged. The opening sentence of the committee's report describes its role and that of technical and further education residually – that left over from the other sectors. The Kangan committee (1974: 2) acknowledged interest in a precise definition of technical and further education but 'it believes that it is beyond human capacity to devise a precise definition of technical or further education that would stand the test of time'.

3.3.5.2 Status quo

The initial residual understanding of vocational education readily develops into another pragmatic construction of identity, the status quo: what happens to be the arrangement in a particular place at a particular time. Thus

Cotgrove (1958: vi) wrote: 'Technical education has been defined, therefore, for the purposes of this study, as those forms of education which have been included in the administrative conception of technical education in England.' Arrangements are commonly identified by institution: the vocational education sector is what the institutions identified as vocational education institutes do. The institutional construction of identity has also been proposed as an analytical basis for the sector's identity and has been adopted by the sector's coordinating body in Australia. Arrangements are also commonly identified by programme. The programmatic construction of vocational education identifies the sector by a characteristic set of programmes.

As will be seen, in Australia the institutional construction of vocational education largely coincides with the programmatic construction of the sector. But this coincidence is unnecessary and indeed is unusual in English-speaking countries. In Canada, the UK and the USA, vocational education institutions offer higher education programmes in addition to vocational education programmes; and in these countries and in Australia, there are higher education institutions that offer vocational education programmes. The institutional construction of identity is unproblematic if practice is consistent, at least within the jurisdiction of interest if not internationally and if it is consistent with other constructions of identity. However, this is rarely the case and is of little use to a comparative study since practice varies so greatly between jurisdictions.

The pragmatic construction of vocational education's identity is considered a strength by some writers. In a paper descriptively titled 'Chameleon or phoenix: the metamorphosis of TAFE', Anderson (1998: 6–7) charted the changes in the identity of Australian technical and further education 'which to date have threatened TAFE's survival as a distinct sector of education and training'. Nonetheless, Anderson considers vocational education and training's adaptation to contemporary needs and circumstances to be a strength. While this may be an institutional strength, it is a weakness analytically and a liability in comparative studies.

3.4 Discussion of the definition of 'vocational education'

Thompson (1973: 105) observed that a major influence on vocational education is the definitions that have been applied to it and that have given it meaning and substance. This is a specific application of Bourdieu's argument that even the act of identifying and naming a group and one may infer by extension an activity, exercises control over that activity:

> To give a name, one single name, to an individual or group of individuals . . . is to adopt one of the possible viewpoints towards them and claim to impose it as the single, legitimate viewpoint. What is at stake in

the symbolic struggle is the monopoly of legitimate nomination, the dominant viewpoint which, in gaining recognition as the legitimate viewpoint, causes its truth as a specific, situated, dated viewpoint to be misconstrued. Thus, to escape the danger of polemical recuperation, we might think of designating each of the sectors of the space by a plurality of concepts designed to remind us that each of the regions of the space can, by definition, only be conceptualised and expressed in its relation to the others.

(Bourdieu 1988 [1984]: 26)

Nonetheless, to most vocational education's lack of a clear identity is a weakness. (Goozee (2001 [1993]: 6) observes that: 'To some extent, technical education in Australia had to be self-defining and it therefore lacked the immediate recognition of roles and structures that characterized both the school and higher education sectors.' Clark (1973: 329) warned that 'The non-universities will fail us if they evolve only as carbon copies of the past or as institutions that zig and zag with the opportunism of the moment. A firm self-concept is essential to their promising new role in society.'

There are a number of difficulties with founding vocational education's identity on a single characteristic. This chapter has found that no single characteristic consistently identifies vocational education in different juris-dictions or even in the same jurisdiction over different historical periods. Since a characteristic used to identify vocational education at one time has had to be changed as vocational education itself adapted and changed, it is unlikely that any single characteristic identified now will be adequate to encompass the next historical shift. It may not even be desirable to fix vocational education on a single characteristic since this may introduce a rigidity that thwarts the very changes in society and the nature of work for which vocational education is meant to be stimulating and equipping communities.

A characteristic such as Rushbrook's (1997: 104) 'abstracted institutional teleology' or Stevenson's (1998a: 155) 'positive purpose . . . characterised by clarity, coherence and continuity' would overcome many of these difficulties. But it has not been possible to identify such a purpose of sufficient generality to encompass vocational education even in the jurisdictions we have con-sidered while at the same time being sufficiently precise to delineate it from other forms of education. Neither has it been possible to found a purpose that encompasses vocational education's past, let alone being a guide for the future.

Yet vocational education is clearly identified when observed on many occasions, presumably using Wittgenstein's (1968) family resemblance. An alternative approach is therefore to establish vocational education's identity not on a unique characteristic, but on a unique combination of character-istics. In its 1996/97 annual report the Australian federal government's vocational education body described vocational education and training as post-compulsory education and training that provides people with the skills and learning required by enterprises and industries, thus combining characteristics of educational level, content and purpose. The Smith-Hughes Act of 1917, which was the first US federal act to fund vocational education, used a compound definition of vocational education; and the current US federal legislation defines vocational and technical education as a combination of several characteristics. White (2001) observes of Ireland that:

> The characteristics of those [technical] colleges have been identified as a) the provision of course programs of shorter duration than universities, b) the practical orientation of curricula, c) responsiveness to industry and business, d) limited ranges of subjects mostly in engineering and business studies, e) little, or only applied research and f) heavy teaching loads for faculty.

These compound definitions are rather too specific and it is unclear whether an activity needs to have all the characteristics precisely to be considered vocational education. The better approach is to define vocational education by the four general characteristics we have considered – epistemological, teleological, hierarchical and pragmatic. Thus, we may deem vocational education to be the development and application of knowledge and skills for middle-level occupations needed by society from time to time. This definition relies on the concept of applied knowledge as if Aristotle's notion of art or applied science (techne) is adequate, which it clearly is not without elaboration. It also locates vocational education by occupational level thus making it subject to shifts in occupational hierarchy and economic structure. While it would be more satisfying to locate vocational education by educational level, this is probably the preference of an educationalist not shared by employers, workers and government.

While considering the definition of 'vocational education' it is useful to note that an apparent cognate 'vocation' has quite a different emphasis, at least originally somewhat similar to the current German concept of *Beruf.*

3.5 Vocation – *Beruf*

The word 'vocation' is derived from the Latin *vocatio* 'summons' and from *vocare* 'to call', which in turn is derived from *vox* 'voice'. One of the earliest uses of 'vocation' or 'calling' was the Christian monastic tradition established in the Middle Ages of novices being called away from normal life to dedicate themselves to prayer and contemplation in monasteries (Dawson 2005: 223). This reflected the view, ultimately derived from the ancient Greeks, that contemplation was of higher value than productive work and manual labour. The Protestant Reformation of the late fifteenth and early sixteenth centuries and the accompanying challenge of the agrarian feudal economies of late medieval Europe by the more entrepreneurial urban economies led to the valuing of daily work as a divine vocation and thus to the Protestant work ethic, a term coined by Max Weber in *The Protestant Ethic and the Spirit of*

Capitalism. As capitalism developed vocation increasingly became associated with careers and occupations in the paid economy, thus adopting a meaning completely opposite from its initial meaning.

The German concept of *Beruf* has some of the initial English connotation of vocation as a way of life. It refers to an occupation that is formally recognized by employers, unions, government and society generally as having a specified place in the economy that is reflected in its wage level, status and general social standing. Each *Beruf* is based on a specified body of systematically related theoretical knowledge (*Wissen* – knowing that), a set of practical skills (*Können* – know-how) and a collection of working life skills. Therefore *Berufsbildung* or vocational education does not entail training young people for a small number of specific tasks at one company immediately on finishing training, but preparing people for a life in an industry including the changing economic and social environments of a whole occupational field. This broader and deeper understanding of *Berufsbildung* should be kept in mind when comparing vocational education in the jurisdictions following the German tradition and is an option for reforming vocational education elsewhere.

4

Countries

This chapter describes tertiary education in the countries compared in this study: Australia, Canada, the UK and the USA. In Chapter 9, we consider student transfer rates for Australia, Scotland and the US states of California, Colorado and Texas, so these jurisdictions are described in some detail to put transfer rates in context. Since the most similar systems design has been adopted for the study, systems are compared that are similar, but which nevertheless have different characteristics which will be the key points compared.

4.1 Tertiary education in its economic and social context

As we observed in Chapter 2, social systems are open. So while we pragmatically choose to study subsystems such as tertiary education, it is important to study them in their broader social and historical context. For a very broad range of factors influence vocational and higher education such as the organization and functioning of the labour markets they serve. The degree to which companies operate internal labour markets rather than rely on external occupational labour markets is of crucial importance in structuring the shape and nature of vocational education. Governments' regulation of occupations such as doctors, electricians, nurses and plumbers affects vocational and higher education considerably. The historical circumstances and processes of industrialization and the structure of countries' economies and industries also shape tertiary education. However, only the most salient factors such as the nature of occupational regulation will be included in this overview. Other factors will be noted where they are directly relevant.

Since the most similar systems design (Przeworski and Teune 1970) has been adopted for the study it compares tertiary education systems that are similar, but which nevertheless have different characteristics which will be the key points compared. The comparators are wealthy Anglo countries:

Australia, Canada, the UK and the USA. Table 4.1 gives an idea of the relative scale of the vocational education and higher education sectors in each country.

The first row in the table is Australia, which has a very high share of total tertiary enrolments in vocational education (65 per cent), largely because of its very high proportion of part-time vocational education students. In the next row is the UK which has a lesser proportion but still a majority of enrolments in further education programmes (56 per cent). Third is the USA, which has a minority of enrolments in 2-year colleges (39 per cent), and finally Canada has the lowest proportion of community college enrolments (37 per cent), largely because of its extraordinarily low proportion of part-time enrolments in community colleges. As is elaborated in the next section, Australian vocational education and training, UK further education, US 2-year college education and Canadian community college education may all be classified as tertiary type B education. This is distinguished from baccalaureate level programmes offered by universities in Australia, Canada and the UK and by 4-year colleges and universities in the USA.

4.2 Australia

Australia is a sparsely populated English-speaking first-world country located on the southwest of the Pacific Rim whose neighbours are densely populated developing countries of diverse Asian and Pacific cultures. Much of its past is in the UK, but many see its future in the USA.

4.2.1 Geography

Australia is 7.7 million square kilometres in area, a little smaller than the USA's 48 contiguous states, located between latitudes 10 and 42° south, at about the same latitude as southern Africa and the middle of South America.

Table 4.1 Proportion of tertiary education enrolments by tertiary type and study load in Australia, Canada, the UK and the USA

	Tertiary type B (vocational) (%)			*Tertiary type A (higher ed.) (%)*			*All (%)*
	Part-time	*Full-time*	*Total*	*Part-time*	*Full-time*	*Total*	
Australia	59	6	**65**	12	22	**35**	**100**
UK	37	20	**56**	14	27	**44**	**100**
US	24	14	**39**	17	44	**61**	**100**
Canada	7	31	**37**	19	44	**63**	**100**

Australia's population is 20 million people and so there are 2.6 people per square kilometre, less than Canada's 3.2, one-tenth of the USA's 31 and almost one-hundredth of the UK's 246 people per square kilometre. Most of Australia is flat and dry, with a mostly temperate fertile coastal strip of up to 500 kilometres wide. Of Australia's population, 83 per cent lives within 50 kilometres of the coastline and almost 80 per cent live in cities and major towns. Australia's geography is similar to Canada's with a big population centre on the southwest coast separated by a large desert from the major population centres on the east coast. However, Australia's desert is hot and dry, while Canada's is, of course, frozen.

Australia was settled from 40,000 to 60,000 years ago, possibly in successive waves of migration that ended from 15,000 to 20,000 years ago. From about 2000 years ago Trepang fishers from the Makassan Straits in present-day Indonesia visited the northern coast of Australia for several months each year until they were outlawed by the newly federated Australian government in 1906 and people from the north still fish in Australian waters. Migrations have continued until the present, alternately subsidized and suppressed by Australian governments.

Australia was forcibly settled by the British in 1788 who over the next century drove indigenous peoples from their lands. For most of the period since then Australia's economy has been based on primary industries: initially wool, gold and wheat. Since the oil shocks of the 1970s Australia has undergone industrial restructuring, in common with other industrialized countries, and Australia's economy has diversified into service industries, including education, which attracts large numbers of international students. In 2006 Australia's biggest exports were coal (exports now valued at Aus$23.3 billion), iron ore ($14.4 billion), transport ($14 billion) and education was Australia's fourth largest export, worth $10.2 billion.

Most of Australia's population of 21 million is concentrated in two widely separated coastal regions. By far the largest of these in area and population is in the southeast and east around Australia's biggest cities Sydney and Melbourne. The smaller of the regions is 3000 kilometres distant in the southwest of the continent around Perth. In both coastal regions, the population is concentrated in urban centres, particularly the state and territory capital cities. Half the area of the continent contains only 0.3 per cent of the population and the most densely populated 1 per cent of the continent contains 84 per cent of the population. Australia's biggest cities are Sydney (4 million), Melbourne (3.7 million), Brisbane (1.8 million), Perth (1.5 million) and Adelaide (1 million).

While 23 per cent of Australia's population was born overseas, the large majority of Australia's population is white: 12.5 per cent of Australians were born in Europe and the former USSR, 6 per cent in the UK, 5.5 per cent in Asia, 2 per cent in Oceania, 1 per cent in the Middle East and North Africa and less than 2 per cent in other regions. Indigenous Australians are some 2.5 per cent of the population. Some 17 per cent of Australia's population speak a language other than English at home. Australia has a gross domestic product of $766.8 billion (purchasing power parity), the 19th biggest in the world. Its GDP per capita is $37,500 (PPP), rank 23 in the world. The Gini index of inequality of Australia's distribution of family income is 30.5, which is above the median of big wealthy countries (Denmark 23.2, USA 45).

4.2.2 Tertiary education overview

Australia's tertiary education is divided into two sectors: higher education and vocational education and training. Most students are enrolled part-time in vocational education and training. Australia has an unusually low proportion of full-time vocational education and training students (6 per cent of Australian vocational education students study full-time compared with 35 per cent in the UK, 37 per cent in the USA and a very high 82 per cent in Canada).

The relative weight of the sectors can be seen by considering students' study load. Study load is recorded in higher education as equivalent full-time student load. Student study load is recorded in Australian vocational education and training as annual contact hours. These are the total nominal hours of student learning supervised by a vocational education provider. The Williams Committee (1979: 55) posited that a normal full-time study load for a vocational education student was 720 hours per annum. This works out at 26 hours of supervised learning over two semesters of 14 weeks each. Annual contact hours may therefore be converted to equivalent full-time students by dividing by 720. This shows that vocational education and training comprises 44 per cent of total tertiary education study load (part-time 28 per cent, full-time 16 per cent). As with other countries, the biggest tertiary education study load in Australia is taken by full-time higher education students, who comprise 42 per cent of total tertiary load. Part-time higher education comprises 14 per cent of total tertiary education load.

4.2.3 Higher education

What is called higher education in Australia has been long dominated by the 37 public universities. Australian higher education also includes two small private universities and five specialist public academies, which together enrol less than 2 per cent of total student load, and 84 private non-university providers. Most of the private non-university providers are religious colleges (49 per cent of private student load), providers of occupational qualifications, mostly in one or two fields (42 per cent) and providers of university preparatory and transfer programmes (7 per cent).

Universities range in size from 3000 to 35,000 equivalent full-time student load, with an average of 17,500 equivalent full-time study load (EFTSL), which is rather large compared with the other countries considered in this study. Some 21 per cent of university student load is in postgraduate programmes but most of this is in coursework or taught programmes; only 5 per cent of higher education load is in research masters or doctorates. Some 67 per cent of students study full-time on campus, 33 per cent study part-time and 13 per cent study externally, mostly part-time.

Eight of the generally oldest and biggest capital city universities have formed themselves into a group of research intensive universities. The Australian Group of Eight, like the UK Russell Group, has no formal standing, even within the universities' peak body, Universities Australia. However, it has a small secretariat and is a useful grouping for some purposes and will be used in this study. Five universities that originated as capital city technology institutes have formed themselves into the Australian Technology Network and six universities established in the 1960s and early 1970s have formed a group, Innovative Research Universities Australia, which compares itself with the UK's 1994 group.

Universities are governed by councils or senates with from 15 to 22 members, one-third of whom are typically internal to the university: the vice-chancellor as chief executive officer and staff and student representatives. All but one public university is established by state or territory acts of parliament and they are formally accountable to their state or territory legislatures. While this remains important for some matters, almost all universities' public funding comes from the Australian government from which derives considerable, albeit formally indirect, power.

4.2.4 *Vocational education and training*

Some 85 per cent of Australian vocational education and training student load is provided by 66 public technical and further education institutes offering courses on 1100 campuses and by five other government providers including agricultural colleges and multisector higher education institutions. Ten per cent of vocational education is provided by 1400 private providers receiving public funds and 4 per cent is provided by 513 community education providers. Five universities are dual-sector institutions, having substantial student load in both higher education and vocational education and training. All dual-sector universities institutions have their origins in technical colleges, all but one in the late nineteenth or early twentieth century. These institutions retained their lower level work while acquiring baccalaureate granting and then doctoral granting status, unlike other former technical colleges, which discarded their lower level programmes as they acquired the right to offer higher level degrees.

As may be expected from the very high proportion of part-time students, 67 per cent of vocational education and training students study while employed. Some 78 per cent of students study for employment-related reasons and 17 per cent for personal development. Only 5 per cent of Australian vocational education students are studying to proceed to further study, which is much lower than the other jurisdictions considered in this chapter.

Some 56 per cent of funding for publicly supported vocational education is provided by state and territory governments, 22 per cent by the Australian government and 13 per cent of revenue is from fee for service, which includes employer charges and full-fee paying programmes, 5 per cent from tuition fees and 5 per cent from other trading activities. Public vocational education and training providers are funded and to varying extents planned and managed through state and territory government departments. Publicly funded vocational education and training programmes are required to conform to the national training framework, which specifies training packages and national recognition of all qualifications that conform to the framework. Training packages specify the competences that a person must achieve to be awarded a registered qualification and the assessment guidelines that must be used to assess whether candidates have achieved the required competences. But training packages do not specify the content of the learning experience or the learning–teaching method or duration. The national training framework was established in 1998 and there are still some variations between the jurisdictions in the way it is administered.

The Australian government has been concerned to ensure that workplace-based education does not wither as the traditional industries for which the older apprenticeships are required disappear or are greatly reduced in size. It has therefore developed new apprenticeships to introduce workplace-based training to newer occupations. The New South Wales vocational education and training accreditation board lists 607 declared traineeships in areas such as community services, entertainment, information technology, office administration and tourism. Apprenticeships and traineeships may taught entirely on the job, perhaps but not necessarily involving technical and further education institutes to assess competences. They may equally have periods of off-the-job training, as typically the apprenticeships do, which is usually but not necessarily taken at TAFE institutes. In 2006 there were 400,000 apprentices and trainees or about 24 per cent of all publicly funded vocational education and training students.

4.2.5 Occupational regulation

When the state regulates a vocation it very often specifies an educational requirement, which, in turn, establishes and often structures a formal education provision. The extent and nature of occupational regulation therefore has an important effect on tertiary education. Almost every occupation regulated in Australia is regulated by each state or territory. Exceptions are aircraft and ship pilots, who are registered by the Australian government. While historically there have been distinct differences between jurisdictions' occupational regulation, there has been a convergence of standards, processes and recognition over the last 5 to 10 years. Annoying differences remain, but the arrangements for Australia's largest state, New South Wales, are a fair representation of the arrangements of the other states.

New South Wales has separate acts to restrict practice to registered practitioners of 19 occupations. These are mostly the higher status occupations such as architects, medical practitioners and surveyors, but also include some newer occupations such as driving instructors, private investigators and real estate valuers. Section 21 of the Industrial and Commercial Training Act 1989 gives the relevant minister power to designate any occupation a declared trade or calling. Section 24 of the act prohibits people under 21 from being employed in declared trades unless they are engaged as apprentices.

The NSW vocational education and training accreditation board lists 111 apprenticeships from aircraft maintenance engineering to wood machining. It is effectively impossible to practise many of these trades without having completed an apprenticeship, either because of another legislative provision proscribing unqualified practitioners or a requirement imposed by employers, unions or both. In addition there are various licensing requirements for businesses such as tow truck operators and travel agents, which are also effectively occupational regulations. In other occupations, there are high proportions of unqualified practitioners, driven largely by a high demand for skilled labour. Unions are often unable to regulate entry to the workforce because they are competing with other unions that have coverage of all or part of their work.

4.3 Canada

Canada is a land of vast distances and rich natural resources. It is almost 10 million square kilometres in area, somewhat larger than the USA and the second largest country in the world after the Russian Federation, mostly plains with mountains in the west and lowlands in the southeast. Its climate varies from temperate in the south to subarctic and arctic in the north. Approximately 90 per cent of its population of 33 million is concentrated within 160 kilometres of the USA/Canada border. Canada has a gross domestic product of $1.181 trillion (purchasing power parity), the 12th biggest in the world. Its GDP per capita is $35,700 (PPP), the 16th highest in the world. The Gini index of inequality of Canada's distribution of family income is 32.6, which is at about the median of big wealthy countries (Denmark 23.2, USA 45).

Canada has one of the highest postsecondary participation rates for 18–21-year-olds and is distinctive in having a very high proportion of full-time students, both in universities and community colleges. Some 75 per cent of Canadian tertiary education students are enrolled full-time, much higher than Australia (where 28 per cent of tertiary education students study full-time), the UK (47 per cent) and the USA (58 per cent).

Canada is a federation of ten provinces and three territories. There is no such thing as a 'Canadian system' of higher education. There is no federal department of education or higher education, nothing equivalent to a national policy for higher education and there is no national standard for either secondary or higher education. Consequently, higher education evolved in different ways in different provinces. The provincial systems of tertiary education comprise a university sector and a community college sector. Universities are relatively similar across provinces. No province has created a stratified university sector and universities are not very specialized by function.

Since the Royal Commission on Industrial Training and Technical Education in 1910 the federal government has provided direct assistance to agricultural, technical and vocational education through capital grants and student financial support. Community colleges developed strongly from the 1960s, although differently in each province. For example, provinces such as Manitoba, New Brunswick and Ontario operate non-degree institutions that offer technical/vocational programmes but do not have a formal university transfer function, while non-degree institutions in Alberta, British Columbia and Quebec have a formal university transfer or pre-university function and these provinces have created formal structures for coordinating the sectors. British Columbia's tertiary education most resembles the archetypal arrangement in the USA, in which community colleges having an important function preparing students to transfer to universities.

In contrast in Quebec, students cannot move directly from secondary school to university but must first complete a 2-year programme in one of the *collèges d'enseignement général et professionnel* (colleges of general and vocational education). The 2-year programme for students seeking to transfer to universities is a diploma of collegial studies (*diplôme d'études collégiales*). Bilingual Quebec is unique among the jurisdictions considered in this study in requiring all students to complete a short-cycle higher education programme before proceeding to medium or long-cycle higher education. Quebec achieved this neatness by a *revolution tranquille* (quiet revolution) in 1967. Quebec's *collèges d'enseignement général et professionnel* also offer a 3-year terminal vocational track.

4.4 United Kingdom

The United Kingdom is 244,820 square kilometres in area and has a population of 61 million. Its strong national government has devolved some powers to the Scottish Parliament, the National Assembly for Wales, and the Northern Ireland Assembly. The UK has a gross domestic product of $1.928 trillion (purchasing power parity), the sixth biggest in the world. Its GDP per capita is $31,800 (PPP), the 28th highest in the world. The Gini index of inequality of the UK's distribution of family income is 36, which is above the median of big wealthy countries (Denmark 23.2, USA 45).

Tertiary education in the UK is divided into two sectors. There are more than 600 further education colleges, which offer English-language programmes, year 12 programmes, vocational programmes (known in the UK as career-based courses), access programmes and some degree programmes by arrangement with higher education institutions. Higher education institutions comprise more than 50 higher education colleges and over 90 universities. Universities tend to be classified by age: ancient, recent and new. An informal self-selected group of 19 'research-led' institutions have formed themselves into the Russell Group and this is also sometimes used to group universities by research intensity.

Part-time further education students are the largest group of tertiary students being 37 per cent of all tertiary education students, but not very much larger than the next largest group, full-time higher education students, who are 27 per cent of the total. These in turn are balanced by the other student categories: full-time further education students (20 per cent) and part-time higher education students (14 per cent).

While there is a formal distinction between further and higher education in the United Kingdom, the unequivocally higher education qualifications of the ordinary baccalaureate and foundation degree are offered by colleges of further education under licence or 'franchise' to a collaborating university or consortium of institutions as well as by universities in their own right and further education colleges have offered higher education programmes in some form for a considerable time. Furthermore, following the adoption of the recommendation of the Dearing Committee, all higher education programmes offered by colleges of further education in England are funded by the Higher Education Funding Council for England. This covers all first-degree, postgraduate, higher national diploma and certificate, diploma of higher education and certificate of education courses offered by colleges of further education.

4.4.1 Scotland

Scotland has a formally unified university sector, but they are informally grouped by age of establishment. The Scottish *ancient universities* – those founded before the nineteenth century – are the University of St Andrews (founded 1411), University of Glasgow (1451), University of Aberdeen (1494) and the University of Edinburgh (1583). (The other British ancient universities are the University of Oxford, which was founded in 1249 and the University of Cambridge, founded in 1284.) The *1960s universities* – those institutions with university status before the Further and Higher Education Act 1992 – are the University of Strathclyde (1964), Heriot Watt University (1966), University of Dundee (granted university status in 1967) and the University of Stirling (1967). The *post-1992 universities* – those institutions redesignated as universities by the Further and Higher Education Act 1992 or founded after the act – are Robert Gordon University (1992), Napier University (1992), University of Paisley (1992), Glasgow Caledonian University (1993), the University of Abertay Dundee (granted university status in 1994) and Queen Margaret University (granted full university status in 2007).

As we shall see in detail when we examine student transfer in Chapter 9, Scottish universities are informally highly differentiated by status. Three universities win about 60 per cent of formula-based research funding, another five win around 30 per cent and the remaining universities gain 10 per cent of research funding. Gallacher (2002: 5) says that further education colleges have moved from being fairly marginal and often having low status to having a much more significant role in Scottish tertiary education. Enrolments have more than doubled from 175,216 in 1985–86 to 383,543 in 1999–2000, most in full-time higher education programmes, which have grown by over 300 per cent over the period. Nonetheless, 70 per cent of all Scottish tertiary education students are enrolled part-time in further education colleges.

Until recently the Scottish Executive funded education by the sector of the provider rather than by the level of programme, so higher education programmes offered by further education colleges were funded by the Scottish Further Education Funding Council, not the Scottish Higher Education Funding Council. As a result, says Gallacher (2002: 14), Scotland has two sectors of higher education that are different in their curriculum, culture, study skills and methods of assessment. The sectors have developed in parallel but with little attempt to plan them as a joint system. Most links and relationships between the sectors are ad hoc arrangements between programmes and institutions. However, as Gallacher acknowledges, Scotland has made considerable progress in systematizing its awards. All Scottish qualifications are built up from modules and in 2001 they were been brought into a single unifying framework, the Scottish credit and qualifications framework. This framework describes each qualification's level and credit value in SCQF points. The Scottish Qualifications Authority is implementing a credit accumulation and transfer framework across further education and higher education. This is described further in Chapter 5.

Scotland introduced income-contingent fees for higher education graduates in the form of the 'graduate endowment' in 2001. It was £2289 (US $4685, €3183) for students who began their degree in session 2006–07, but the Scottish government planned to scrap the fee in 2007. The Scottish Executive is consulting on a review of occupational standards and national guidelines on programmes leading to the further education teaching qualification. Since 2002 the Scottish Executive has been conducting an extensive review of higher education, which has considered the performance of the Scottish Higher Education Funding Council, the future of higher education in Scotland and the competitiveness of higher education in Scotland.

4.5 United States of America

The United States of America is 9,629,091 square kilometres in area and has a population of 301 million. The USA has a gross domestic product of $13.06 trillion (purchasing power parity), the biggest in the world. Its GDP per capita is $43,800 (PPP), the 10th highest in the world. The Gini index of inequality of the USA's distribution of family income is 45, which is the highest of big wealthy countries. Denmark's Gini index is 23.2 and countries with higher indices are China 46.9, Chile 54.9, Brazil 56.7 and South Africa 57.8.

The USA is a federation of 50 states. In comparison with Australia and the UK, education is highly decentralized. State legislation establishes school rating districts which raise funds for school education and determine their distribution within their district. Since districts differ greatly in economic and cultural wealth schools in different districts have very different resources. A large amount of vocational education in the USA is conducted by industries' internal training and educational programmes which range from trade apprenticeships to the highest levels of collegiate graduate work.

4.5.1 Community or 2-year colleges

Perhaps the USA's most distinctive higher education institution is the institution known successively as the junior, community and 2-year college. Junior colleges were first proposed in 1831 by Henry Tappan, president of the University of Michigan and were further prominently promulgated by William Mitchell, a trustee of the University of Georgia, and William Folwell, president of the University of Minnesota. They proposed that their universities foster the development of strong academies and high schools, which would complete a student's general education near their home, so that their universities may develop 'high-order scholarship' as did the universities of France and Germany.

The model for the 'lower schools' was the German gymnasium, which offers 2 additional years for those planning to pursue higher studies. In 1892 president William Rainey Harper reconstituted the University of Chicago into a lower division providing general education and an upper division providing professional education. While this structural change has been enduring, Martorana (1973: 96) notes that Harper considered it a stage to a more radical repositioning of his university, 'aiming at the eventual abolition of the lower division or "junior college" ' (first use of the term, as he named it, in 1896).

Thus, 2-year colleges were first proposed in the USA in the middle of the nineteenth century as a way of allowing 4-year colleges to emulate the Germany research universities, symbolized by Wilhelm von Humboldt's founding of the University of Berlin in 1810. However, these early proposals were not followed. The first institution recognized as a 2-year college was a high school in Joliet, Illinois, which added years 13 and 14 in 1901 and a similar development followed in Fresno in California in 1910. Thus, as Clark (1960) observes, the public junior college is entirely a twentieth-century phenomenon. None existed at the turn of the twentieth century. While there were 19 units that could be considered public junior colleges by 1915, their total enrolment did not exceed 600 students. Two-year colleges did not grow rapidly until after World War I. While universities were not successful in relinquishing their lower divisions, they did establish a formal division between the general education lower division and the professional education upper division.

A second major force for the establishment of 2-year colleges, advanced in the middle of the twentieth century by University of California system president Clark Kerr, was to cater for the great expansion of higher education to accommodate the post-World War II baby boomers. That is, 2-year colleges were proposed to protect the selectivity of the universities that had by that time established themselves as research institutions.

Since 2-year colleges originated as 2-year extensions of secondary school they were administered, staffed and funded as extensions of the secondary school systems. Communities formed themselves into 2-year college rating districts, sometimes co-extensive with school districts, but often larger. In the early twentieth century states would typically provide assistance in the form of a capital or foundation grant and perhaps a small continuing subsidy, but the responsibility for financing and therefore managing 2-year colleges remained with local districts. State contributions increased over the century so that by the end of the century state governments assumed full responsibility for financing and by extension managing 2-year colleges.

The New York State Board of Regents stated four major functions of 2-year colleges in 1964: general education, transfer education, occupational or terminal education and adult or continuing education. These were expanded by the Oklahoma State Regents for Higher Education in its guidelines for the role and scope of Oklahoma higher education issued in 1970. These provided that the functions for 2-year colleges in the state are to:

1) provide general education for all students,
2) provide education in several basic fields of study for the freshman and sophomore years for students who plan to transfer to senior college and complete requirements for the bachelor's degree,
3) provide terminal education in several fields of vocational and technical study, and
4) provide both formal and informal programs of study especially designed for adults and out of school youth in order to serve the community generally with a continuing education opportunity.
(Oklahoma State Regents for Higher Education 1970: 47)

These functions remain current today, although the emphasis on each function differs in different states and colleges and changes over time. Thus, the transfer function became the dominant purpose for many 2-year colleges by the mid-twentieth century, fell in importance by the end of the century and there are indications that it started growing in significance again at the start of the twenty-first century.

4.5.2 Types of institution

The standard description of US higher education institutions is the Carnegie classification of colleges and universities, which is described briefly in Chapter 7. However, the two primary distinctions are between 2- and 4-year colleges and between public and private colleges. Four-year institutions are authorized to offer at least a 4-year programme of college-level studies wholly or principally creditable toward a baccalaureate degree, although many also offer masters and some also offer doctorates. Two-year institutions are authorized to offer at least a 2-year programme of college-level studies, which terminates in an associate degree or is principally creditable toward a baccalaureate degree.

Public schools or institutions are those controlled and operated by publicly elected or appointed officials and derive their primary support from public funds. Private schools or institutions are controlled by an individual or agency other than a state, a subdivision of a state or the federal government and are usually supported primarily by other than public funds. Private schools and institutions include both non-profit and proprietary or for-profit institutions. This distinction notwithstanding, states provide 46 per cent of the financial support for public institutions and approximately 29 per cent of the total support for all public and private colleges. Most of the balance is from tuition fees, often supported by federal and state financial aid for students at public and private institutions.

In 2003 some 39 per cent of US tertiary education students were enrolled in public 4-year institutions and 22 per cent were enrolled in private 4-year colleges, so almost two-thirds (62 per cent) were enrolled in 4-year colleges. This is similar to Canada (where 61 per cent of tertiary students are enrolled in universities), but much higher than the UK (44 per cent) and Australia (35 per cent). This probably reflects a greater range in type of 4-year institutions in the USA, most of which do not offer doctorates and many of which do not offer masters. Some 37 per cent of US tertiary education students were enrolled in public 2-year colleges and 2 per cent were enrolled in private 2-year colleges.

4.5.3 Different enrolment patterns in different states

There are considerable differences in enrolment patterns between states. However, it is possible to discern patterns and four are suggested here:

New England: a higher than average proportion of enrolments in private 4-year colleges.

West: a higher than average proportion of enrolments in public 2-year colleges.

South: a higher than average proportion of enrolments in public 4-year colleges.

Middle America: average proportions in all sectors.

The *New England* pattern is a lower than average proportion of students in public colleges – typically 20 per cent less than the national average – and a corresponding high proportion of students in private, mostly 4-year colleges. These states also typically have 20 per cent higher than average enrolment in 4-year colleges. Many of the states that fit this pattern are in New England:

Connecticut, Massachusetts, New Hampshire, Rhode Island and Vermont. The nearby mid-Atlantic states of New York and Pennsylvania also follow this pattern. Typically these states have above average median household income and above average college participation. The New England state of Maine and Utah in the western mountain region are similar to the New England pattern in having an unusually high proportion of students in 4-year colleges, but unlike the New England group, they do not have such a high proportion in private 4-year colleges.

A second pattern shared by states in the *west* is an unusually high proportion of enrolments in public 2-year colleges, typically at least 10 per cent and for many states as much as 15 per cent above average. This is combined with about average enrolments in public 4-year colleges to give an unusually high proportion of students enrolled in public institutions. Many of the states with this pattern are in the west – Arizona, California, New Mexico, Oregon, Washington and Wyoming – but the pattern is also shared by Florida, Mississippi and Texas in the south. These states typically have participation rates around the median, but their median household incomes are spread from relatively low to relatively high. Illinois in the Midwest is similar in having a high proportion of students enrolled in 2-year public colleges, but has a lower proportion enrolled in public 4-year colleges.

A third pattern in the *south* and with its variants the most common, is a very high proportion of enrolments in public 4-year colleges – from 10 per cent to 25 per cent higher than the US average – with corresponding lower than average proportions of enrolments in public 2-year colleges and private colleges. Many of these states are from the south (Alabama, Arkansas, Delaware, Kentucky, Louisiana, Oklahoma and West Virginia), but others are from the west (Colorado, Idaho, Montana), Midwest (Kansas, North Dakota, South Dakota) and Delaware, in the north. While Idaho in the west fits this pattern, it is unique among US states in having such a high proportion of students enrolled in private 2-year colleges – 17 per cent compared with the national average of 2 per cent. These states range from high participation to low participation. Most have lower than average median household incomes, although Colorado and Delaware have considerably higher than average median household incomes.

There are two variants on the southern pattern. Some states have about 10 per cent higher shares of enrolment in public 4-year colleges which is at the expense of private 4-year colleges, with the other proportions being about average: Maryland, Michigan, Nevada, South Carolina, Virginia and Wisconsin. These states have a spread of participation rates but all except South Carolina have considerably higher than average median household incomes. A second variation on this pattern formed by some Midwest (Indiana, Ohio) and southern (Georgia, Tennessee) states is moderately higher than average share of enrolments in public 4-year colleges balanced by lower than average shares in public 2-year colleges and average proportions of enrolments in private colleges. These states tend to have average median household incomes but below average participation.

The fourth discernible pattern is *middle America* – shares of enrolments close to the US average – which is followed by Iowa, Minnesota, Missouri, New Jersey and North Carolina. All but Missouri have higher than average participation rates and all but Iowa and North Carolina higher median household income, some considerably higher.

Douglass (2004: 9) argues that these enrolment patterns reflect different patterns of economic development and political culture and, in turn, different patterns of state building. Most states along the eastern seaboard and centred in the northeast first developed private institutions that remain major providers of higher education. The south developed higher education institutions slowly and participation rates have historically been lower than the nation as a whole. Douglass says that a vibrant mix of public universities and small denominational colleges emerged in the midwest by the late 1800s and remains. In the expansive west, as territorial governments vied for statehood they developed schemes to invest almost exclusively in public higher education institutions and they sought their rapid development to encourage economic development and socioeconomic mobility (Douglass 2004: 9).

4.5.4 California

California – the home of Hollywood, Silicon Valley, Berkeley, CalTech, Stanford and UCLA – is a state of international significance. California, 411,015 square kilometres in area, is located in the southwest corner of the USA, spanning latitudes 42 to almost 32° north. It is about four times longer than it is broad, bordered by the Pacific Ocean on the west and Nevada in the east and, importantly, sharing a border with Mexico in the south. California's large and diverse landscape is defined by patterns of mountains and valleys creating four major natural ecosystems: the coast, the Central Valley which is one of the most productive agricultural areas in the world and the largest of any US state, the Sierra Nevada mountain range and the deserts in the east.

Numerous indigenous peoples had settled in Californian regions for thousands of years before 1769, when the Spanish forcefully settled what is now San Diego, a large coastal city in the south of California. Spanish rule was replaced by that of the Mexican Republic in 1823, which in turn was replaced by the United States in 1847, California being admitted as the 31st state in 1850. Gold was discovered in 1848, starting a massive rush of immigrants from around the world.

Mining was replaced as the state's main industry in the 1870s by agriculture, which was further developed by large dam and irrigation projects around the turn of the century. Military spending on aircraft production in California in the first decades of the twentieth century lead to the development of an aviation industry, which, in turn, lead to the development of aerospace technologies and a research and development environment at Stanford University in Palo Alto and surrounding communities. That

77-kilometre stretch of Highway 101, halfway between San Francisco 70 kilometres to the north of Palo Alto and San José to the south, became Silicon Valley, the cradle of the information and communication technologies. California had a gross state product of $1.62 trillion in 2005 which, if it were a country, would be the ninth biggest in the world.

California has a population of 37.7 million, making it the most populous US state. The biggest conurbations are the Los Angeles metropolitan area in the south (17.8 million), the San Francisco metropolitan area (7.2 million), the Riverside–San Bernardino–Ontario metropolitan area (the 'Inland Empire') inland from Los Angeles (4 million), the San Diego metropolitan area on the Mexico border (2.9 million) and the Sacramento metropolitan area which includes the state's capital northeast of San Francisco (1.8 million). California has one of the most diverse populations of the US states: 43.8 per cent of its population is non-Hispanic white (who are 66.9 per cent of the USA as a whole), 35.2 per cent is Hispanic (US 14.4), 12.2 per cent Asian (US 4.3) and 6.7 per cent of its population is black or African American (US 12.8). California will be the first mainland US state to have a majority of non-white population, predicted to be around 2010.

4.5.4.1 Tertiary education overview
Descriptions of higher education in California usually start with the master plan for higher education enshrined in the Donahoe Act of 1960, however Douglass (2004: 11) points out that the state developed three distinct and geographically dispersed and multicampus public segments as early as 1920. The University of California at Berkeley became the USA's biggest university in 1910, and it 'became the first multicampus state university in the nation with the inclusion of a "southern branch" in Los Angeles in 1919 – what became UCLA' (Douglass 2004: 15). 'California was the first state to develop the public community college, passing legislation in 1907 for their creation as an extension of public high schools' (Douglass 2004: 15). Graduates of community colleges were guaranteed admission to the University of California Berkeley campus from 1910 and 'in the 1930s, some 40 to 50 percent of all admissions to both Berkeley and what became UCLA were transfer students from local community colleges' (Douglass 2004: 13–14). Community colleges expanded rapidly: almost two new colleges were established in California each year from 1910 until 1970 (Douglass 2004: 15). According to Douglass (2004: 15) the California state university system did not grow substantially until the 1950s, after it gained authority to offer the masters degree in 1948 and with the introduction of new undergraduate education in fields such as engineering.

Douglass (2004: 21) reports that the state maintained a tripartite structure well before the master plan. In the 1940s, for example, the state rejected pressure from local communities to develop a number of community colleges into 4-year institutions and in the 1950s it rejected attempts to merge the missions of California State University and the University of California to expand the number of research universities. The 1960 California master plan for higher education ended these aspirations for institutional elevation. As Douglass (2004: 21) says: 'The master plan was more important for what it prevented . . . than what it created.'

Public higher education in California is formally organized in three sectors or segments. At the peak is the University of California, which has ten campuses throughout the state, the most famous of which are Berkeley, which Shanghai Jiao Tong University's Institute of Higher Education ranks as fourth best in the world, and Los Angeles, which is ranked 14th best in the world. The University of California's intake is restricted by legislation to the top 12.5 per cent of high school graduates. The University of California system enrols 160,000 students, 10 per cent of the total public tripartite system. The state funds the university at about $18,200 per student (Turnage and Yatooma 2006: v).

The middle tier of California's public higher education system is the California State University, which has its origins in teachers' colleges ('normal schools') established in the late nineteenth century. California State University has 23 campuses offering a comprehensive range of bachelors and masters degrees, some professional degrees and has areas of research strength. California State University does not have authority to offer PhDs and while many of its campuses compete for federal and other extramural research funds, relatively little research is done in the system and teaching loads are about double those of the University of California. California State University's intake is restricted to the top 33.3 per cent of high school graduates. The university teaches 332,000 students, 22 per cent of the tripartite system's total. The state funds the university at about $11,600 per student (Turnage and Yatooma 2006: v).

The lower and by far the largest sector is the California community colleges, which have open admission. The sector's 109 campuses include some of North America's oldest community colleges established in the first decades of the twentieth century and include what is now called the San José City College, which was the subject of Burton Clark's *The Open Door College: A Case Study* (1960). Community colleges offer associates in arts and science which require 2 years' full-time study and allow students who achieve a grade point average of 2.0 (CSU) or 2.4 (UC) to transfer, mostly with full credit, towards the 4-year baccalaureate awarded by universities and university-level colleges. Community colleges also offer occupational certificates and various community education and bridging programmes.

Community colleges enrol 2.6 million students, but because so many study part-time, it has 1.0 million full-time equivalent students or 68 per cent of the tripartite system's total. California's high proportion of higher education enrolments in community colleges reflects its early and strong support for the establishment of the sector and its mandated restrictions on the proportion of high school graduates who may be admitted to the more selective sectors. The state funds community colleges at $5400 per full-time equivalent student (Turnage and Yatooma 2006: v). Shulock (2004: 69) observes that the 'disparity' in funding rate between community colleges and

4-year colleges in California is far greater than in other states and 'deficient by any standard' in her view. Community colleges have a strong legacy of local control through locally elected boards and are subject to detailed prescriptive statutes and regulations.

Some 240,000 or 11 per cent of all California higher education students are enrolled in 255 private universities and colleges. These are very varied institutions of different types: 2- and 4-year specialized schools in the arts and sciences, traditional liberal arts colleges, small comprehensive universities, major research universities such as the California Institute of Technology (CalTech) and Stanford University, free-standing graduate and professional schools and campuses for working adults. There are, in addition, more than 300 institutions that are not regionally accredited but have been approved by the state to offer various degree programmes. There are also more than 3000 non-degree-granting institutions offering vocational and occupational training programmes. State-approved schools and colleges enrol an estimated 400,000 students.

The three tiers of public higher education are managed as largely separate systems within the sectoral boundaries established by the master plan. The University of California system is governed by a board of regents established with considerable autonomy by the state's constitution in 1880. Section 9 of article 9 of the constitution invests the regents of the University of California 'with full powers of organization and government' of the university, subject to limited legislative controls to ensure the security of its funds, compliance with endowments and competitive bidding for letting contracts and purchasing. This level of autonomy is unusual in the USA, shared by public universities in only five other states (Douglass 2000: 6).

The California State University is governed by a board of trustees established by an act of the state's legislature. But the constitutional amendment establishing the California State University board of trustees gave it little autonomy. While the University of California is allocated a block grant, CSU is granted funds for specific programmes and has limited flexibility to change priorities. Broad policy and guidance of Californian Community Colleges is provided by a board of governors established by the legislature. More detailed oversight of the colleges in each of 72 districts is provided by a locally elected board of trustees for each district. The two levels of board operate what is known as 'shared governance' (Douglass 2000: 8).

The three systems of higher education in California are coordinated by the California Postsecondary Education Commission established by statute in 1974. The commission is required to 'assure the effective utilization of public postsecondary resources, thereby eliminating waste and unnecessary duplication, and to promote diversity, innovation and responsiveness to student and societal needs'. The commission's responsibilities are long-range planning, policy development and analysis, programme administration, review of new campuses and off-campus centres and to be a state clearinghouse for information on higher education. Its priorities are to improve the use of resources by promoting better coordination and collaboration between California's systems of postsecondary education, increase the public accountability of postsecondary institutions and plan for a better California future by ensuring postsecondary education opportunities for all students. Douglass (2000: 9) says that the commission has little legislated authority and is not influential. Hayward and colleagues (2004: 18) say that the commission is 'relatively weak' and that California does not have an effective mechanism for dealing with issues that transcend segments.

4.5.4.2 Occupational regulation

The California department of consumer affairs regulates more than 200 occupations, many of which have licensing requirements. Typically registration requires a minimum period of work experience and passing assessment. Credit towards work experience but less usually the assessment is often given for technical training, apprenticeship training, or education (Department of Consumer Affairs 2001).

4.5.4.3 Vocational education

Vocational education, or 'occupationally related training' in California is offered by some 200 public secondary schools with occupational programmes, 240 public adult schools with occupational programmes, 140 2-year technical and community colleges, 360 4-year colleges and universities, 1400 private business and technical schools (many of which offer only one or two programmes), 86 schools offering apprenticeships, 14 schools offering hospital and health programmes and 200 various other educational providers including job corps centres and community-based organizations.

4.5.5 Colorado

The Columbine High School massacre occurred in suburban Denver, the capital of Colorado and South Park in the Rockies southwest of Denver is the inspiration for the eponymous cartoon. The Rockies give Colorado the highest average elevation of US states, of 6800 feet or over a mile high. Colorado has some fine higher education institutions within a system more heavily regulated than other US states. Hence Colorado is a state with regulation a mile high.

4.5.5.1 Geography

Colorado is almost a perfect rectangle of 270,000 square kilometres in area located just southwest of the geographic centre of the USA. The eastern half of the state has flat, high plains rising to the Rocky Mountains that run north–south through the centre and west of the state. Colorado's average elevation is 2073 metres. Gold was discovered in Colorado in 1858, leading to a gold rush and the foundation of the state's economy on mining, which expanded to silver, uranium, coal, molybdenum and petroleum. Colorado's main agricultural products are grains, beef, fruit and vegetables. Much of its economy is now built on high technology and on providing transport and other services to its greater region.

Colorado has a population of 4.8 million, most located on the front range along the Denver metropolitan/I-25 corridor that runs north–south through the state where the eastern plains meet the Rockies: 2.9 million in Denver-Aurora-Boulder, 600,000 in Colorado Springs, 275,000 in Fort Collins, 240,000 in Greeley and 150,000 in Pueblo. Some 72.1 per cent of Colorado's population is non-Hispanic white (who are 66.9 per cent of the USA as a whole), 19.5 per cent is Hispanic (US 14.4), 4.1 per cent is black or African American (US 12.8) and 2.6 is Asian (US 4.3).

4.5.5.2 Tertiary education overview
Some 250,000 students are enrolled in Colorado postsecondary education institutions. Almost half of Colorado's higher education students are enrolled in public 4-year colleges, 34 per cent are enrolled in public 2-year colleges, 14 per cent in private 4-year colleges and 4 per cent in private 2-year colleges. Colorado's premier research university is the University of Colorado at Boulder, which Shanghai Jiao Tong University's Institute of Higher Education ranks as the 34th best university in the world. The 2001 Nobel Prize in physics was shared by Carl E. Wieman of the University of Colorado at Boulder and his colleague Eric A. Cornell of the National Institute of Standards and Technology also in Boulder and Wolfgang Ketterle of MIT. Previous CU-Boulder laureates are Thomas Cech (chemistry 1989) and William Phillips (physics 1997).

Higher education in Colorado is coordinated by the Colorado Commission on Higher Education, an agency of the Department of Higher Education. The commission has dual functions – executive policy and legislative implementation. By statute, the commission is responsible for higher education finance and appropriations, academic programmes and system-wide planning, capital construction and long-range planning, and for overseeing the administration of a research grant programme to develop new technologies and materials in the universities' research laboratories and bringing them into the marketplace. The director of the commission is appointed by the state governor, one of the few in the USA (Northwest Education Research Center 2000: 14). Colorado's higher education institutions are governed by a mixture of multicampus, single campus, elected and appointed boards. The Northwest Education Research Center (2000: 6) suggests that Colorado may be unique among the US states in its mixture of governance arrangements.

The community college missions are stated in fairly conventional terms: open-door, associate degree, liberal arts transfer, occupational and technical programmes and personal and vocational programmes for adults. However, adult basic education, which is a fairly significant community college responsibility in most states, is the responsibility of the department of education in Colorado. Local district colleges raise a proportion of their funds from local rates and are governed by community boards elected locally.

The Colorado Commission on Higher Education (2002) Blue Ribbon Panel recommended the missions for Colorado's 4-year colleges, set out in Table 4.2. Also shown is the proportion of undergraduate students in each institution who transferred from a 2-year college. These data are analysed and compared with other jurisdictions in Chapter 9.

Table 4.2 Proportion of undergraduate students at Colorado 4-year public institutions who transferred from a 2-year institution, by institution's selectivity, 2001

Institution	Transfer students
Highly selective – competitive admission to students who at minimum have an index of 110, rank in the top 10% of high school class and earn 27 or above on the ACT composite test	
Colorado School of Mines	1%
Campus of the University of Colorado associated with the University of Colorado Hospital (UCHSC)	0%
Selective – competitive admission to high school graduates with an index score that meets or exceeds the institutional admission index or who earn the specified high school GPA or specified ACT score. Minimum index score is 90	
Colorado State University	4%
University of Colorado, Boulder	2%
University of Colorado, Colorado Springs	7%
University of Colorado, Denver	9%
University of Northern Colorado	5%
Moderately selective – guaranteed admission to high school graduates who achieve a high school GPA of 2.5 or ACT score of 20 or above. Competitive admission with index score of 80 or above. Admission into selected degree programmes is based on programme admission standards (e.g., teacher education, business)	
Adams State College	3%
Fort Lewis College	3%
Mesa State College	2%
University of Southern Colorado	7%
Western State College of Colorado	2%
Modified open admission standards – guaranteed admission to students over 20, admission to students who have an index of 76	
Metropolitan State College of Denver	7%
Open admissions programme – guaranteed admission based on a high school diploma or its equivalent	
Community and technical colleges – Aims Community College, Colorado Mountain College	0%

Source: Jacobs (2002)

4.5.5.3 Occupational regulation

The Colorado department of regulatory agencies regulates 41 occupations and legal practice is regulated by the Colorado Supreme Court board of law examiners. There is no licensing requirement and in many cases seem to be no apprenticeship for bricklayers, car mechanics, carpenters, fitters and turners, painters and decorators, riggers or welders (Department of Regulatory Agencies 2001).

4.5.5.4 Vocational education

Vocational education in Colorado is provided by six public area vocational/technical schools and several private occupational and trade schools. Most of these offer a few programmes in one or two areas of specialization, but the private for-profit Colorado Technical University offers programmes from associate degrees to doctorates.

4.5.6 Texas

Texas is a mixture of rural fundamentalism, aggressive entrepreneurialism and sophisticated technology.

4.5.6.1 Geography

Texas has an area of 692,244 square kilometres of varied geography, extending from sea level at the Gulf of Mexico to over 2438 metres in the Guadalupe Mountains of far West Texas and from the semitropical Lower Rio Grande Valley to the High Plains of the Panhandle. At its longest, Texas is 1300 kilometres north–south and 1200 kilometres miles east–west.

The area that is now Texas was first settled around 10,000 BC. At the time of European settlement by the Spanish in the late seventeenth century Texas was occupied by Kiowas, Comanches, Southern Cheyennes and Arapahoes. Texas joined the United States Union in 1845. The cattle drives that are so prominent in US myth had been occasional in the 1830s sporadic during the 1840s and 1850s and almost non-existent during the Civil War, but began in earnest in the 1860s, mostly to markets and railheads in the Midwest. They were at their peak for only about 20 years until the proliferation of railroads made them unnecessary.

Oil was discovered in Texas in 1894. In 1958 Jack Kilby of Texas Instruments developed the integrated circuit and in 1962 the National Aeronautics and Space Administration (NASA) opened its Spacecraft Center in Houston. The siege in Waco was in 1993. Texas' main industries are manufactures, chemicals and allied products, petroleum and coal products cattle, cotton, dairy products and transport equipment.

Texas has a population of 23.5 million, almost 85 per cent of whom live in metropolitan areas. Its biggest cities are Dallas-Fort Worth metropolitan area (6.4), Houston metropolitan area (5.6 million), San Antonio (1.9 million), Austin-Round Rock (1.5 million) and El Paso (735,000). Much of Texas' character is shaped by its origins as a part of the former Spanish colony of Mexico and its sharing of an extensive border with Mexico.

4.5.6.2 *Tertiary education overview*

Some 46 per cent of students are enrolled in 4-year institutions. While Texas has the very prominent private Rice University (ranked 87 in the world by Shanghai Jiao Tong University's Institute of Higher Education), this has a relatively small enrolment of 4800 students and only 10 per cent of students are enrolled in private 4-year colleges. Private 2-year colleges enrol 2 per cent of Texas students. So 88 per cent of Texas tertiary education students are enrolled in public institutions.

Higher education in Texas is coordinated by the Texas Higher Education Coordinating Board, which was established by the Texas Legislature in 1965 to 'provide leadership and coordination for the Texas higher education system to achieve excellence for the college education of Texas students' (Texas Higher Education Coordinating Board 2001a). The board has a strong role.

The Texas education code requires the Texas Higher Education Coordinating Board to review periodically the role and mission statements, the table of programmes and all degree and certificate programmes offered by the public institutions of higher education to assure that they meet the present and future needs of the state and the counties in which they are located. The code also requires the board to order the initiation, consolidation or elimination of degree or certificate programmes where that action is in the best interest of the public institutions themselves or the general requirements of the state of Texas, the counties in which they are located or when that action offers hope of achieving excellence by a concentration of available resources. Furthermore, no new department, school, degree programme or certificate programme may be added at any public institution of higher education except with specific prior approval of the board (Texas Legislative Council 2001).

Texas has four public university systems: Texas A&M University system, Texas State University system, the University of Texas system and the University of Houston system. Texas A&M University is a land grant, sea grant and space grant institution. The TAMU system has ten institutions, most of which are comprehensive masters-granting institutions, but three of which are research doctoral-granting universities. Texas A&M University, College Station, is ranked 91 in the world by Shanghai Jiao Tong University's Institute of Higher Education. It was the state's first public institution of higher education, established in 1876 as the Agricultural and Mechanical College of Texas.

The Texas State University system has eight institutions, all masters comprehensive. It was established in 1911 to consolidate the management of teachers' colleges, but now the components offer a comprehensive range of programmes. The system is governed by a board of regents comprising nine members appointed by the governor with the advice and consent of the state senate. An administrative staff headed by a board-appointed chancellor administers the central activities of the system and provides support to the system components.

The University of Texas system comprises nine institutions, five of which are masters-comprehensive institutions and four of which are research doctoral-granting institutions. The oldest institution, the University of Texas, Austin, was founded in 1883 and is ranked 38 in the world by Shanghai Jiao Tong University's Institute of Higher Education. The University of Houston system has four institutions, ranging from a general baccalaureate-granting institution to an extensive research doctoral-granting institution. The oldest component was established in 1927. In addition to the university systems there are six separate universities serving specialist needs.

Texas has 74 public community and technical colleges. Most 2-year colleges are established by their district. Each district is formed by a local community and governed by a locally elected board. Colleges are funded through a combination of locally assessed taxes, tuition fees and state-general revenue appropriations. Subsection 130.003 (e) of the Texas Education Code provides that public community colleges primarily serve their local taxing districts and service areas by offering technical programmes leading to associate degrees or certificates; vocational programmes leading directly to employment in semi-skilled and skilled occupations; freshman and sophomore courses in arts and sciences; continuing adult education programmes for occupational or cultural upgrading; compensatory education programmes; workforce development programmes; and adult literacy and other basic skills programmes for adults (Texas Higher Education Coordinating Board 2000).

Two per cent of 2-year college enrolments are in the Texas State Technical College System, a system of public 2-year institutions of higher education that includes four colleges and three extension centres located throughout Texas. The technical college system's role is described in section 135.01 of the Texas Education Code as

> offering courses of study in vocational and technical education for which there is demand within the state of Texas' and 'emphasizing highly specialized advanced and emerging technical and vocational areas ... The emphasis of each TSTC system campus shall be on advanced and emerging technical programs not commonly offered by public junior colleges.

The Texas State Technical College System institutions and the Lamar University lower division institutions have no taxing authority and are funded by local tuition fees and state general revenue appropriations. As a result, the service area for these colleges is the whole state and their profiles vary slightly in content from the community colleges' profiles. TSTC offers more than 75 associate degree and certificate programmes ranging from laser electro-optics to telecommunications, from environmental science to aircraft pilot training, from biomedical equipment to webmaster, from culinary arts to automotive.

The Texas charter for public higher education adopted by the legislature in 1987 provides that: 'Each postsecondary educational institution should be assigned a distinct role. Each college and university should strive to excel in selected academic or technical areas and to achieve distinction among peers nationwide' (Texas Higher Education Coordinating Board 2005: principle III). The Texas Higher Education Coordinating Board has interpreted this as encouraging each college and university to have at least one programme or service of nationally recognized excellence. However, Texas does not have an explicit policy of distinguishing public 4-year colleges by selectivity of student admissions. A measure of the selectivity of institutions is the proportion of their first-time undergraduates who were in the top 10 per cent of their high school class.

The most selective public institution on this measure is Texas A&M University, College Station: 39 per cent of its admissions were in the top 10 per cent of their high school class. The Texas Higher Education Coordinating Board defines a transfer student as an undergraduate student who enrolled in 30 semester credit hours or more in the past 6 years at a public community or technical college. By this definition, 17 per cent of College Station students in 2000 were transfer students. The next most selective public institution is the University of Texas at Austin, which had 31 per cent of its admissions in the top 10 per cent of their high school class and 13 per cent transfer students.

There is a gap to the group of moderately selective institutions that are of gradually lesser selectivity but which have very variable transfer rates apparently unrelated to their selectivity and probably heavily influence by local factors. Finally, there is a group of not so selective institutions, which, again, have variable transfer student admission rates. But the average transfer student admission rate for not so selective institutions is a little less than the average for the moderately selective institutions, probably because they are less attractive institutions for transfer students. The distinction between moderately selective and not so selective institutions is not so significant for transfer student admission rates so it is convenient to treat them as one group.

4.5.6.3 Occupational regulation

Texas Higher Education Coordinating Board Community and Technical Colleges Division's 2001 Statewide Annual Licensure Report includes data on 23 licensure examinations for occupations such as aircraft mechanic, court reporting, funeral directing, law enforcement (academy, corrections, criminal justice), nursing (nurse aide, licensed vocational nurse and registered nurse) and radiation therapy. In addition, at least a further 20 occupations are licensed by specialist agencies and boards, such as accountants, air conditioning and refrigeration, architects, chemical dependency counsellor, childcare administration, (building) code enforcement, dental hygienist, engineer, fitting and dispensing of hearing instruments, marriage and family therapists, medication aide, optometrists, pharmacists, plumbers, polygraph examiners, real estate appraiser, real estate sales agent and respiratory care practitioner and veterinary medical examiners.

By virtue of the Texas Public Accountancy Act of 1991 Texas is one of 36 states to require candidates for the certified public accountancy exam to have a baccalaureate or graduate degree and a minimum of 150 semester credit hours of recognized courses or subjects. Since the normal full-time study load is 15 hours per semester or 30 hour per annum, this requirement is normally met after 5 years' full-time study, often leading to the joint award of a bachelor of business in accounting and a master of business administration.

5

Qualifications frameworks

A qualifications framework is one way of depicting the relations between vocational and higher education and facilitating students' transfer between sectors. This chapter reviews the development of qualifications frameworks and considers their future.

5.1 Overview

A qualifications framework is a representation of the relations between types of qualification. Qualifications are official, validated statements of successful completion of education or training or of having fulfilled the requirements to enter or progress within an occupation, discharge a function or hold an office (Coles and Oates 2005: 26). This definition and most qualifications frameworks are designed to include occupational as well as academic qualifications, but all current qualifications frameworks are dominated by academic qualifications. Qualifications frameworks represent the relations between qualifications in a diagram, typically a table showing the levels of qualifications in rows and the strands or routes through the levels in columns. Ireland is distinctive in representing its qualifications in a fan diagram, which is like a dial ranging from level 1 certificates at the bottom left of the dial through level 5 certificates in the middle of the dial to the highest qualifications in the frameworks, doctorates, which are shown at the bottom right of the dial.

Qualifications frameworks are developed by governments to support the coordination, correspondence, coherence, integration or harmonization of alternative, sometimes competing, qualifications. Qualifications frameworks are sometimes introduced as part of a wider systematization or reorganisation of education, but, more commonly, recently to show students and employers the relations between qualifications. For whatever reasons they are introduced, qualifications frameworks seek to relate qualifications that had hitherto not been widely related, often because the qualifications are in different domains, are of different types, are offered by different types of institution or are achieved after completing different pathways or programmes. A central question is therefore how qualifications in different domains may be compared with each other. The almost universal answer is to try to compare qualifications by their outcomes rather than by the institutions that offer them or the learning pathways or programs ('inputs') that lead to them. Outcomes in turn are most commonly expresses as competences which holders of the qualifications are expected to have.

5.2 Outline of the most prominent frameworks

Tuck (2007: 1) charts the accelerating introduction of national qualifications frameworks in three stages. In the first generation which started between the late 1980s and the mid-1990s were Australia, England and Northern Ireland, New Zealand, Scotland and South Africa. The second generation started from the late to the early 2000s and comprised Ireland, Malaysia, Maldives, Mauritius, Mexico, Namibia, the Philippines, Singapore, Trinidad and Tobago and Wales. Some 24 countries are in the third generation, which are currently considering introducing national qualifications frameworks. These countries include Brazil, China and some smaller countries of Europe, Latin America and sub-Saharan Africa. In addition, regional qualifications frameworks are being developed in the Caribbean, European Union, Pacific Islands and the Southern African Development Community.

5.2.1 National qualifications framework for England, Wales and Northern Ireland

Michael Young (2003: 199), a prominent analyst of qualifications frameworks, traces the origin of the idea of a qualification framework based on outcomes to the UK's national vocational qualifications framework introduced by the National Council for Vocational Qualifications in late 1987, which he believes was the first attempt to establish a national qualifications framework based on criteria and levels and independent of any institutions providing programmes of study. However, the national qualifications framework for England, Wales and Northern Ireland was not introduced until 2000. The framework contains entry-level qualifications, schools qualifications, vocational and occupational qualifications but not higher education qualifications, which are included in a separate framework.

The national qualifications framework has eight levels. Its lowest, level 1, includes the general certificate of secondary education, which pupils normally start studying at age 14 (called year 10 in England and Wales and year 11 in Northern Ireland) and take final examinations at age 16 (year 11/year 12). The advanced level or A-level general certificate of education, which students normally study during the optional final 2 years of secondary school (years 12 and 13), are level 3 on the national qualifications framework.

Higher national diplomas are at level 5, with which foundation degrees are aligned. Bachelor degrees and graduate certificates and diplomas from the framework for higher education qualifications are aligned with level 6 of the national qualifications framework, masters with level 7 and doctorates are aligned with level 8 of the national qualifications framework.

The national qualifications framework is maintained by the Qualifications and Curriculum Authority which includes in the framework only qualifications it accredits. The framework currently does not include units and thus does not support credit accumulation. However, the authority is developing a new qualifications and credit framework, which will be based on units and support credit accumulation and transfer. The framework will have three sizes of qualification: awards that require from ten to 120 hours of learning time, certificates that require from 130 to 360 hours of learning time and diplomas, requiring at least 370 hours of learning time. A peculiar challenge of the English qualifications framework is that it seeks to include qualifications awarded by over 100 bodies, some of which are private for profit and thus have a proprietary interest in their qualifications.

5.2.2 Scottish credit and qualifications framework

The Scottish credit and qualifications framework was launched in 2001. However, as Raffe (2003: 242) points out, the framework launched in 2001 originated as a federation of sub-frameworks that had been developed over the previous two decades. The first framework was a national system of portable modules of non-advanced vocational education introduced in 1984 as a result of the Scottish Education Department's 16-plus action plan. Modules were defined by their learning outcomes. The main advanced vocational education programmes were reformed in 1989 to create a single, unit-based national framework in Scottish vocational qualifications. Scottish Credit Accumulation and Transfer (SCOTCAT) was established as the national credit framework for higher education in Scotland in 1991. SCOTCAT was based on credits and levels. Post-compulsory academic and vocational qualifications were incorporated in a unified system of qualifications in the Higher Still changes of 1999. The Scottish credit and qualifications framework was formed by incorporating within one framework SCOTCAT and the national qualifications introduced by Higher Still. Thus the Scottish framework was developed incrementally in building on earlier unifying reforms and bringing together existing sub-frameworks. Raffe (2003: 251) says that the Scottish framework was also developed pragmatically by the voluntary participation of partners.

The Scottish credit and qualifications framework therefore covers all areas of post-compulsory education although not all qualifications are yet included in the framework. It has 12 levels. The normal school leaving certificate and university entrance qualification in Scotland are highers, taken at year 12 of schooling. Highers are level 6 on the Scottish credit and qualifications framework. Advanced highers are considered for university entry on the same footing as A-levels and are level 7 on the framework. Higher national diplomas are level 8, ordinary degrees are level 9, honours are level 10, masters level are 11 and doctorates are level 12 on the framework.

The Scottish credit and qualifications framework includes only qualifications – it does not include units. However, it records the credits or volume of learning in each qualification as well as its level to maximize students' transfer of credit between programmes and qualifications. The Scottish framework is also enabling or descriptive rather than regulatory – a qualification must have quality assured assessment of learner achievement to be included in the framework, but the quality assurance is the responsibility of the institution or the sector awarding the qualification, not of the body overseeing the framework.

5.2.3 South African national qualifications framework

The South African national qualifications framework was formally established under the South African Qualifications Act of 1995, the first act of the democratic post-apartheid parliament. South Africa's framework covers all education and training qualifications. The framework has eight levels based on levels of cognitive complexity. Level 1 is the equivalent to the end of junior secondary school. Further education and training certificates are at levels 2 to 3 and the senior secondary qualification – the general education and training certificate – is at level four. Higher education and training are at levels 5 to 8: national certificates and diplomas at level 5, higher diplomas and first degrees at level 6, honours degrees and professional qualifications at level 7 and masters and doctorates at level 8.

South Africa's framework comprises unit standards as well as qualifications. These are defined by outcomes that are independent of the inputs and processes that may lead to them. Qualifications and unit standards are generated and evaluated by engaging stakeholders in a complex process of consultation that is separate from educational institutions, which are associated with the previous apartheid regime. The South African Qualifications Authority then formally ratifies each qualification and unit standard and puts it on one of the eight levels of the framework, a process known as registering. The authority has specified a complicated format and specifications for the qualifications and unit standards to be registered. Unit standards are long documents, comprising up to 25 pages of specifications. A qualification might comprise 20 unit standards and so its specification can be very long. The South African system seems to be mainly concerned with credit accumulation and not so much with transfer. All unit standards and qualifications are accredited for registration on the framework. So South Africa has a very strong qualifications framework: it is comprehensive in scope, based on units, is regulatory as well as communicative and is mandated by government.

By August 2007 some 11,489 unit standards and approximately 818 outcomes-based qualifications had been developed and registered on the framework (Allais 2007: 525), but the framework has not been successful (yet). Allais (2007: 532) reported in 2007 that in the 12 years since the passage of the legislation implementing the framework an estimated 0.3 per cent of qualifications awarded in South Africa were registered on the framework. Conversely, only 10 per cent of the new qualifications registered on the framework had ever been awarded. 'In other words, the qualifications framework is a castle in cyberspace – a list of qualifications and unit standards with very little relationship with the real world of educational provision' (Allais 2007: 532). This may be due at least partly to the objections of universities and senior secondary schools to the qualifications framework's specification of qualifications as outcomes, especially competences that are particularly reductive expressions of outcomes.

5.2.4 Australian qualifications framework

The Australian qualifications framework was introduced in 1995 to locate within an overall system of qualifications the national training framework, which comprises national qualifications based on industry standards of competence introduced in vocational education and training from 1996. However, the Australian qualifications framework is a continuation of a well-established system of national tertiary awards that originated in 1971 to systematize the development of a sector of colleges of advanced education that was established in 1965. The Australian framework is a unified system of national post-compulsory qualifications in schools, vocational education and training and higher education, mainly universities. It comprises 14 qualifications from senior secondary certificate of education to the doctoral degree. The framework describes the qualifications as 'differentiated' between three sectors: schools, vocational education and training and higher education.

While the Australian qualifications framework does not formally allocate levels, they are readily derived from the framework's diagram. The framework has 11 levels. The final year of secondary school, year 12, would be level three on the framework. Associate degrees would be at level 6, bachelors at level 7, graduate certificates at level 8, graduate diplomas at level 9, masters at level 10 and doctorates at level 11. The framework does not play a role in the accreditation of awards or in quality assurance. However, the Australian framework has guidelines on each qualification, which include statements of learning outcomes, responsibility for assessment, pathways to the qualification and the issue of certificates. The framework also has guidelines for cross-sectoral links and national principles and operational guidelines for the recognition of prior uncertified learning.

The Australian qualifications framework does not include the subjects or units that comprise qualifications and it is not a credit accumulation scheme. It is not established by legislation but is maintained by agreement of the sectors that have their own separate and independent legislative authority. The Commonwealth, state and territory ministers responsible for each sector have established a board to maintain the qualifications guidelines and to promote and monitor national implementation of the framework. The Australian qualifications framework advisory board is the only official cross-sectoral body in Australia. While the Australian qualifications framework is enabling in form, it is given regulatory force indirectly by regulation of vocational education provision, the legislation governing the offering of programmes to international students and by the Australian government's conditions for the award of institutional grants and student loans for higher education programmes.

5.2.5 New Zealand national qualifications framework

The New Zealand national qualifications framework was developed pursuant to subsection 253(1) of the Education Act 1989 and was launched in 1991. It covers all post-compulsory education, although as we shall see many higher education qualifications are not registered on the framework. Qualifications are classified by subject matter in a hierarchy of 17 fields, 185 subfields and an unspecified number of domains.

The New Zealand framework has ten levels. The lowest, level 1, is equivalent to year 11 and level 3 is the final year of secondary education year 13, like England's qualification framework. However, New Zealand's qualifications framework is more expanded at the higher levels than the English framework: bachelors and graduate diplomas that do not assume prior undergraduate knowledge are level 7, bachelor with honours and post-graduate certificates and diplomas that assume prior undergraduate knowledge are level 8, masters are level 9 and doctorates are level 10.

New Zealand's framework includes qualifications and their components 'unit standards' for all qualifications other than university qualifications. While some university qualifications are included in the framework they are described by their programme objectives and learning profiles, but are not defined by NQF standards. Neither does the framework include other university qualifications and qualifications offered by polytechnics, colleges of education, *wānanga* (tertiary education institutions that provide education in a Maori cultural context) and private training establishments.

5.2.6 European qualifications framework

On 24 October 2007 the European Parliament (2007) recommended that member states use the European qualifications framework as a reference tool to compare the qualification levels of the different qualifications systems and relate their national qualifications systems to the European qualifications framework by 2010. The European parliament said that the objective of its recommendation 'is to create a common reference framework which should serve as a translation device between different qualifications systems and their levels, whether for general and higher education or for vocational education and training'. The framework covers all post-compulsory education and training. Each of its eight levels is defined by a set of descriptors of learning outcomes of knowledge (what the person knows), skills (the ability to apply knowledge to complete tasks) and competence (the ability to use knowledge and skills in work or study and in professional/personal development, described in terms of responsibility and autonomy). The balance between these elements varies from qualification to qualification.

Levels 1 and 2 indicate basic general and factual knowledge, level 3 indicates knowledge of general concepts and level 4 is at the same level as the senior secondary qualification. Level 5 is the short-cycle qualification – such as the diploma or associate or foundation degree – within the first cycle of higher education, which is the bachelor degree at level 6 of the European qualification framework. Level 7 is the second cycle or masters degree and the highest level 8 is the third-cycle doctoral degree.

The European qualifications framework for lifelong learning involves 25 members of the European Union and 7 other European countries. It further incorporates the higher education qualifications framework being developed by the 45 countries of the European higher education area that have signed the Bologna declaration. The qualifications framework is being developed by an open method of coordination described in the next chapter: it is proposed as a non-binding European Union recommendation and other members of the European higher education area subscribe voluntarily.

While the qualifications framework comprises qualifications only, it uses as a measure of workload the existing European credit transfer system for higher education (ECTS) and the European credit transfer system for vocational education and training which the ministers responsible for vocational training in 32 European countries agreed to develop in the Maastricht communiqué of 14 December 2004. The ECTS was introduced in 1989 and so is already reasonably well-established. It allocates 60 credits for 1 year of full-time study, which is equivalent to 1500–1800 hours of study, 30 credits for one semester and 20 credits for a term of 3 months. ECTS is currently designed for the transfer of credit and there are a number of projects to investigate the feasibility of developing it into a scheme for credit accumulation as well as transfer. ECTS also includes a standard grading scale, intended to be shown in addition to national grades. The grades are awarded as a proportion of all passing grades:

A: best 10%, outstanding performance.
B: next 25%, very good performance.
C: next 30%, good performance.

D: next 25%, passable performance.
E: next 10%, adequate performance.
FX: 'fail – some more work required before the credit can be awarded'.
F: 'fail – considerable further work required'.

5.3 Types of qualifications framework

Young (2005: 15) observes that qualifications frameworks are based on two tensions. The first tension is between the principles of difference and similarity. The traditional, 'tracked' qualifications systems of northern Europe emphasize the different purposes of qualifications in vocational and higher education and the different occupational destinations they serve. Tracked systems therefore use the principle of difference to construct qualifications. However, tracked systems may make it harder for holders to progress and transfer between tracks. This may be a distinct disadvantage in labour markets that have become more fluid as a consequence of global markets and technological change. This leads governments to base qualifications on the other pole on this continuum, of similarity. On this analysis, the boundaries between occupational sectors are more permeable and they are supported by common knowledge and skill requirements. Thus some policies require qualifications to include general or generic skills so that the similarities shared by qualifications are putatively more important than their differences. The principle of similarity supports the qualifications frameworks in the 'unified' systems in Anglophone countries that emphasize progression to and from general and vocational education.

The second tension Young observes within qualifications frameworks is between specifying qualifications by their inputs and by their outputs. Process-based or institutional systems specify qualifications by their inputs such as their syllabus, learning–teaching processes, institutional setting and assessment. Young (2003: 206) notes that process-based or institutional qualifications systems usually require a high level of trust between all stakeholders. Governments have sought to release qualifications from requirements for institutional inputs by specifying qualifications by their outputs and more specifically by learning outcomes that, in principle, can be applied to any kind of learning. Outcomes in turn are most commonly expressed as competences which holders of the qualifications are expected to have. The tracked systems of northern Europe tend to be based on processes or institutions while the unified systems of Anglophone countries tend to be based on outcomes.

An important distinction is between enabling frameworks whose main purpose is to communicate the relations between qualifications and regulatory frameworks which also seek to prescribe what qualifications may be offered (Young 2005: 12). All qualifications frameworks have a communicative role in showing the relations between qualifications and indicating the progression routes between levels and, at least in principle, between sectors.

Most frameworks with only a communicative role are based on agreement and they do not prescribe many conditions for including qualifications in the framework. They are therefore reasonably straightforward to introduce but have limited effect in, for example, reducing the barriers to progression up levels and transfer between sectors. Scotland's is an enabling framework, as is the framework for higher education qualifications in England, Wales and Northern Ireland.

Some frameworks also have a regulatory role such as the South Africa national qualifications framework and the national qualifications framework of England, Wales and Northern Ireland. These set standards and conditions for qualifications to be registered on the framework and may also accredit bodies to award certificates. Regulatory frameworks seek to control the growing and increasingly complex post-compulsory education, they impose consistency between qualifications and seek to reduce barriers to progression and transfer. However, they are harder to impose on all levels and sectors of education, particularly on higher education and general secondary education which have traditionally high status and greater autonomy from the state. Regulatory frameworks are also harder to impose on institutions that do not depend heavily on government for their revenue. So what regulatory frameworks gain in consistency they often lose in comprehensiveness.

A related distinction is the extent to which qualifications frameworks are just descriptive, passively accommodating existing arrangements and the extent to which they seek to actively change the status quo. Accommodating frameworks tend to have a larger number of levels and more general descriptors or simply equate qualifications without trying to fit them into descriptors. Normative and therefore active frameworks tend to be more prescriptive (Coles and Oates 2005: 16). Raffe (2005: 21) argues that the literature on qualifications frameworks suggests that they are most successful when they are modest in ambition and incremental in approach: when they build on existing structures and practices and on the trust, the mutual understandings and the power relationships that are embedded within them. This argues for governments to make frameworks descriptive and accommodating, at least in the early years of their establishment.

Qualifications frameworks also differ importantly by the size of their building blocks, normally whether they are based on units or qualifications (Young 2005: 14). The simplest frameworks comprise only qualifications, perhaps also indicating their normal duration in the equivalent full-time years of study normally needed to complete the qualification. These frameworks have the considerable advantage of simplicity and clarity, but it is commonly held that it should be possible to transfer credit from one, perhaps partly completed qualification, to another. To do so traditionally requires the awarders of the destination qualification to assess the level, amount and quality of the previous study.

Advocates of unit-based qualifications frameworks argue that if each qualification comprises units of a standard size and specified level these need not be assessed individually by the awarders of qualifications, thus facilitating credit transfer and making it more efficient. Advocates of strong unit-based qualifications frameworks argue further that if each unit is required to meet standard quality criteria the awarders of qualifications need not assess the quality of prior study, thus making the transfer of credit almost 'automatic' or at least subject to little if any individual judgement. If the conditions for the award of qualifications are specified in rules it should be possible for a student, employer or indeed a computer program to determine a candidate's eligibility for the award of a qualification. This underlies the credit accumulation and transfer schemes of Scotland, New Zealand, South Africa and the state of Victoria in Australia. Credit accumulation and transfer schemes also maximize students and employers' potential flexibility and choice in assembling units in ways that suit their interests. However, what unit-based qualifications frameworks gain in potential flexibility they lose in complexity and opacity: they are often very difficult to understand and follow and few if any have yet realized their potential to improve the accumulation and transfer of credit.

Qualifications frameworks differ by their scope. Some such as those for Australia, Ireland, Scotland and South Africa are comprehensive in including all post-compulsory qualifications while others such as those for England and New Zealand are limited to one or two sectors and thus normally are normally also limited in the levels they cover. Coles and Oates (2005: 16) note that qualifications frameworks may also have levels without descriptors (equating framework) while the levels in others are based on descriptors (descriptor framework); and frameworks may vary in their number of levels or sublevels, some of which may be vacant.

5.4 Future of qualifications frameworks

A framework is literally a structure supporting or containing something, most commonly used in construction. Some extend the physical meaning of framework to characterize qualifications frameworks as climbing frames which allow students to extend their learning in three dimensions. By extension 'framework' can mean an analytic structure of a complex entity or process and this is also a common understanding of the term in 'qualifications framework'. Qualifications frameworks are commonly represented as a diagram, which is frequently referred to as 'the framework'. But as Coles and Oates (2005: 44) observe, such a diagram is an abstraction – a representation of real arrangements. Frameworks are operationalized by the arrangements that register qualifications and in the way in which they are used by people and this is different for different users. Students and their parents see qualifications frameworks as a diagram, teachers and careers advisers see it as a concept and regulators and awarding bodies see it as a quality assurance process (Coles and Oates 2005: 44).

Frameworks are also described in metaphor. Qualifications frameworks have been characterized as a 'common language' and a 'bridge' between qualifications. The European Union often refers to its qualifications framework as a 'map' to guide students in locating qualifications and their destinations. In a 1997 green paper on education, the New Zealand minister of education proposed a qualifications framework to establish a 'common currency' to recognize students' achievements over time, across sectors and through different institutions, a metaphor also used by Norman Sharp, Director of the Scottish Office of the Quality Assurance Agency for Higher Education.

The economic role of qualifications frameworks is most frequently said to be to improve qualifications' links with labour markets. In particular, reformers hope that qualifications frameworks will improve the capacity of qualifications to signal the knowledge, skills and competences of job applicants, thus reducing the costs of recruitment for employers and more generally enhancing people's employability. However, the metaphor of qualifications frameworks as a 'common currency' suggests that they are also used to establish a market in qualifications, a point made by Strathdee (2003: 157). A currency, or more generally money, is commonly understood to have four functions: 'a medium, a measure, a standard and a store' (Wikipedia, 2008).

To be effective, a medium of exchange or intermediary in trade should be recognizable as something of value, easily transportable and durable. The certificates recording qualifications are durable and easily transportable but their value is not necessarily recognized outside the jurisdiction or even sector in which they are issued.

So the development of the diploma supplement as part of the Bologna process can be understood as a means for improving the recognition of the value of European qualifications. A medium of exchange should also be a store of value, that is, be reliably saved, stored, retrieved and have a predictable value when retrieved (Wikipedia, 2008). Qualifications already mostly meet the conditions for being a store of value: they are long lasting and durable, they have a stable value and they can be made difficult to counterfeit, for example by requiring verification by the awarding body.

A medium of exchange also needs to have a standard numerical unit of measure of relative worth. An effective measure should be divisible into small units without destroying its value and it should be verifiable. A measure should also be fungible; that is, one unit must be exactly equivalent to or at least indistinguishable from another (Wikipedia, 2008). This explains the concern of designers of many qualifications frameworks to base them on standard units of learning of standard and verifiable quality. It also explains the importance of the European credit transfer and accumulation system, the unit of measure of learning that is gaining increasing acceptance in European higher education. The standard measure of student learning in the USA is the Carnegie unit or credit hour. A normal full-time academic year is 30 credits. The USA also has a common grading scheme to report the quality of student achievement, which is frequently summarized as a grade point average. The standard US grading scheme has a five-point scale, with 4 being the highest score and 0 for fail.

Clearly, there must be widespread and high confidence in qualifications frameworks for them to serve any useful role, including as a medium of exchange. This led Young (2002: 60; 2003: 208) to posit that qualifications must be founded on 'communities of trust' based on the shared values and practices of occupational, subject and disciplinary communities. Coles and Oates (2005: 12) develop this into the concept of a zone of mutual trust, which is an understanding between individuals, enterprises and other organizations about the teaching, assessment and recognition of learning outcomes. Zones of mutual trust may vary in scope, formality and stability.

Coles and Oates (2005: 14) categorize mechanisms for establishing and maintaining zones of mutual trust. Direct formal mechanisms include legislation, licensing, labour market agreements, national accreditation systems and targeted funding. They categorize qualifications frameworks as indirect formal mechanisms for zones of mutual trust with credit structures and mechanisms for recognizing and accrediting prior learning. Informal mechanisms include recruitment drives, employer–candidate information exchange, guidance processes and local validation systems. A good example of a zone of mutual trust is the European higher education area, which comprises a formal agreement in the Bologna declaration of 19 June 1999; the collaboration of institutions in restructuring their qualifications in the three cycles of bachelors, masters and doctorates; the tuning project on curricula agreements in higher education; and the European credit transfer and accumulation system.

Zones of mutual trust are therefore developed by a properly functioning qualifications system, which comprises all aspects of a country's activity that result in the recognition of learning. These systems include the means of developing and operationalizing national or regional policy on qualifications, institutional arrangements, quality assurance processes, assessment and awarding processes, skills recognition and other mechanisms that link education and training to the labour market and civil society (Coles and Werquin 2007: 22). A related concept is policy breadth, which describes the extent to which a qualification framework is directly and explicitly linked with the conditions for its implementation, such as assessment systems and teacher retraining (Raffe 2003: 242). The existence and strength of a country's zones of mutual trust are related to its type of economy.

In Chapter 1, we noted that northern continental Europe tends to have market economies coordinated by their social partners: governments at national and regional levels, business and labour. The mechanisms differ in different economies, but in Germany, the federal government in consultation with the social partners sets the national framework and the provision of vocational schooling by the state governments (*Länder*) and the provision of on the job training by employers is coordinated by local chambers of industry and commerce (*Kammer*) and chambers of crafts (*Handwerkskammer*) and their vocational training committees. The coordinated market economies thus tend to have strong communities or zones of mutual trust. In contrast in the liberal market economies, employers invest less and are less involved in vocational education because they are less confident that their newly trained employees will not be poached by employers who do not invest in vocational training. Zones of mutual trust therefore tend to be weaker in the unpredictable liberal market economy.

It will be noted that all the countries that established a qualifications framework in the first phase have a liberal market economy – Australia, England and Northern Ireland, New Zealand, Scotland and South Africa – and that most of the countries that established a qualifications framework in the second phase also have a liberal market economy. Conversely, it will be noted that the countries with a strongly coordinated market economy – such as Germany, the Scandinavian countries, France and other countries of northern continental Europe – do not have a qualifications framework and, further, are not contemplating one. This reflects the importance of qualifications in sorting and matching graduates and employment in liberal market economies and hence the utility of a qualifications framework in establishing a 'common currency' or medium of exchange between qualifications and between qualifications and employment opportunities. But in coordinated market economies this sorting and matching is done by the education systems and employer groups cooperatively, often tracking students from a relatively young age.

However, the coordination mechanisms of coordinated market economies are national and regional – few if any cross national borders. So the European higher education area – the 45 countries that signed the Bologna declaration – does not have the coordination mechanisms of an integrated coordinated market economy 'to promote citizens' mobility and employability and the Continent's overall development' as the Bologna declaration says in its preamble on its first page. A European qualifications framework may form part of a mechanism to promote people's mobility and employability, but this posits a role for qualifications across Europe somewhat different from the role they have within many European countries, particularly those with coordinated market economies.

Even larger issues will arise should tertiary education become further internationalized. National qualifications frameworks were the natural and adequate development when education was largely self-contained within nations or component regions. However, since at least the turn of the century, education has become increasingly internationalized: increasing numbers of students are studying in countries other than their own, institutions are increasingly establishing teaching sites in countries other than their country of establishment, graduates are seeking to have their qualifications recognized for employment in other countries and governments are increasingly comparing the performance of their own education systems with systems of other countries. As a result regional qualifications frameworks are being developed for the Southern African Development Community, the Caribbean and the Pacific Islands as well as Europe. But students, institutions, graduates and governments do not restrict their international links to the regions that were established for other reasons. This suggests that regional qualifications frameworks are an interim or possibly transitional stage to an international reference for qualifications.

Coles and Oates (2005: 15) argue that the obvious international reference for qualifications is UNESCO's international standard classification of education (ISCED) which is widely used to report and compare educational statistics within and between countries. The classification is described further in Chapter 3, but for present purposes it is sufficient to note that its most recent version, ISCED-97 classifies formal education into seven levels. Upper secondary education is level 3, what ISCED-97 terms the first stage of tertiary education is level 5 and the highest level is the second stage of tertiary education, level 6. ISCED-97 therefore has only three levels between the final year of secondary education and the doctorate, whereas most qualifications frameworks have from six to eight levels from the final year of secondary education and the doctorate. ISCED-97 is therefore too coarse at least at the upper levels to be useful as an international reference for qualifications frameworks.

However, if a qualifications framework or an international comparator has a large number of levels to accommodate every possible variation it becomes too complicated to be useful. Coles and Oates (2005: 19) suggest that the number of classificatory levels be kept reasonably modest and that variations be recorded as sublevels. They suggest that each major level have a possible three sublevels:

- *partial*: indicates that the qualification, training programme or job experience, while predominantly matching the specific descriptors, has some significant gaps that need to be acknowledged;
- *modal*: indicates that there is a good match of the qualification, training programme or job experience to specific descriptors;
- *exceeds*: indicates that there is a complete match of the qualification, training programme or job experience to the requirements of the specific descriptors at this level and some additional elements that exceed the requirements of the descriptors at this level.

National qualifications frameworks benefit from a variety of institutional supports. Yet they have taken a long time to achieve success that has been modest although worthwhile. International frameworks have much less developed institutional structures for consultation, consensus building, decision making, encouragement and enforcement. It therefore seems likely that it will be some time before international qualifications frameworks are well established and widely accepted. In the mean time, governments, institutions, employers and students will have to continue to broker international transfer and other relations between qualifications individually.

6

European integration in vocational and higher education

This chapter considers the Bologna declaration to establish the European area of higher education and the Copenhagen declaration on enhanced European cooperation in vocational education and training. It considers their antecedents, elements and prospects. The chapter concludes by considering the place of tertiary education in the European project.

6.1 The European project

All agree on the significance of the Bologna declaration on higher education of 19 June 1999. While it is admirably clear if a little general in its expression, there is marked disagreement over its motivation, implications and value. Arguably, this is because the Bologna declaration is part of the European project that operates concurrently and interchangeably at several levels:

- the integration of Europe;
- the pursuit of common economic, social, diplomatic and legal interests;
- the reform of specific sectors of economic and social activity.

6.1.1 The integration of Europe

While European powers had fought wars against each other for centuries, the European wars of the twentieth century and in particular World War II were distinctive in using industrial and mechanized means and in applying those against civilian populations and facilities. Never before had Europe visited on itself such mass devastation from war and the European project was established to ensure that it would never do so again. The origin of the European Union is the declaration delivered with the agreement of the chancellor of West Germany, Konrad Adenaur, by the French minister for foreign affairs, Robert Schuman. The Schuman (1950) declaration, which was prepared or at least inspired by the French economic advisor and politician Jean Monnet, looked behind the causes of war – be it the nationalism of the twentieth century or the religious disputes that animated previous European wars – to the means for the conduct of modern industrialized war. It proposed that French and German production of coal and steel be placed under what it called a common 'high authority', which was to become the European Coal and Steel Community. The Schuman declaration argued that:

> The pooling of coal and steel production should immediately provide for the setting up of common foundations for economic development as a first step in the federation of Europe, and will change the destinies of those regions which have long been devoted to the manufacture of munitions of war, of which they have been the most constant victims.
>
> The solidarity in production thus established will make it plain that any war between France and Germany becomes not merely unthinkable, but materially impossible. The setting up of this powerful productive unit, open to all countries willing to take part and bound ultimately to provide all the member countries with the basic elements of industrial production on the same terms, will lay a true foundation for their economic unification.
>
> (Schuman declaration 1950)

So, at its highest level, the European project is to integrate the continent, initially in coal and steel, then in nuclear energy and customs (1957) and subsequently in many other areas including a common passport (1985) and currency (2002).

6.1.2 Pursuit of common interests

The second level of the European project of the pursuit of common economic, social, diplomatic and legal interests is evident from article two of the Treaty of the European Union (Maastricht Treaty) signed in 1992 which sets out its objectives. The Union's first object is to promote economic and social progress:

> The Union shall set itself the following objectives:
>
> – to promote economic and social progress and a high level of employment and to achieve balanced and sustainable development, in particular through the creation of an area without internal frontiers, through the strengthening of economic and social cohesion and through the establishment of economic and monetary union, ultimately including a single currency in accordance with the provisions of this Treaty
>
> (European Communities 2002b [1992]: 10)

The union's other objectives are to establish an international identity through a common foreign and security policy; to strengthen the protection of human rights; to develop the union as an area of freedom, security and justice; and to maintain the *acquis communautaire* or the union's law.

6.1.3 Reform of specific sectors

The third level of the European project is to reform several sectors of economic and social activity. Part three of the Treaty of Rome establishing the European Community signed in 1957 as subsequently amended has 21 titles dealing with sectors. Thus, title I deals with customs, II agriculture, IV visas and V transport. Title XI is about social policy, education, vocational training and youth. Chapter 3 of title XI is about education, vocational training and youth. Clause 2 of article 149 provides that community action shall be aimed at, among five other things, 'encouraging mobility of students and teachers, by encouraging *inter alia*, the academic recognition of diplomas and periods of study' (European Communities 2002a [1957]: 98). Article 150 provides for the community to 'implement a vocational training policy which shall support and supplement the action of the Member States, while fully respecting the responsibility of the Member States for the content and organization of vocational training'. Title XVIII is about research and technological development.

6.1.4 Bologna's encouragement of student mobility

An example of the multiple levels at which the European project works is the Bologna declaration's encouragement of student mobility. As will be elaborated later, the Bologna declaration specifies six objectives. The fourth objective is 'promotion of *mobility* by overcoming obstacles to the effective exercise of free movement' (European Ministers of Education 2003 [1999], original emphasis). The Bologna declaration's promotion of student mobility can be understood to contribute to the European project's highest level of European integration since one of the declaration's introductory remarks posits the paramount importance of education and educational cooperation in developing and strengthening stable, peaceful and democratic societies. Student mobility can equally be considered to contribute to the European Union's pursuit of common economic and social interests since the declaration's introduction also posits that:

> a Europe of knowledge is now widely recognized as an irreplaceable factor for social and human growth and as an indispensable component to consolidate and enrich the European citizenship, capable of giving its citizens the necessary competences to face the challenges of the new millennium, together with an awareness of shared values and belonging to a common social and cultural space.

Some have understood Bologna's promotion of student mobility as part of a policy to increase trade in higher education by seeking to make European higher education more attractive to international students. This interpretation is supported by the exhortation in the introduction to the declaration:

> We must in particular look at the objective of increasing the international competitiveness of the European system of higher education. The vitality and efficiency of any civilisation can be measured by the appeal that its culture has for other countries. We need to ensure that the European higher education system acquires a world wide degree of attraction equal to our extraordinary cultural and scientific traditions.

When this is combined with the Bologna declaration's objects of shortening higher education's first cycle or qualification and increasing the transfer of credit one may reasonably argue that Bologna is concerned with reforming continental European higher education on a somewhat mythical Anglo-US model of commercialized or at least marketized higher education.

I suggest that all three interpretations of the Bologna declaration are correct. This does not make the declaration internally inconsistent because it operates concurrently at three levels. A mild marketization of higher education may contribute to the economic goal of a more productive community and the social goal of a more aware and tolerant community and the establishment of a common European market in higher education may contribute to European integration. Neither does this necessarily compromise the broader or idealistic objects of education: students, teachers and governments engage in and support education for multiple reasons. A bachelor of commerce may both educate its graduates and increase human capital.

6.2 The Bologna declaration

The Bologna declaration (European Ministers of Education 2003 [1999]) opens with an introduction of 500 words and then sets six objectives, shown in Box 6.1.

The declaration closes with 30 words about implementation and an agreement to meet again within 2 years. The declaration was initially signed by 29 European ministers of education, all the then members of the European Union and Iceland, Norway and the Swiss Confederation, which are not members of the Union. Since then there has been a steady flow of more countries joining the process, including Turkey, which joined in 2001, and the Russian Federation in 2003. By 2007 there were 46 signatories, so the European area of higher education created by the Bologna declaration is far bigger than the 27 countries of the European Union. The Bologna process is monitored by biannual ministerial conferences held in Prague in 2001, Berlin 2003, Bergen 2005, London 2007 and Leuven/Louvain-la-Neuve 2009.

Box 6.1   Extract from the Bologna declaration of 19 June 1999

While affirming our support to the general principles laid down in the Sorbonne declaration, we engage in co-ordinating our policies to reach in the short term, and in any case within the first decade of the third millennium, the following objectives, which we consider to be of primary relevance in order to establish the European area of higher education and to promote the European system of higher education world-wide:

Adoption of a system of *easily readable and comparable degrees*, also through the implementation of the Diploma Supplement, in order to promote European citizens employability and the international competitiveness of the European higher education system.

Adoption of a system essentially based on *two main cycles*, undergraduate and graduate. Access to the second cycle shall require successful completion of first cycle studies, lasting a minimum of three years. The degree awarded after the first cycle shall also be relevant to the European labour market as an appropriate level of qualification. The second cycle should lead to the master and/or doctorate degree as in many European countries.

Establishment of a *system of credits* – such as in the ECTS system – as a proper means of promoting the most widespread student mobility. Credits could also be acquired in non-higher education contexts, including lifelong learning, provided they are recognised by receiving Universities concerned.

Promotion of *mobility* by overcoming obstacles to the effective exercise of free movement with particular attention to:

- for students, access to study and training opportunities and to related services
- for teachers, researchers and administrative staff, recognition and valorisation of periods spent in a European context researching, teaching and training, without prejudicing their statutory rights.

Promotion of *European co-operation in quality assurance* with a view to developing comparable criteria and methodologies.

Promotion of the *necessary European dimensions in higher education*, particularly with regards to curricular development, inter-institutional co-operation, mobility schemes and integrated programmes of study, training and research.

(European Ministers of Education 2003 [1999], original emphasis)

6.2.1 Antecedents of the Bologna declaration

The Bologna declaration refers to its antecedent, the Sorbonne joint declaration 'on harmonisation of the architecture of the European higher education system', adopted on 25 May 1998 by the ministers responsible for higher education in France, Germany, Italy and the United Kingdom (European Ministers of Education 2004 [1998]). The Sorbonne declaration refers to the Lisbon convention of 1997, which in turn refers to six previous conventions on the equivalent periods of university study and on the academic recognition of university qualifications dating back to 1956 (Council of Europe 2004 [1997]). The Bologna process, therefore, is, importantly, part of the European project of integration. Indeed, one of the founders of the European Union, Jean Monnet, is reported to have said: 'If I had to do it again, I would start with education' (Watson 1997: 1).

6.2.2 Diploma supplement

To an English reader the diploma supplement through which the declaration seeks to promote European citizens' employability appears to be a combination of a degree certificate or testamur and an academic transcript. In addition to the information one would expect in a testamur and transcript, the diploma supplement includes information on the programme's entry requirements, mode of study, duration and any eligibility it provides for further study and professional status. The 2003 Berlin communiqué committed countries to ensure that that all students would be issued a diploma supplement free of charge by 2005. However, in 2007 *Trends V* (Crosier *et al.* 2007: 8) found that slightly fewer than half of the 908 institutions responding to their survey confirmed that they issue a diploma supplement to all graduating students.

6.2.3 Degree structure

Most of the very considerable attention devoted to the Bologna process in continental Europe has concentrated on the establishment of the two-tier qualification structure of bachelors and masters, often abbreviated as BA/MA. This was a radical change for many countries, whose first university qualification took from 5 to 7 years' full-time study before the two-tier structure was introduced. In their Berlin communiqué in 2003 the European ministers responsible for higher education said that they 'consider it necessary to go beyond the present focus on two main cycles of higher education to include the doctoral level as the third cycle in the Bologna Process'. In 2007 *Trends V* found that 82 per cent of the 908 institutions responding to the survey had the three cycles of bachelors, masters and doctorates. However, the new structure had not yet been implemented fully. It seems that in many institutions nearly all students who complete the first cycle continue to the second cycle. In many countries, especially Germany, the new degree structure was introduced in parallel with the old and in 2007 many universities were still enrolling students in the old programmes.

6.2.4 System of credits

The ECTS through which the Bologna declaration seeks to promote student mobility is the European credit transfer system, which was introduced in 1989 as part of the Erasmus student and staff mobility programme, which is now part of the Socrates programme to develop the European dimension in higher education described later. Sixty ECTS credits represents the workload of a full-time student for 1 academic year. ECTS was established initially to support the recognition of periods of study abroad and thus enhance the quality and volume of student mobility in Europe. That is, ECTS was a credit transfer scheme. Recently ECTS has been developing into an accumulation system to be implemented at institutional, regional, national and European levels. ECTS is described further in Chapter 4, section 4.2.6. In 2007 *Trends V* found that almost three-quarters of institutions responding to its survey reported the use of ECTS as a transfer system and over two-thirds as an accumulation system.

6.2.5 Student and staff mobility

The Bologna declaration's objectives to promote student and staff mobility have tended to be subsumed within, or at least overshadowed by the European Union's programmes, which have prominently promoted student and staff mobility since 1976. The union started with a pilot joint studies programme, which provided financial support for networks of departments that exchanged students for a period of up to 1 year and also included some modest funds to support mobile students. The joint studies programme was widely considered successful and was replaced and expanded in 1987 by the Erasmus programme. More than half of Erasmus funds support students whose study abroad for 3 to 12 months is recognized by their home institution. Erasmus was soon considered the flagship of the educational programmes administered by the European Union.

In 2001 the European Union established the Erasmus Mundus programme, which supports masters programmes involving consortia of at least three European universities. In 2007 nearly 2000 students and academics participated in Erasmus Mundus programmes. Erasmus also supports short intensive programmes of study lasting between 10 days and 3 months which bring together students and staff from institutions in at least three countries. These programmes support the efficient teaching of specialist topics, students working in multinational groups and teaching staff exchanging views on teaching content and approaches. The Erasmus programme also supports academics' assignments of short duration (1 to 8 weeks) and fellowships of medium duration (2 to 6 months) provided they are fully integrated in to the department or faculty of their host institution where they are required to make a substantial contribution to the host institution's teaching. In 1997 the Erasmus programmes were brought together with several other education programmes under the Socrates programme.

In its first year of operation 3244 students participated in the Erasmus programme. By 2007 this had increased to 150,000 annually or almost 1 per cent of the European student population. While this has been a considerable expansion, it is well short of the union's ambitious target for 10 per cent of students to study temporarily in another European country. Some 20,877 teachers or 1.9 per cent of the European teacher population participate in Erasmus teacher mobility.

Trends V reported institutions' perceptions of sustained and cumulative annual growth in student mobility from 2000 to 2007. However, the mobility of students within Europe is often not distinguished from international students who travel to study to or from countries beyond Europe. While European student mobility is meant to be revenue neutral for institutions and the numbers of incoming and outgoing Erasmus students are meant to be balanced, non-EU international students pay full tuition fees in many countries to provide substantial revenue for many institutions. There is also a longstanding and strong east–west imbalance in international students, with countries in western Europe having significantly more incoming than outgoing international students and countries in eastern Europe having significantly more outgoing than incoming international students.

6.2.6 Quality assurance

In the Berlin communiqué of 19 September 2003 the ministers of the Bologna process signatory states invited the European Network for Quality Assurance in Higher Education to develop 'an agreed set of standards, procedures and guidelines on quality assurance' and to 'explore ways of ensuring an adequate peer review system for quality assurance and/or accreditation agencies or bodies and to report back through the Bologna follow-up group to ministers in 2005'. As a result in 2005 the European Association for Quality Assurance in Higher Education and their ministers adopted standards and guidelines for quality assurance in the European higher education area. These provide:

- European standards and guidelines for internal and external quality assurance and for external quality assurance agencies;
- for European quality assurance agencies to submit themselves to a cyclical review;
- an emphasis on subsidiarity, the principle that matters are handled by the

competent authority closest to the citizen; accordingly, reviews will be
undertaken nationally where possible;
- a European register of quality assurance agencies;
- a European register committee, which will decide on the inclusion of
  agencies in the register;
- a European consultative forum for quality assurance in higher education.

6.2.7 European dimension

There are several European associations of higher education institutions,
students and staff promoting European cooperation. The European Union's
Socrates programme develops the European dimension at all levels of education. The Socrates programme encourages European educational cooperation in mobility, organizing joint projects, joint curriculum development,
establishing European networks to disseminate ideas and good practice and
conducting studies and comparative analyses. *Trends V* reported in 2007 that
while 60 per cent of institutions state that they have joint programmes in at
least one of the three cycles, mostly the second cycle, there was evidence that
only a small minority of students enrolled in these programmes.

6.2.8 Recognition of qualifications

The convention on the recognition of qualifications concerning higher education in the European region was developed by the Council of Europe
and UNESCO and adopted by a meeting of 27 national representatives in
Lisbon on 11 April 1997. By 2007 it had been ratified by 45 countries. The
Lisbon convention provides for each country to recognize qualifications –
whether for access to higher education, for periods of study or for higher
education degrees – as similar to the corresponding qualifications in its own
system unless it can show that there are substantial differences between its
own qualifications and the qualifications for which recognition is sought.
There are several other provisions for processes protecting applicants seeking
recognition of their qualifications.

The convention refers to six previous Council of Europe and UNESCO
conventions about academic recognition in Europe going back to the
European convention on the equivalence of diplomas leading to admission
to universities adopted in 1953. The Lisbon convention was adopted 2 years
before the Bologna declaration yet the latter makes no reference to the
recognition of qualifications. This may have been an oversight, but that
seems unlikely since most of the countries that initially signed the Bologna
declaration had attended and signed the Lisbon convention 2 years previously. It seems more likely that the signatories to the Bologna declaration
could not agree on a text about the recognition of qualifications. However, the Bologna process official website 2007–09 says that the mutual

recognition of degrees and other higher education qualifications is a 'cornerstone' of the European higher education area in which the Lisbon convention plays a 'crucial' role.

6.2.9 Prospects of the Bologna process

As was observed by Pavel Zgaga (2004: 15) in a paper based on his report to the 2003 Berlin conference of the ministers of education of the Bologna signatory countries, it is unlikely that the signatories at Bologna in 1999 expected that the process established or at least stimulated by the declaration would be as extensive and expeditious as it became. The Bologna process may have developed so strongly and quickly at least partly because European governments and institutions attached to the Bologna process changes that they believed were desirable in any case. The Bologna process was therefore a trigger and focus for many changes that had already been contemplated.

While the UK is a signatory of the Bologna declaration, and indeed it is a signatory of the antecedent Sorbonne joint declaration, until recently there has been little interest in the Bologna process either from the UK government or its institutions. Instead, the UK government has been concerned with its own far-reaching changes to higher education, starting with the National Committee of Inquiry into Higher Education chaired by Sir Ron, now Lord, Dearing. The Dearing committee reported in 1997, 2 years before the Bologna declaration was signed and arguably its implementation extended until variable tuition or 'top-up' fees were introduced in the 2006–07 academic year. More recently the UK government has shown more interest in the Bologna process and indeed hosted the Bologna fifth ministerial conference in London in May 2007.

Zgaga (2004: 4) also observes a growing convergence between the Bologna process and the European Union processes to strengthen European cooperation in higher education. Furthermore, Zgaga notes that decisions of a series of European Union councils have gradually altered the status of the Bologna declaration for Union members from a voluntary action to a set of commitments. While this seems a good observation, since Zgaga formed those views the Russian Federation became a full member of the Bologna process in 2003. Russia is vast, with a population almost as big as Germany and France's combined and with a gross domestic product almost as big as that of France. Some 50 Russian institutions responded to the *Trends V* questionnaire, only 4 per cent of the 1146 accredited higher education institutions in the Russian Federation. As the Russian Federation engages fully with the Bologna process it may change its dynamic so that it develops differently from the European Union.

6.3 The Copenhagen declaration

On 30 November 2002 the ministers for vocational education and training of 31 European countries including the original signatories of the Bologna declaration, the members of the European Union and the European Commission (2002) adopted the Copenhagen declaration on enhanced cooperation in European vocational education and training. The introduction to the declaration of almost 700 words refers to the Bologna declaration which was probably an incentive for the Copenhagen declaration. It also refers to the presidency conclusions of the Lisbon European Council of March 2000, which will be elaborated later. The Copenhagen declaration then states eight priorities, which are set out in Box 6.2.

Box 6.2 Extract from the Copenhagen declaration of 30 November 2002

On the basis of these priorities we aim to increase voluntary cooperation in vocational education and training, in order to promote mutual trust, transparency and recognition of competences and qualifications, and thereby establishing a basis for increasing mobility and facilitating access to lifelong learning.

European dimension
- Strengthening the European dimension in vocational education and training with the aim of improving closer cooperation in order to facilitate and promote mobility and the development of inter-institutional cooperation, partnerships and other transnational initiatives, all in order to raise the profile of the European education and training area in an international context so that Europe will be recognised as a world-wide reference for learners.

Transparency, information and guidance
- Increasing transparency in vocational education and training through the implementation and rationalization of information tools and networks, including the integration of existing instruments such as the European CV, certificate and diploma supplements, the Common European framework of reference for languages and the EUROPASS into one single framework.
- Strengthening policies, systems and practices that support information, guidance and counselling in the Member States, at all levels of education, training and employment, particularly on issues concerning access to learning, vocational education and training, and the transferability and recognition of competences and qualifications, in order to support occupational and geographical mobility of citizens in Europe.

Recognition of competences and qualifications
- Investigating how transparency, comparability, transferability and recognition of competences and/or qualifications, between different countries and at different levels, could be promoted by developing reference levels, common principles for certification, and common measures, including a credit transfer system for vocational education and training.
- Increasing support to the development of competences and qualifications at sectoral level, by reinforcing cooperation and co-ordination especially involving the social partners. Several initiatives on a Community, bilateral and multilateral basis, including those already identified in various sectors aiming at mutually recognised qualifications, illustrate this approach.
- Developing a set of common principles regarding validation of non-formal and informal learning with the aim of ensuring greater compatibility between approaches in different countries and at different levels.

Quality assurance
- Promoting cooperation in quality assurance with particular focus on exchange of models and methods, as well as common criteria and principles for quality in vocational education and training.
- Giving attention to the learning needs of teachers and trainers within all forms of vocational education and training.

(European Ministers of Vocational Education and
Training and the European Commission 2002)

The Copenhagen declaration concludes with four principles to underpin enhanced cooperation in vocational education and training and three directions on implementing the declaration. The Copenhagen process is monitored by biannual ministerial meetings and updates, which have been held in Maastricht in 2004 and Helsinki in 2006.

6.3.1 Antecedents of the Copenhagen declaration

Vocational education has been a subject of the European Union from its foundation, but as a support, enabler or extension of economic policy rather than a policy in its own right. The Treaty of Paris signed on 18 April 1951 establishing the European Coal and Steel Community, the antecedent to the European Union, did not refer to vocational education. However, the community's governing body, the High Authority, undertook intensive work on training from its foundation and in its first general report it identified vocational training as a strategic element that, in improving the possibility of workers adapting to technical change, would promote the 'attainment of higher productivity' (Mechi 2004: 12–13). The authority published numerous reports on vocational education in member countries and exchanged training materials between members.

'Vocational training' was explicitly mentioned in the Treaty of Rome signed on 25 March 1957 establishing the European Economic Community. Article 41 of the treaty said that to enable the objectives of the common agricultural policy to be attained there should be 'effective coordination of efforts in the sphere of vocational training' and basic and advanced vocational training was one of the matters for which the commission had 'the task of promoting close cooperation between Member States' provided by article 118. Article 128 provided that the Council would 'lay down general principles for implementing a common vocational training policy capable of contributing to the harmonious development both of the national economies and of the common market'. While the implementation of this article was delayed because of national sensitivities in vocational education, by 1968 after 7 years' operation of the European social fund, 92 per cent had been allocated to national vocational retraining programmes.

One of the first specialized and decentralized agencies the European Community established to provide scientific and technical know-how in a specific field was Cedefop, the European Centre for the Development of Vocational Training, which was established in 1975. The community's role in vocational education was broadened by the Maastricht Treaty on the European Union signed on 7 February 1992 which established community policies in six new areas, including education and vocational training.

The decisive step towards the Copenhagen declaration in 2002 was taken the year before at a meeting of the directors general for vocational training for members of the European Union held in Bruges in October 2001. The meeting initiated a political process aimed at developing transparency and mutual trust in vocational education and training, which was adopted and elaborated by ministers for vocational education in the Copenhagen declaration. However, this was done in the light of the Lisbon European Council in March 2000 which, as the introduction to the Copenhagen declaration says, 'recognised the important role of education as an integral part of economic and social policies, as an instrument for strengthening Europe's competitive power worldwide, and as a guarantee for ensuring the cohesion of our societies and the full development of its citizens'. The presidency conclusions of the Lisbon European Council are known as the Lisbon strategy.

6.3.2 Lisbon strategy

The European Council comprises the heads of government of the European Union members and the president of the European Commission. The council held a special meeting on 23–4 March 2000 in Lisbon to agree on a new strategic goal for the union 'to strengthen employment, economic reform and social cohesion as part of a knowledge-based economy' as the preamble to the presidency conclusions says. There are six chapters in the presidency conclusions. Chapter 1 is on employment, economic reform and social cohesion and paragraph 1 observes: 'The European Union is confronted with a quantum shift resulting from globalisation and the challenges of a new knowledge driven economy. These changes are affecting every aspect of people's lives and require a radical transformation of the European economy.' Paragraph 5 of the presidency conclusions says:

5. The Union has today set itself a ***new strategic goal*** for the next decade: *to become the most competitive and dynamic knowledge-based economy in the world, capable of sustainable economic growth with more and better jobs and greater social cohesion.* Achieving this goal requires an ***overall strategy*** aimed at:

– preparing the transition to a knowledge-based economy and society by better policies for the information society and R&D, as well as by stepping up the process of structural reform for competitiveness and innovation and by completing the internal market;
– modernising the European social model, investing in people and combating social exclusion;
– sustaining the healthy economic outlook and favourable growth prospects by applying an appropriate macro-economic policy mix.
(Lisbon European Council 2000, original emphases)

In paragraph 26, the European Council called on the member states and the European Council and the commission to take the necessary steps to

define, by the end of 2000, the means for fostering the mobility of students, teachers and training and research staff both through making the best use of existing Community programmes (Socrates, Leonardo, Youth), by removing obstacles and through greater transparency in the recognition of qualifications and periods of study and training; to take steps to remove obstacles to teachers' mobility by 2002 and to attract high-quality teachers.

The Council also said that a common European format should be developed for curricula vitae to facilitate mobility.

6.3.3 European dimension

Early progress has not been made with strengthening the European dimension in vocational education and training or as the Copenhagen coordinating group's stocktaking report (European Commission 2003: 16) puts it: 'The specific modalities for follow-up of this priority have not yet been decided.'

6.3.4 Transparency, information and guidance

The European CV has been developed as the Europass, which comprises five documents (European Communities 2007). The Europass curriculum vitae (CV) is in a standard format with a web tool for users to create their own. The Europass language passport is also in a standard format and has a web tool for users to create their own passport in which they rate their language proficiency on the common European framework of reference for languages that has levels in each of listening, reading, spoken interaction, spoken production and writing. The Europass certificate supplement augments the information provided in a vocational education and training certificate and the diploma supplement augments information provided in a higher education award. Both supplements are issued by the body that issued the original award. The final document making up Europass is the Europass Mobility, which is a record of any organized experience that a person spends in another European country for the purpose of learning or training. A Europass Mobility experience might be a work placement in a company, an academic term as part of an exchange programme or a voluntary placement in a non government organization. The Europass Mobility is completed in a common format by the home and host organizations involved in the mobility project.

6.3.5 Recognition of formal learning

The European Commission (Commission of the European Communities 2006) proposes a European Credit system for Vocational Education and Training (ECVET), as a system for the transfer, accumulation and recognition of learning outcomes in Europe. The system would be based on the description of qualifications as learning outcomes of knowledge, skills and competence; the expression of qualifications in units of learning outcomes that can be transferred and accumulated; and the representation of the weight and value of each unit in ECVET credit points. The commission says that since the credit system would be based on learning outcomes it can be implemented irrespective of whether the learning context is non-formal, informal or different kinds of formal training programme and modules of various durations and involving various arrangements.

In the previous chapter on qualifications frameworks, we noted the difficulties in implementing frameworks based on learning outcomes, particularly those based on competences. The European Union's attempt will be much more difficult and much less likely to succeed, for two reasons. First, the experience of the South African national qualifications framework shows the difficulty of specifying learning outcomes with the precision needed to be operationalized even within one country. The task will be much more complex for the 31 signatories of the Copenhagen declaration working in over a dozen languages. Rainbird (1996: 117) argues that terms such as 'skill', 'qualification' and 'apprenticeship' derive from distinctive historical traditions and do not necessarily have equivalents from one country to another. And as Clarke and Winch (2006) and Brockmann *et al.* (2007) demonstrate, outwardly similar terms have different understandings and meanings in Dutch, English and German societies and presumably other cultures. Second, the tertiary education and particularly the vocational education systems of many countries of continental Europe such as Austria, France, Germany and the Swiss Federation are grounded deeply in their processes or institutions and specify qualifications by their inputs such as their syllabus, learning–teaching processes, institutional setting and assessment. These would be very difficult to change, even if those communities considered it desirable. This suggests that the European attempt to specify qualifications and units as outcomes will take a very long time to achieve, if it succeeds at all. It also seems highly improbable that the European credit system will be implemented irrespective of whether the learning context is non-formal, informal or different kinds of formal training programme.

To implement the system, a country's competent bodies will need to describe qualifications in terms of units of learning outcome. Specifications for a unit should typically give the generic title of the unit; the knowledge, skills and competence contained in a unit; and the criteria for assessing the corresponding learning outcomes. Competent bodies will also need to allocate ECVET credit points to qualifications and units and the commission proposes that 120 ECVET credit points represent the average learning outcomes achieved by a student in a normal full-time year of vocational education study. This is inconsistent with the European credit transfer system for higher education (ECTS) which allocates 60 credits for one year of full-time study, although the Copenhagen coordinating group's stocktaking report says that the vocational education European credit system should, in the medium term, be made compatible with the existing European credit transfer system in higher education.

6.3.6 Recognition of non-formal and informal learning

The European Union and the OECD distinguish three contexts of learning. Formal learning is learning through a programme of instruction in an educational institution, adult training centre or in the workplace that is evaluated and generally recognized in a qualification or a certificate. Non-formal learning is learning through a programme that is not usually evaluated and does not lead to certification. Informal learning is learning in daily activities of work, family or leisure. The union adopted a set of common European principles for validating non-formal and informal learning in 2004 that are organized in six themes: purpose of validation, individual entitlements, responsibilities of institutions and stakeholders, confidence and trust, impartiality and credibility and legitimacy.

In its progress report on the Copenhagen process to the ministerial meeting in Helsinki in December 2006 Cedefop, the European centre for the development of vocational training, noted that some countries were still debating and planning the validation (identification, assessment and recognition) of non-formal and informal learning. Cedefop used the European Commission's inventory of the validation of non-formal and informal learning to categorize countries' development in three stages:

- *experimental:* ad hoc methods and approaches have been set up to gain experience; a more permanent approach has still to be formulated and decided;
- *emerging:* a national approach has been decided; full implementation has yet to take place;
- *established:* permanent systems have been established and are in use.

Cedefop (Lipinska *et al.* 2007: 75) reported that the number of countries categorized as 'emerging' or 'established' has increased steadily in the last few years. They observed three methods being used. Portfolios are most common. Declarative methods such as inviting and supporting individuals to record their learning outcomes are gaining importance. The third method is for educational institutions to allow people with non-formal and informal learning experiences to sit tests, often known as challenge tests.

6.3.7 Quality assurance

In January 2003 the European Commission established a technical working group on quality assurance that examined existing national and international standards and norms, their application, strengths and weaknesses and identified a common core of criteria and a set of indicators for European quality development. This led to the preparation of a proposal on a common quality assurance framework that can be applied at both the level of the vocational education and training system and of individual providers. The framework has four interrelated parts:

1. a model that includes four steps of planning (i.e. setting goals), implementation, evaluation of programme provision by objectives including learners, assessment of students' achievement of outcomes and review (i.e. feedback and procedures for change);
2. a self-assessment method;
3. a monitoring system;
4. a measurement tool to contrast, compare and benchmark member states' systems.

The European Union's technical working group on quality proposed ten quality indicators for vocational education and training:

1. share of vocational education and training providers applying quality management systems consistent with the common quality assurance framework;

2. investment in training of trainers;
3. unemployment by population groups;
4. prevalence of vulnerable groups;
5. participation in initial vocational training and lifelong learning;
6. successful completion of training;
7. destination of trainees 6 months after training: further training; employed in a job related to training; unemployed etc.;
8. use of acquired skills at the workplace and it proposed two descriptive indicators;
9. mechanisms for forecasting skills development;
10. guidance, support and other schemes to promote better access.

Cedefop (Lipinska *et al.* 2007: 77) reported countries tend to adopt one of two approaches to quality assurance in vocational education and training. One provides common frameworks, recommendations and/or standards for individual vocational education providers to apply. The other is a centralized approach that involves national inspection, audits and quality labels or awards. Cedefop reported that countries are giving increasing importance to qualifications registers, mandatory quality assurance plans and provider accreditation.

6.3.8 Prospects of the Copenhagen process

While higher education has vocational outcomes and is often associated with high-status occupations, vocational education and training is often much more strongly associated with the economy and with industry's interests. This is true both in the European project and in individual countries and it is both a strength and a weakness. It is a strength because vocational education is often given importance in economic policies as well as social polices, as we have seen in the European Coal and Steel Community's early attention to vocational education and in its prominence in the Lisbon strategy. However, vocational education's close association with the economy and industry is a weakness because they sometimes subjugate the educational values and interests that should inform vocational education.

Vocational education's close association with the economy and industry is a weakness particularly for the European project in vocational education because changes to vocational education to implement European approaches have implications for nations' economies and industrial structures that are very close to the interests of nations and their powerful economic and industrial groups. Countries' vocational education systems may therefore continue to be as diverse as their economies and industrial structures, which would reduce the scope for the European project in vocational education. In many countries of continental Europe, the social partners – employers and unions – are closely involved in vocational education policy and programmes, often through regional vocational training bodies. However, while the social partners are consulted in European policy development, they have no formal role in European bodies. Any transfer of initiative in vocational education from national to European mechanisms is therefore likely to reduce the involvement of the social partners. This is not only likely to be resisted by the social partners, but may also undermine the implementation of vocational education policies that do not involve the social partners closely.

6.4 Prospects of tertiary education in the European project

The Sorbonne declaration of 1998 signed by four ministers of education concluded:

> The anniversary of the University of Paris, today here in the Sorbonne, offers us a solemn opportunity to engage in the endeavour to create a European area of higher education, where national identities and common interests can interact and strengthen each other for the benefit of Europe, of its students, and more generally of its citizens. We call on other Member States of the Union and other European countries to join us in this objective and on all European Universities to consolidate Europe's standing in the world through continuously improved and updated education for its citizens.
>
> (European Ministers of Education 2004 [1998])

The subsequent Bologna declaration's commitment 'to consolidate the European area of higher education' was initially adopted by 29 European ministers of education and by 2007 there were 46 signatories. Substantial progress has been achieved in establishing a common degree structure, adopting a diploma supplement and consolidating the European credit transfer system for higher education and a start has been made on promoting European cooperation in quality assurance. The Bologna process has developed a substantial momentum in the number of countries involved, the range of activities conducted, the depth in which they are pursued and the thoroughness of implementation and follow-up. This momentum therefore seems likely to carry the Bologna process forward some distance further.

The Copenhagen declaration is a little younger in being adopted in 2002 and its 31 signatories are hardly broader than the European Union's 27 members. Since its antecedents, the European Union has been active in vocational education and thus had established projects and machinery to implement them. Substantial progress has been made with the European CV Europass, progress has been made with a European credit system for vocational education and training and quality assurance and a start has been made on the recognition of non-formal and informal learning. Vocational education's close engagement with the economy and industry seem likely to ensure that it will remain prominent in the union for the foreseeable future.

As we observed earlier, there has been a growing convergence between the Bologna process to establish the European higher education area and the European Union's processes to strengthen European cooperation in higher education. If this continues despite the number of signatories that are not members of the European Union, especially the recent addition of the Russian Federation, the future of both the Bologna and the Copenhagen processes will depend on how the European Union develops. That in turn will depend on how the subsidiarity principle is implemented.

6.4.1 Subsidiarity

Subsidiarity is the principle that a central authority should have a subsidiary role, performing only those functions that cannot be performed effectively at a more immediate or local level. It originates in Catholic social teaching and was developed in *Rerum Novarum* (of new things), the encyclical or letter to bishops issued by Pope Leo XIII in 1891. The principle was elaborated in *Quadragesimo Anno* (in the 40th year), an encyclical by Pope Pius XI issued in 1931, 40 years after *Rerum Novarum*. Paragraph 79 of *Quadragesimo Anno* states the principle of 'subsidiary function':

> Just as it is gravely wrong to take from individuals what they can accomplish by their own initiative and industry and give it to the community, so also it is an injustice and at the same time a grave evil and disturbance of right order to assign to a greater and higher association what lesser and subordinate organizations can do.

The principle of subsidiarity is stated in section 1883 of the catechism or summary or exposition of *doctrine* of the Catholic Church.

In the European Union, the subsidiarty principle is that decisions must be taken as close as possible to the citizen. The principle was established in the Treaty of Maastricht in 1992. Article 3 of the consolidated treaty establishing the European Community lists its activities, including a customs union, common market, a common agriculture policy and several other matters. Article 5 states the principle of subsidiarity:

> The Community shall act within the limits of the powers conferred upon it by this Treaty and of the objectives assigned to it therein.
>
> In areas which do not fall within its exclusive competence, the Community shall take action, in accordance with the principle of subsidiarity, only if and in so far as the objectives of the proposed action cannot be sufficiently achieved by the Member States and can therefore, by reason of the scale or effects of the proposed action, be better achieved by the Community.
>
> Any action by the Community shall not go beyond what is necessary to achieve the objectives of this Treaty.
>
> (European Communities 2002b [1992]: 9–10)

This is elaborated in the treaty's protocol 30 on the application of the principles of subsidiarity and proportionality. The principle of proportionality is that no action by the community shall go beyond what is necessary to achieve the objectives of the treaty. Paragraph 5 of the protocol 3 guidelines to test whether the principle of subsidiarity is fulfilled: the issue has transnational aspects that cannot be handled satisfactorily by member states, the issue involves a conflict with the treaty such as a restriction of trade which requires community action to address or action at community level would produce clear benefits by reason of its scale or effects compared with action at the level of the member states. Paragraph 3 provides that subsidiarity is a dynamic concept that allows community action to be expanded or contracted in accordance with circumstances.

While paragraph 1 (q) of the consolidated treaty provides that the community's activities shall include 'a contribution to education and training of quality and to the flowering of the cultures of the Member States', education is clearly subject to the principle of subsidiarity. This means that most European Union policy on education is voluntary and community action can be achieved only by the open method of coordination.

6.4.2 Open method of coordination

The open method of coordination is sharing information and monitoring performance to align national policies either with each other or with a framework adopted by the European Union. It was first applied to employment policy by the Amsterdam Treaty of 1997. This inserted into the European Union treaty a new title VIa of provisions on closer cooperation, which explicitly did not include the harmonization of the laws and regulations of the member states. The open method of coordination was first named and described in paragraph 37 of the presidency conclusions of the Lisbon European Council (2000). It involves:

- fixing European guidelines and goals and short-, medium and long-term timetables for their achievement;
- establishing quantitative and qualitative indicators;
- translating European guidelines into national and regional policies and targets;
- periodic monitoring, evaluation and peer review.

Paragraph 38 of the presidency conclusions says that the method will be implemented with a fully decentralized approach in line with the principle of subsidiarity. It will be seen that both the Bologna and Copenhagen processes have been implemented by the open method of coordination, with countries' progress towards European guidelines monitored in biannual ministerial meetings. It is likely that the open method of coordination will be continued for both the Bologna and Copenhagen processes, but for different reasons. While both are about tertiary education and thus are subject to the principle of subsidiarity, vocational and higher education have different dynamics that make more directive coordination or harmonization unlikely.

Universities have a deep and old tradition of institutional autonomy and their teachers and researchers have an even older tradition of intellectual freedom. The close involvement of the state in managing universities in France, Germany, Russia and many other countries notwithstanding, universities and their academics stoutly resist encroachment on their decision-making privileges. Governments and the union will therefore need to continue to rely on the open method of coordination has succeeded in bringing universities into line.

In contrast, vocational education institutions and their staff typically do not have unusual discretion that would allow them to resist national or European harmonization. Vocational education is, however, closely engaged with national economies and industries and harmonization of vocational education would require either its disengagement from national economies and industries or a harmonization of economies and industries. Either outcome seems remote, so the open method of coordination will continue to be necessary in vocational education and training.

6.4.3 Separation of vocational and higher education

The starkest point about the prospects of tertiary education in the European project is the separation and, indeed, inconsistency between the objectives for vocational and higher education. The qualifications frameworks, credit systems and quality assurance for each sector are different and in some aspects inconsistent. While some of these differences appropriately reflect the differences between the sectors and their purposes, others seem contingent and arbitrary, but no less unresolvable for that. The Bologna process for higher education anticipated the Copenhagen process for vocational education, but while Copenhagen was probably inspired by Bologna, in almost all its actions it has declined to follow Bologna's example. Instead, Copenhagen has built on the work of the European Union in vocational education that extends back half a century, work that Bologna has almost completely ignored. While rapporteurs and analysts occasionally note the almost complete separation of the Bologna and Copenhagen processes some suggest the desirability of coordinating them but that prospect seems remote.

7

Sectors

This chapter considers why sectors of tertiary education emerged and whether it is desirable to maintain them. The chapter posits a division of tertiary education into four tiers, segments or sectors: world research universities, selecting universities or colleges, recruiting universities or colleges and vocational institutes.

7.1 Overview

The dominant use of 'sector' is in economics where it refers to a subdivision of economic activity. Thus modern diversified economies have three main areas of activity: a primary sector that extracts and produces raw materials, a secondary sector that transforms materials into goods and a tertiary sector that provides services. On this classification, education is in the tertiary sector. Mixed economies may also be divided into public, private and voluntary sectors and education is typically found in all three sectors, albeit predominantly in the public sector. 'Sector' is also used in economics to refer to producers that produce similar goods or services, such as the housing sector or the education sector.

In education, 'sector' refers to institutions that offer broadly similar types of education. The main divisions are primary, secondary and tertiary. Primary and secondary education are readily identified by the age of their pupils, although the age of transfer from primary to secondary education differs in each jurisdiction. The description of the sector that follows secondary education is less well settled. Some describe it as 'post-compulsory' since this is said to describe an important characteristic. However, in most jurisdictions post-compulsory senior secondary education is offered in the same institutions under similar conditions as compulsory secondary education, so this characteristic is not as important as others. Some describe the sector as 'postsecondary'. While this is descriptive, the synonym 'tertiary' is preferred here because it is in the same linguistic sequence as 'primary' and 'secondary'.

This chapter is about subdivisions within tertiary education, which are also often called sectors, although in California they are called segments. Burton Clark (1983: 53) observed that: 'If there is a single structural key in the negotiating of effective modern systems, it appears to lie in sectoral differentiation.' This chapter starts with the division of tertiary education into vocational and higher education. It traces the origins of this division to both employers' and unions' resistance to state involvement in apprenticeships and to the state's concern to expand higher education beyond its initial restricted social and disciplinary coverage. The chapter then critically examines arguments for segmenting tertiary education into sectors and common binary and tripartite arrangements.

The second part of the chapter considers numerous mechanisms for bridging the sectoral divide between vocational and higher education. These are analysed in a matrix: one dimension is levels of association from unified to partnership, collaboration and separation; the other dimension is levels of organization from supra-institutional to institutional, sub-institutional and personal (manager, teacher, student). This framework systematizes the numerous examples of cross-sectoral associations described.

7.2 Historical development of vocational education

Formal education in Europe during the Middle Ages was provided by monasteries, which educated their pupils for religious duties and by apprenticeships. Craft skills were passed from parent to child with little collective instruction until the establishment of guilds, which had among their purposes some forms of vocational education. One of the earliest was the Candlemakers' Guild founded in 1061 (Barlow 1965: 1). England established a national system of apprenticeships remarkably early with the Statute of Artificers of 1563. The US colonies were strongly committed to education to teach people to read and thus receive the authority of the Bible directly, unmediated by the teaching of the church (Thompson 1973: 58). Apprenticeships soon followed, supported by laws and rules adopted by towns and counties but without the support of guilds and other craft organizations that fostered the apprenticeship system in England.

Apprenticeships had three characteristics which became anachronistic after the Industrial Revolution (Bennett 1926: 266). Apprenticeships were based on the handicraft mode of production. The first Industrial Revolution was distinctive not in its introduction of power and mechanization, but in its introduction of the division of labour ('the Babbage principle', Berg 1993: 287, fn 20) and its introduction of a new organization of work in the factory system of production (Berg 1993: 191). As many contemporary commentaries observed, this made redundant craftsworkers trained with multiple skills to produce a whole product. Second, the apprenticeship as with all other relations of the trade was long-term, normally 7 years, and terms including price were based on 'custom' or those traditionally accepted as just. One of the critical changes in England from the Napoleonic Wars was to set prices by supply and demand and establish terms by contract 'freely' negotiated separately and for the rather short duration of each transaction (Thompson 1980: 260).

Third, apprentices normally lived with their master's family. The relationship between a master and his apprentice established by the indenture was of guardianship or custodian of the apprentice's whole development rather than the narrow employment relationship of the factory. So masters were expected to give their apprentices moral, religious and civic instruction as well as teaching their craft's technical skills and introducing their charges to the 'mysteries' of their trade (Bennett 1926: 21). Some guilds even required masters to teach their apprentices how to read and write and masters who did not have the ability or time to fulfill this responsibility personally did so by sending their charges to continuation schools established for this purpose.

Among the upheavals of the Industrial Revolution was the collapse of the apprenticeship system and in 1814 the repeal of the apprenticeship clauses of the Statute of Artificers, which had been on the statute books for 252 years. As contemporaries observed, the division of labour in the new factories did not develop workers' skills or their knowledge of the whole production process, yet skilled workers were still needed and were not being produced by the 'now almost obsolete' apprenticeships (Magnus 1888: 21–2). Magnus (1888: 21, 23) concluded that workers' 'only opportunity of acquiring such knowledge is outside the workshop or factory – in a technical school . . . or some other substitute for apprenticeship'.

Apprenticeships were therefore replaced, at least partly, by Sunday schools, part-time schools and factory schools. In 1791 'schools of industry' were established in England as a substitute for apprenticeships (Bennett 1937: 46). France established its *écoles nationales d'arts et métiers* (national schools of arts and crafts) in 1799 and its *École Centrale des Arts et Manufactures* (Central School of Arts and Industries) in 1829. A very influential model was Russia's School of Trades and Industries established in 1830, which became the Imperial Technical School in 1868. Magnus (1888: 23) also argued for the establishment of a system of technical education for social reasons, to occupy and train children factory workers who were dismissed when they mature. 'Numbers of young men are thus thrown upon the labour market, competent to do nothing more than children's work, and to earn children's wages, and knowing no trade to which they can apply their hands' (Magnus 1888: 23). The Industrial Revolution was not as quick and extensive in Germany, hence its guilds and apprenticeship system remained to form Germany's modern dual system of tertiary education.

The London Mechanics Institution was established during this period in 1824 inspired by George Birkbeck's lectures in Glasgow and London 20 years earlier. The main purpose of these institutions was to disseminate 'useful knowledge' but even so their courses were limited to instruction in the scientific principles underlying a craft and did not include instruction in the craft itself (Magnus 1888: 20). Practical trade instruction in workshops was opposed both by employers, who feared that they would sell their output at subsidized prices, and by unions, which feared that they would produce too many and too cheaply skilled workers who would depress wages and working conditions. Governments were also wary of favouring particular industries by supporting technical education. The Australian colonies followed the UK example remarkably quickly, establishing the Van Dieman's Land Mechanics Institute in 1827, the Sydney Mechanics' School of Arts in 1833 and similar institutes in Adelaide in 1838, in Melbourne in 1839, Brisbane in 1849 and in Perth 1850 (Murray-Smith 1965: 174). Again following the UK example: 'All of these institutions placed emphasis on "Instruction in the principles of the Arts and in the various branches of science, and useful knowledge" as the objects of the Van Dieman's Land Mechanics Institution had it' (Murray-Smith 1965: 174). Their emphasis on the principles underlying a craft rather than the craft itself separates theory from practice.

While the mechanics institutes did not survive their original purpose beyond 25 years, they 'were particularly important as early examples of further technical instruction for their influence on later developments' (Cotgrove 1958: 13). 'Moreover the teaching of the scientific principles underlying a craft in the mechanics' institutes and the separation of theory from practice became an established tradition which set the pattern for later provision and persisted in its influence over technical education throughout the century' (Cotgrove 1958: 13–14). Thus the Technical Instruction Act of 1889 defined technical instruction as 'instruction in the principles of science and art applicable to industries, and in the application of special branches of science and art to specific industries or employments. It shall not include teaching the practice of any trade of industry or employment' (quoted in Pratt 1970: 14).

The early success of the mechanics institutes encouraged the philanthropist Quintin Hogg to open his polytechnic in Regent Street in 1881. This was a great success and by 1897 another eight polytechnics had been established with a total enrolment of 26,000 students, a large proportion of whom were manual workers (Cotgrove 1958: 60). But manufacturers doubted that trades could be taught satisfactorily outside a workshop and largely ignored the new institutions. Cotgrove argues that polytechnics were established to serve social, not industrial or business interests. Only later was vocational education redirected from serving individuals' needs to those of an industrial economy:

> The extension of technical instruction in the polytechnics and else-
> where was the outcome of efforts to elevate the working classes, rather
> than any concern with the contribution of education to industrial pro-
> ficiency. It was the child of educationists, philanthropy, and the demands
> of students, and received little blessing or guidance from the manu-
> facturing and business community.
>
> (Cotgrove 1958: 65)

From this quick review two analytic distinctions can be posited. First, one may distinguish training for a job, for a vocation, for a career and training for life. Medieval apprenticeships were clearly training for a vocation – from apprentice to journeyman and then to master – but also training for life in their inclusion of moral, religious and civic instruction. Second, educational institutions may provide education and training that complements, substitutes or is an alternative to training for a job. Thus the pre-Industrial Revolution continuation schools complemented the on-the-job training of apprenticeships, but in teaching literacy they provided education for life as well as enhanced career prospects. By the same token, England's schools of industry and France's *écoles nationales d'arts et métiers* were substitutes for apprenticeship systems heavily eroded if not completely destroyed by the Industrial Revolution. The mechanics institutes provided education for a career and for life as alternatives to apprenticeships.

From its antecedents there was no obvious reason in principle for systematic vocational education to be separated from general and higher education. It was established for social and moral improvement rather than to contribute to industrial efficiency, it provided education for life as much as developing technical skills and it taught the principles underlying crafts rather than the crafts themselves. Nonetheless, as we shall see in the next section, vocational education was separated from general education much further than might be warranted by its different subject matter.

7.3 Historical separation of vocational education from general education

Despite their being established to offer lower level education, polytechnic students expressed strong demand for more advanced studies. By 1904 some six polytechnics were offering baccalaureates and 50 of their teachers were recognized as university teachers, teaching 500 undergraduates. By 1909 this had increased to 100 recognized teachers and 836 matriculated students (Cotgrove 1958: 64). Some 80 per cent of polytechnic undergraduates attended lectures part-time in the evening, indicating that then UK universities did not make much of an effort to accommodate part-time students. However, there was considerable resistance to polytechnics offering higher academic studies, from, for example Millis, Principal of the Borough Polytechnic, and Quintin Hogg himself. Hogg argued that polytechnics were intended mainly for artisans and workers and 'I did not include the [cultural] subjects you mention for fear of attracting a class of young men of a higher educational status than those for whom the institute was intended' (Cotgrove 1958: 63). Nonetheless, technical colleges maintained baccalaureate programmes as a substantial part of their offerings.

Central governments' antipathy to vocational education also contributed to its deep separation from general education. Sir Robert Morant, the UK's permanent secretary for education from 1902 and the main architect of the

English educational system, separated 'technical' from 'secondary' education under the Education Act of 1902 rather than develop them as an integrated whole. Morant redirected resources, attention and prominence from vocational education to classical education in the grammar schools he promoted (Vlaeminke 1990: 64) although Sanderson (1999: 12) argues that Morant's effect on vocational education was equivocal rather than as harmful as Vlaeminke claimed. The other countries covered in this study followed similar patterns.

The separation of technical colleges and universities was established in Australia by the 1880s. It was reinforced by the Murray Committee of 1957, which criticized the blurring of responsibilities in many places between universities and technical colleges, but emerged again after 1964 when the bigger technical colleges were promoted to colleges of advanced education and did not relinquish all their vocational education programmes. Education authorities' comparative neglect of vocational education provoked a defensive reaction from its champions. Thus in 1917 the US federal government became involved in education, a state responsibility under the US constitution, to fund vocational education under the Smith-Hughes Act. The champions of vocational education and the act sought to protect it from encroachment by general education by encouraging separate administration of the programme.

The rest of this chapter considers the desirability of establishing tertiary education sectors and how they may be constructed.

7.4 Why have sectors?

Clark (1983: 51–71) gives three arguments for dividing tertiary education into sectors. First, it greatly facilitates student access, at least to the lower tier. Second, Clark argues that a lack of sectors leads to an overload of activities and conflicting priorities. This in turn leads to the burdens of mass teaching and counselling crowding out research and advanced training according to Clark. But this depends on which activities are taken as given and which are variable. Clark seems to assume that universities will retain a comprehensive range of disciplines while the activities of teaching, counselling, research and advanced training are opportunities for specialization. But in many ways it would be more logical for institutions to specialize by discipline but conduct a comprehensive range of activities for their specialized disciplines. An example is the former Soviet Union and communist countries of central and eastern Europe, which unified vocational and higher education within sectors defined by field. Thus monotechnics in agriculture, economics, engineering, fine arts, medicine, pedagogy and physical education offered both types of tertiary education.

Third, Clark argues that new sectors should be established to discharge major new functions. Thus, junior or community colleges were created in the USA to handle mass participation and the UK established its Open

University to offer mass distance education. According to Clark adding new types of institution to handle new functions makes the system as a whole more adaptive than trying to get the old sectors to discharge new functions in addition to their current functions. But this overlooks the fact that in the USA the mass higher education function was grafted on to the upper stream of secondary education which until then already had an important role in providing occupational training. Consequently, 2-year colleges were expected to fulfil dual and then multiple purposes. They offer a large variety of programmes ranging from less than 6 months to up to 2 years and from continuing education to vocational education and to academic education in the first 2 years of baccalaureate studies. This, in turn, has caused competing and in some cases conflicting roles and priorities within 2-year colleges. Arguably Clark's (1983) functional segmentation in the USA has simply shifted role overload from the more powerful and better resourced higher education institutions to the more vulnerable and lesser resourced vocational education institutions.

Furthermore, on this argument research should not have been added to the then mostly teaching-only universities in the nineteenth century, but a new sector should have been established specifically to discharge this new function, and indeed this was argued by Newman (1959 [1853]) in *The Idea of a University*. Depending on what is considered a major activity or contradictory operation, graduate professional education, part-time study, distance education, mature age entry and online learning should not have been added to universities throughout the twentieth century which, at least until World War II, were then dominated by full-time face-to-face undergraduate education for school leavers.

Even granting the need or desirability for organizational specialization, Clark's argument does not help in deciding the organizational level at which specialization should occur. Consider graduate programmes such as the master of business administration. These could be made the specialized responsibility of a sector such as France's *grandes écoles*; of an institution such as Quebec's *École des Hautes Études Commerciales*; the responsibility of part of an institution such as the graduate schools of management common in the UK and the USA; or of part of a faculty also responsible for undergraduate teaching and research as is common in Australia. Likewise baccalaureates are variously the specialized responsibility of sectors, of institutions, in the USA of undergraduate colleges within institutions and of programme coordinators within faculties within institutions. As will be seen later, in parts of continental Europe mode 1 (Gibbons *et al.* 1994) investigator-initiated and discipline-based research is mainly the responsibility of what might be considered a fourth sector of research only institutes and in other jurisdictions such as California research is concentrated in research intensive universities. It is also commonplace for research centres to be established within institutions and within faculties and departments within institutions. It is not obvious that labour is better divided at one level of organization rather than any other.

A modern variant of this argument of Clark's is that formally prescribed institutional diversity supports programmatic diversity – the capacity of the system to offer a diversity of programmes for a diversity of learners and for a diversity of outcomes. However, Huisman *et al.* (2003: 14) found exactly the opposite: 'High levels of diversity are not related to high levels of participation. On the contrary: the results indicate that the lower the level of diversity, the higher the level of participation.' Huisman *et al.* claim that this is consistent with what little empirical research there is in the area. They cite Teichler's (1997: 225) conclusion: 'The data made available in the six country studies [USA, Japan, Switzerland, Singapore, China and Germany] do not suffice to draw any conclusions about the relationship between massification and structural diversification.'

Others argue for the maintenance of sectors to promote excellence in the more selective sector or to protect 'elite segments' from the pressures of more and more diverse students. Scott (2000: 198) observes that the differentiation that was initially based on a distinction between academic and vocational programmes which was closely aligned with social class hierarchies is now based on a distinction by research activity. Scott does not quite disentangle three successive drivers of segmentation:

1. *cognitive*, when academic education was differentiated from vocational education which, in turn, is related to different labour force needs and outcomes;
2. *access*, when open-entry sectors were established to preserve selective entry of the 'noble' sector;
3. research, when support for research is concentrated in a sector.

These drivers have been overlayed on existing structures, so that top-tier institutions in the jurisdictions in this study are academic, have selective student entry and are research intensive. While most arguments for the establishment of sectors are from or on behalf of the more selective institutions, some argue for the maintenance of sectors to protect vulnerable vocational education institutions from predation by universities, echoing vocational education's defensive position early in the century. James (2007: 10) argues that whatever the merits of the stratification of tertiary education into sectors, it is an almost inevitable outcome of massification.

7.5 Two sectors

As was outlined in Chapter 3, the international standard classification of education distinguishes between two types of tertiary education. Tertiary type A programmes typically require a minimum of 3 years' full-time study. They are theoretically based and prepare students for research in basic disciplines or provide access to professions with high-skills requirements. Tertiary type B programmes are typically shorter than type A programmes and are practical, technical or occupationally specific. This distinction also often coincides with a distinction between programmes leading to the award of a baccalaureate or bachelor's degree and programmes leading to sub-baccalaureate awards such as certificate, diplomas and associate or foundation degrees. The distinction also often coincides with students' social origins, occupational destinations and manner of attendance. Tertiary type A institutions are also distinctive in having at least a significant proportion of students in residence, whereas tertiary type B students commute. These institutional types are also sometimes referred to as 'noble' and 'less noble' (OECD 1971), referring to their status or esteem.

Thus there is a general pattern of tertiary type B education that offers shorter vocational programmes that do not lead to the baccalaureate, it has open or at least less selective entry, students come from a broad range of backgrounds, most attend part time, most commute to study and most proceed to middle-level occupations. Tertiary type B institutions are known as further education colleges in the UK, community or 2-year colleges in the USA and vocational education and training institutions in Australia. The general pattern of tertiary type A education is to offer longer programmes that are broader and more general in orientation, the first qualification typically leads to the baccalaureate, it has more selective entry, most students come from middle to upper social backgrounds, most attend full-time, many are in residence and most proceed to professional and higher level occupations. Tertiary type A institutions are known as universities in most jurisdictions.

These distinctions between tertiary type B and tertiary type A can be tabulated and mapped onto the arrangements in different jurisdictions, as shown in Table 7.1.

The proportions differ in different provinces and states, but in the USA, associate degrees typically comprise from 20 per cent to 40 per cent of total tertiary education load, with the national average being 30 per cent (US Department of Education 2000). Some 11 per cent of higher education load in England and 27 per cent of tertiary education load in Scotland is taken in colleges of further education (Parry and Thompson 2002). Vocational education is 17 per cent of tertiary education in Australia, 37 per cent in Canada, 9 per cent in France and 15 per cent in Germany (Grubb 2005: 19).

7.6 Three sectors

We have seen that California formally segments its tertiary type A or public 4-year colleges and universities into two segments. The more selective segment is the University of California which has a formal research role, offers doctorates in a wide range of disciplines and is restricted to admitting the top 12.5 per cent of high school graduates. The other sector is the California State University, which does not have a formal research role (although research is conducted in the university), does not offer doctorates in its own right and is restricted to admitting the top 33.3 per cent of high school graduates.

In some other jurisdictions, there is no formal segmentation of tertiary

Table 7.1 Tertiary type B and tertiary type A

Characteristic	Tertiary type B	Tertiary type A
Award baccalaureate?	No	Yes
Programme duration	Short	Medium–long
Student admissions	Less selective – open entry	More – highly selective
Student class	Broad	Weighted to middle-upper
Student attendance	Most part-time	Most full-time
Student residents	All commute	Significant residents
Status	Less noble	Noble
Jurisdiction *Australia*		
Institutions	Vocational education and training providers	Universities/higher education institutions
Sectoral tag	Vocational education and training providers	Higher education
UK		
Institutions	Colleges of further education	Universities
Sectoral tag	Learning and skills sector	Higher education
USA		
Institutions	Two-year/community colleges	Four-year colleges/ universities
Sectoral tag	Higher education	

type A institutions but the older, more research intensive and more selective institutions have formed themselves into a group. One of the oldest of such groups is the Association of American Universities, which was formed in 1900 by a group of 14 universities offering the PhD. The association currently comprises 60 US and two Canadian universities. In the UK, an informal self selected body of 20 research-led institutions formed itself into the Russell Group in 1994. In the same year in Australia, the eight universities with the biggest research expenditure formed itself into the Group of Eight.

In other jurisdictions, there is no formal or informal segmentation of tertiary type A institutions but it is still possible to discern two groupings. The most prominent grouping is of institutions having a big research expenditure, are at least 50 years old but most are much older and are highly selective and thus are also elite. These institutions might be classified as tertiary type A1 institutions or called world research universities. The other institutions are generally younger, have less research expenditure and are moderately and less selective and thus are less socially elite. These might be classified as tertiary type A2 institutions.

For students, staff, businesses and governments that are not geographically mobile the national indicators of institutional standing are sufficient. However, students, research funding and staff are increasingly mobile across national boarders. Because education is a positional good, international students as well as domestic students choose institutions within their financial and educational reach that have the highest status. Multinational businesses commission research from the institutions that have the highest standing in their field of interest in the world or at least in the countries in which they have operations or a market. Governments are also increasingly allocating research funds to the institutions with the highest international standing. Staff, in turn, are attracted to institutions with the best research facilities and working conditions and therefore the highest funding, as well as to institutions with the best prepared students and highest status.

Simply comparing the national groupings of world research universities is not satisfactory for internationally mobile students, staff and business. Many countries have no formal groupings of highly selective universities. Of those that do, the balance between A1 and A2 institutions differs in each country. Thus the Association of American Universities is 2 per cent of US universities, the Russell Group is 12 per cent of UK universities and the Group of Eight is 21 per cent of Australian universities. Since the markers of distinction differ in each country it is not possible to compare directly a member of the Association of American Universities and a member of the Russell Group, for example. An international distinction between A1 and A2 institutions is therefore useful and salient because it affects the international flow of students, research funding and staff. The most methodologically sound and authoritative world ranking of universities is the Shanghai Jiao Tong University's Institute of Higher Education's academic ranking of world universities. This ranking is, however, of research only, it is dominated by research in the physical sciences and it privileges English over other languages of science.

The level of selectivity of membership of the Association of American Universities, the Russell Group and the Group of Eight is similar to being in the top 200 of Shanghai Jiao Tong University's academic ranking of world universities. Inclusion in the top 200 of this rank is therefore arguably an appropriate working definition of world research universities. It is, however, very selective and would mean that these countries would not have a world research university despite having very fine universities: Chile, Czech Republic, Egypt, Greece, Hungary, India, Ireland, New Zealand, Poland, Portugal and South Africa. All universities in Shanghai Jiao Tong University's academic ranking of world universities compete against each other on similar grounds, so it may be appropriate as well as convenient to define the world research universities as those that are ranked in Shanghai Jiao Tong University's academic ranking of world universities. Some 500 universities are ranked in Shanghai Jiao Tong University's academic ranking of world universities, which is 5 per cent of the approximately 9760 universities in the world. So the more inclusive working definition of world research universities is still very selective.

7.7 Four sectors

While the more inclusive definition of world research universities would include in one category universities with considerable differences, arguably there is even greater variation among the universities not included in the rank. The USA has 166 universities in the 2007 academic ranking of world universities, which is 6 per cent of its 2580 institutions offering 4-year or bachelor degrees. The UK has 42 universities in the Shanghai Jiao Tong rank which is 25 per cent of its 170 universities and higher education colleges. Canada's 22 universities in the Shanghai Jiao Tong rank are 24 per cent of its 92 public and private not-for-profit universities and university degree-level colleges and 47 per cent of its 47 universities. Australia's 17 ranked universities are 44 per cent of its 39 universities. So from 60 per cent to 80 per cent of countries' universities are not world research universities and by virtue of their much greater number one may expect at least as much if not greater variation among non-world research universities as there is among world research universities.

The considerable variation among universities not included in Shanghai Jiao Tong University's academic ranking of world universities is evident from the various university categorizations within countries. The USA's Carnegie classification of colleges and universities published in 1973 is well-known. The substantially revised 2005 Carnegie classification of institutions of higher education has a basic categorization of institutions by level of highest award into associate's colleges, baccalaureate colleges, master's colleges and universities, doctorate-granting universities, special focus institutions and tribal colleges. Each basic category has subcategories. Thus doctorate-granting universities are divided by level of research activity into three subcategories and masters colleges and universities are divided into three subcategories by size of their masters programmes. The UK has subgroupings of universities based broadly on age and research intensity, with the 1994 Group being the next prestigious after the Russell Group. There is a broader divide in UK universities between the pre-1992 universities and the post-1992 universities, most of which were formed by redesignating former polytechnics. The Canadian weekly news magazine *Maclean's* categorizes Canadian universities into medical doctoral universities, comprehensive universities and primarily undergraduate universities. Like the UK, Australia also has subgroupings of universities based largely on research intensity and age, and also like the UK, Australia has a broad divide between pre-1987 universities and post-1987 universities, which were largely formed by redesignating former colleges of advanced education.

While these distinctions between non-world research universities differ in detail between countries, arguably it is possible to draw a common distinction between them based on Maclennan and colleagues' (2000) distinction between selecting and recruiting universities. Maclennan *et al.* (2000: 12) observe that post-1992 higher education institutions often promote themselves more prominently seeking to recruit students to fill their enrolment targets. In contrast, pre-1992 higher education institutions have traditionally followed a softer approach, relying more on liaison with schools. A recruiting university might be defined as one that has fewer than two applications for each student place to be filled while a selecting university would have two or more applications for every place to be filled. Recruiting universities have a demand problem and therefore operate in a buyers' market in which the competition is between institutions for eligible students. In contrast, there is a supply problem with selecting universities which therefore operate in a sellers' market in which the competition is between students for admission to desirable institutions (Marginson 1997: 251).

We may thus posit four tiers, segments or sectors of tertiary education. At the top is tertiary type A1 – world research universities. These are the universities listed in Shanghai Jiao Tong University's academic ranking of world universities or, if a more selective sector is sought, in the top 200 of the Shanghai Jiao Tong rank. These institutions are at least 50 years old, but most are much older and some are as much as 500 years old. They are very research intensive, which is supported by considerable research funding from government and often from philanthropists, business and alumni. They compete internationally for staff, students and research funding.

The second tier or sector is selecting universities and colleges. These institutions offer at least bachelor degrees but probably also masters and doctorates. Most conduct research and some have areas of international research strength. However, their research strengths are not sufficient to win them a place in the Shanghai Jiao Tong rank or a place in the top 200 of that rank. These institutions, nonetheless, have very high standing at least in their region if not nationally and internationally and thus enjoy strong demand for their programmes.

The third sector of recruiting universities and colleges comprises institutions that may be similar in many ways to selecting universities and colleges but they do not have the national or perhaps even the regional standing of their selecting counterparts, probably because they are distinctly younger. The fourth tier is of vocational institutes which enrol 75 per cent or more of their load in vocational education programmes such as vocational associate's degree in the USA, higher national certificate and diplomas and diplomas of higher education in the UK and diplomas and associate degrees in Australia. This categorization of tertiary education institutions is shown in Table 7.2.

It should be noted that unlike some national categorizations such as the USA's Carnegie classification and Canada's Maclean's categorization, the categorization proposed here does not distinguish institutions by size or breadth or even by nomenclature. The California Institute of Technology, widely known as CalTech, is clearly a world research university, being ranked 6th in Shanghai Jiao Tong University's 2007 academic ranking of world universities. Yet it has only just over 2000 students concentrated in engineering and sciences and is not even called a university. Imperial College London has 12,500 students concentrated in engineering, natural sciences and

Table 7.2 Four sectors of tertiary education

Characteristic	Tertiary type A1	Tertiary type A2	Tertiary type A3	Tertiary type B
Description	World research university	Selecting university	Recruiting university	Vocational institute
Rank	SHJT/top 200	High in national ranks	Middle to low in national ranks	Unranked
Research	Intensive	Strong	Active	None
Typical age	50–500 years	50–500 years	< 50 years	< 100 years
Award baccalaureate?	Yes	Yes	Yes	No
Program duration	3–7 years	3–7 years	3–7 years	3 months–2 years
Student admissions	Highly selective	Highly selective	Selective–less selective	Less selective –open entry
Student class	Weighted to middle-upper	Weighted to middle-upper	Weighted to middle-lower	Broad
Student attendance	Most full-time	Most full-time	Most full-time, many part-time	Most part-time
Student residents	Significant residents	Significant residents	Some residents	All commute
Status	Elite	Selecting	Recruiting	Less noble

medicine. Yet Imperial College is also clearly a world research university, being ranked 23 in 2007.

The distinguishing characteristic of world research universities is their research strength, the distinguishing characteristic of selecting universities is their strong student demand, the distinguishing characteristic of recruiting universities is their lower student demand and the distinguishing characteristic of vocational institutes is their predominance of vocational programmes. Yet there is one general characteristic that underlies the whole classification: positional value. The sectors or tiers are organized in order of their positional value from world research universities, which have the highest positional value, in descending order to vocational institutes, which generally have the lowest positional value in tertiary education, although they still have markedly more positional value than secondary education. This is illustrated by the OECD's *Education at a Glance*. Table A9.1a of the 2007 edition reports populations' relative earnings from employment by level of educational attainment. Employees without upper secondary education in OECD countries earned on average 78 per cent of the income of employees with upper secondary education. Employees with vocational education qualifications earned on average 24 per cent more than those with upper secondary education. And employees with a tertiary education type A qualification had an earnings premium of 63 per cent above workers with upper secondary education qualifications.

These four tiers manifest differently in different countries and systems. For example, Labaree (2006: 7) also posits four tiers in US tertiary education, but notes the parallel hierarchies of religious institutions and liberal arts. There are also exceptions to these generalizations. Employees with vocational education qualifications earn 54 per cent more than upper secondary graduates in Norway, 19 per cent higher than the earning premium of Norwegian university graduates. Since Norwegian vocational institutes confer greater economic value on their graduates than universities they are likely to also have more positional value. Arguably, in France most *grandes écoles*, which would be classified as selecting universities, are more selective and have higher positional value than the French world research universities. And, again in France, the *instituts universitaires de technologie* are vocational institutes but are more selective and arguably have higher positional value than many universities. Presumably, there are other exceptions in other countries, but the broad generalization certainly holds.

8

Relations between vocational and higher education

This chapter describes patterns for organizing vocational and higher education and ways of overcoming the main disadvantages of sharp divisions between the sectors. The chapter gives numerous examples of various forms of association of the sectors from unification, partnership, collaboration to separatism. These are considered by level of organization from supra-institutional levels to the level of individual manager, teacher and student.

8.1 Different patterns of vocational education provision

Different motives for establishing a vocational education sector posit different models of vocational education institutions. If the purpose is to support cognitive differentiation between academic and vocational education then an appropriate model is of a specialized vocational institutes such as the *instituts universitaires de technologie* in France, *više škole* in Yugoslavia, *Fachhochschulen* in Germany, regional colleges in Norway and *hogescholen* (higher vocational institutes) in the Netherlands.

However, if the main function of vocational institutes is to provide scope for higher education to expand to mass participation without reducing universities' selectivity, then an appropriate model is a sector that is 'equal to but different from' higher education. This, often described as the binary model, was best instanced by the UK polytechnics but other examples are New Zealand's polytechnics and Australia's former colleges of advanced education. Following the dismantling of the binary divide in the UK in 1994 colleges of further education have taken on the role of providing mass participation.

Providing for mass participation was the initial motive of University of Chicago President William Rainey Harper and of University of California system President Clark Kerr in advancing in the USA what are now commonly referred to as 2-year colleges. However, providing mass participation in the USA was grafted on to the upper stream of secondary education which until then had provided vocational education. A similar procedure of upgrading secondary institutions or marginal tertiary institutions was adopted in England and Wales, Spain and in the then Federal Republic of Germany with the upgrading of the *Fachschulen* to *Fachhochschulen*.

In Chapter 1, we observed two broad patterns or tendencies for structuring tertiary education into two sectors: the tracked systems of northern continental Europe exemplified by Germany and the generalist systems of English-speaking countries exemplified by the USA but also seen to greater and lesser extents in Canada, New Zealand and the UK. In the tracked systems vocational and higher education are likely to be sharply differentiated, they are likely to share less curriculum and fewer programmes and there is likely to be less exchange of students, staff and methods. But, as we shall see in the generalist systems, the sectors are more likely to merge and overlap.

8.2 Divide between vocational and higher education

Australia followed the Anglo pattern of giving tertiary education institutions general roles until 1965. However, vocational institutions were confined to sub-diploma programmes following the Martin report of 1964. Since then Australia has followed the western continental European pattern of keeping largely separate its vocational and higher education sectors, institutions, programmes and students. So Australia is anomalous or at least distinctive in formally distinguishing its vocational and higher education sectors as deeply as many western continental European countries, but it does so within a liberal market economy that, in other Anglophone countries, is associated with merged and overlapping vocational and higher education sectors.

The different roles served by tertiary vocational and higher education require different curricula, student entry requirements and different staff qualifications. But the differences between the sectors in Australia go far beyond what may be required to discharge their different roles and are closer to the tracking that is characteristic of Europe. Responsibility for financing and coordinating vocational institutes is mostly with state and territory governments, students pay tuition fees upfront, the curriculum framework is set by training packages and qualifications are accredited in accordance with the Australian quality training framework. Conversely, almost all distinctively higher education qualifications are offered by universities for which the Commonwealth has primary responsibility for financing and coordinating, fees are collected mostly through the higher education contribution scheme and higher education's curriculum is based largely on content that the universities accredit themselves.

Teaching staff in the two sectors in Australia think of themselves very differently and construct their industrial interests differently. Teaching staff in vocational education and training are represented by the Australian

Education Union, which also represents schoolteachers, while higher education teaching staff are represented by the National Tertiary Education Industry Union, which also represents general staff in higher education. Some of the tensions in inter-sectoral relations and obstacles to closer integration of the sectors can be traced to teaching staff of one sector protecting work and conditions from alternatively undermining or encroachment by staff of the other sector. The state branches of both unions are particularly jealous – or vigilant – in maintaining the sectoral boundaries. The alignment of vocational education's identity with distinctive organizational arrangements also leads the sector's supporters to resist the harmonization of organizational arrangements between the sectors despite obvious advantages.

In contrast, the organizational division between the sectors is less distinct in the other English-speaking jurisdictions we are considering and the sectors share more organizational characteristics. While tuition fees for programmes in vocational institutes are lower than in higher education institutions, they are set within the same financing framework. This is partly because the sectors are now the responsibility of the same level of government in these jurisdictions. Vocational institutions have been brought within the same financing framework since US state governments gradually took over more responsibility for financing community colleges from local government districts from the 1980s and since the English government took over responsibility for financing colleges of further education from local government in 1992. Greatest variability remains in curriculum frameworks (see Table 8.1).

While the exchange between vocational and higher education is currently not very big in Australia, they share diplomas and advanced diplomas that may be vocational or higher education qualifications. The overlap of these qualifications and the almost complete separation of the sectors in almost all characteristics generates a host of anomalies and inconsistencies. Students pay different fees under different arrangements and with different levels of subsidy by different levels of government depending on whether they are taking the programme in vocational education and training or a higher education institution. This may have some rationale were programmes substantially different in each sector, but they are described almost identically by the Australian qualifications framework advisory board and there is considerable overlap between the sectors.

8.3 Mechanisms for bridging the sectoral divide

It is important for liberal market economies to have a ready exchange between vocational and higher education. Obstacles to that exchange have been investigated extensively in the USA, where the issue is mostly cast as the problem of student transfer from 2- to 4-year colleges, which is the subject of Chapter 9. In the UK and Australia, the sectoral divide has been problematized in mainly institutional terms. This chapter reviews mechanisms for

Table 8.1 Sectoral divide in selected jurisdictions

Jurisdiction/ administration	Vocational education	Higher education
Australia		
Financing	States	Commonwealth
Fees	Upfront	Deferred income-related loans
Curriculum	Training packages	Content
California		
Financing	State government	State government
Fees	Upfront and loans	Upfront and loans
Curriculum	Mandated core	Mandated core at junior level
Canada		
Financing	Provinces	Provinces
Fees	Upfront and loans	Upfront and loans
Curriculum	Mandated in some provinces; unregulated in others	Mandated in some provinces; unregulated in others
England		
Financing	National	National
Fees	Upfront and loans	Upfront and loans
Curriculum	National vocational qualifications	Content

bridging the sectoral divide at five levels, from the supra-institutional to the individual.

Australia's former National Board of Employment, Education and Training (NBEET 1994: 9–11) identified seven types of cross-sectoral collaboration between vocational and higher education: strategic alliances, pathways, co-location and joint developments, specialized education and training facilities, joint programmes, cross-sectoral institutions and cross-sectoral provision of subjects. Young and colleagues (1997) systematize these relations in what they subsequently call a 'matrix of unification', which classifies systems as unified, linked and those that operate on separate tracks. Their matrix maps systems on four dimensions – content and process, system architecture, delivery and government and regulation. So, one of the four aspects of content and process is curriculum, which can be unified, linked or completely separate on different tracks. Likewise delivery may be by institutions that are unified, linked or tracked. Sommerlad *et al.* (1998: li) position institutions as largely conforming to, or tending towards, one of four approaches to cross-sector collaboration: amalgamation, partnership, association and separation. They observe that collaboration might occur in teaching, research and development, professional development, consultancy, promotion, marketing and recruitment and shared use and development of infrastructure.

This chapter considers four levels of collaboration, but at different levels of organization, from the jurisdiction (which in a federation may be a state or nation depending on the issue) through sectors, subsystems, institutions and faculties to basic units of organization, departments, programmes and subjects and, finally, to individual teachers and students. At each organizational level, vocational and higher education may be unified, there may be a formal legal association of independent bodies, which I will call a partnership, there may be collaboration or the two types may be quite separate. Table 8.2 maps the possibilities.

This typology is perhaps simplistic in ignoring pedagogy and considering only levels of organization, some of which may have been overlooked. The levels of association could certainly be elaborated, but at the price of clarity. This table is the framework for the literature and practices reviewed in this chapter. The review starts with the top level of organization and considers examples of levels of association of vocational and higher education from unified to separate. The review proceeds sequentially down the levels of organization.

Table 8.2 Template of levels of association of vocational and higher education at levels of organization

Level of organization	Level of association			
	Unified	*Partnership*	*Collaboration*	*Separate*
Supra-institutional				
Jurisdiction				
Sector				
Subsystem				
Network				
Institution-wide				
Institution				
Campus				
Division				
Organizational unit				
Group				
Faculty				
Department				
Curriculum				
Programme				
Subject				
Person				
Manager				
Teacher				
Student				

8.3.1 Supra-institutional levels

So starting at the highest level of organization, the jurisdiction, vocational and higher education may be unified, there may be a formal legal association or partnership of independent bodies, there may be collaboration or the two types may be quite separate.

8.3.1.1 Jurisdiction

The powerful – and dynamic – arguments promoting formal segmentation of tertiary education systems notwithstanding, there are good reasons for establishing unitary systems. It is very expensive to establish in each small town separate institutions discharging the specialized functions of each sector. Therefore, people in smaller population centres are either deprived access to whichever sector is not represented in their town or comprehensive institutions should be established in the smaller centres. This has been tried in several countries, but hybrid systems of functionally differentiated sectors in the major cities and comprehensive institutions in the smaller population centres are unstable and rarely work beyond the enthusiasm of their initial founders.

Clark (1983: 66) observes that a unitary system encourages greater similarity in practices and more equal funding of its components since unitary systems encourages ' "coercive comparisons" in which "have-nots" exercise strong leverage for equity against the "haves", the less-noble against the noble'. This may be an advantage or disadvantage depending on a prior position. Clark observes that sectors quickly become hierarchies. He therefore concedes that a unitary system probably advances equity, at least in the short term. Stevenson (1998b: 140) argues more radically for 'the paradigm shifts needed to unify and redefine the tertiary sector', a position that has been also advocated by several others. Scott (2000: 192) argues that in any case the development of new modes of knowledge production appears to be making higher education an anachronism as a distinctive category of institutions.

One alternative is to give students opportunities to transfer between sectors; this is the subject of Chapter 9. Nonetheless, Furth (1992: 1222) remains sceptical of institutional differentiation because of the risks of developing limited and rigid sector structures. Skilbeck *et al.* (1998: 25) argue that coherent policies are facilitated by unitary systems or at least a strong bridging mechanisms between sectors. Raffe and colleagues (1998: 171–2) argue that the sectors are based on an industrial division of labour that is now outmoded. However, Clark (1983: 52) observes that the equitable motives for establishing a unitary tertiary education system may be thwarted by internal differentiation within the system. Just such a phenomenon will be observed in Chapter 9, which reports and examines rates of transfer from vocational to different types of higher education institution.

In the USA, Wisconsin and Georgia have the most comprehensive systems that incorporate all their state's vocational and higher education institutions except 'non-collegiate technical institutes'. Technical institutes are separate from 2-year colleges: they award certificates and diplomas of 2 or fewer years' duration and few if any of the credits are transferable to 4-year degrees. In 1996 Minnesota combined three hitherto separate systems (4-year colleges, 2-year colleges and vocational-technical institutes) into the single state university system of Minnesota, but this still excludes the flagship University of Minnesota and its branches. So only part of these systems is unified.

There are many examples of jurisdictions in which vocational and higher education are associated in partnerships and collaborations, although again they are often smaller and it may not be possible to apply their example to bigger jurisdictions. Arguably, at the level of national jurisdiction, Australia separates its tertiary sectors. With the limited exception of the ministerial council on education, employment, training and youth affairs, there is only one national public cross-sectoral body, the Australian qualifications framework advisory board. This board has been a forum for dispute between rather than cooperation of the sectors recently (over associate degrees) and arguably its long-term role has been to separate, not unify the sectors (Wheelahan and Moodie 2005).

8.3.1.2 Sector
At the next level of organization, which is most commonly the sector, the former Soviet Union established monotechnics in pedagogy, agriculture, medicine, economics, fine arts, physical education and engineering that included both vocational and higher education. Sectors based on the distinction between vocational and higher education may form partnerships or they may collaborate as is common but by no means pervasive in the USA. On this typology, the vocational and higher education sectors of continental western Europe would be shown as quite separate; they would be coordinated, however, or more precisely their role in the economy would be coordinated through regional councils.

8.3.1.3 Subsystem
'System' is often used ambiguously. It has been used so far in this chapter to refer to all tertiary education coordinated or operated under a single high-level policy. It is, however, also often used to refer parts of the larger system when probably 'subsystem' would be more correct. Thus one may observe that the Victorian 'system' of technical and further education has from its foundation in the middle of the nineteenth century been less closely coordinated than, for example, the NSW Tafe system which is rather tightly coordinated. Some (sub)systems in the USA and Canada integrate vocational and higher education, mostly by including what in the UK would be considered further education and higher education institutions within one subsystem.

An example of subsystem collaboration is NSW TAFE (an acronym for technical and further education), which had a credit transfer agreement with all NSW universities from 1991 to 1996. The NSW TAFE educational service divisions, which are the groups responsible for curriculum development in each broad field, negotiated credit for programmes with each NSW university. Because the TAFE curriculum was based on content and was uniform throughout the state, universities could confidently award the same credit for a programme offered throughout the NSW TAFE system.

8.3.1.4 Network
Networks are rather more common in the USA than in other jurisdictions, but the Victorian College of Agriculture and Horticulture was a network before it was incorporated within the University of Melbourne's Institute of Land and Food Resources and, arguably, the Australian Catholic University has many characteristics of a network as well as of the unified multicampus institution that it presents itself as. Harvey (1996: 4) has proposed a variant of Clark Kerr's (1963) multiversity, the 'federal omniversity', which would combine all further and higher education institutions in a region within a single institutional framework. The vice-chancellor of the University of Derby has proposed just such an arrangement for Derbyshire (Waterhouse 1998; 2000).

The UHI Millennium Institute is a partnership of 15 colleges and research institutions in the Highlands and Islands of Scotland. The partners enrolled 3000 full-time equivalent higher education students and 5000 full-time equivalent further education students. A similar arrangement has been proposed for Cornwall.

8.3.2 Institution-wide levels

8.3.2.1 Institution
Familiar in Australia is the institution, which unifies vocational and higher education, called dual-sector universities. Of Australia's five dual-sector universities Swinburne University of Technology unifies vocational and higher education at the institutional level but not at lower levels except for central services, which are mostly fully integrated. Sweden has had a formally unified system of tertiary education since 1977, but within that there are a number of different types of institution, including universities, university colleges and specialized institutions for fields such as health sciences, so Sweden is not a strong example of a unified system.

The USA has over 400 institutions that offer both vocational and higher education programmes. These include institutions that offer vocational and higher education programmes on the same campus, those that vocational and higher education programmes on different campuses and three large state systems that incorporated vocational institutions. Some 13 institutions allocate responsibility for vocational programmes to a separate division (these include Brandywine College of Widener University, University of the District of Columbia, Kentucky State University, University of Chicago at Illinois, University of New Hampshire, Southern Illinois University at Carbondale, Virginia Commonwealth University and Youngstown State University).

Several US institutions include both types of programme within faculties or departments. There are 36 such public institutions including Ball State, Colorado State, Indiana, Purdue, the University of Georgia, the University of Maine, the University of Pittsburgh and Western Michigan. Other institutions that integrate vocational and higher education programmes at the faculty or department level are Colorado Technical University, a private for-profit institution that was founded as a technical training school in Colorado Springs in 1965, small private liberal arts schools (Gwynedd-Mercy College, Huron University, Lincoln Memorial University and Salem College) and two are related to a church (Concordia University, Wisconsin, and Gannon University). The University of Rio Grande is a private institution offering vocational programmes under contract from the state government. Vocational programmes are offered at branch campuses of Pennsylvania State University, the University of Connecticut, the New Mexico State University, the University of South Carolina and several others.

Windham *et al.* (2001: 39) argue that by having 2- and 4-year institutions share what they call a 'concurrent-use campus' students are able to complete their lower division requirements in a community college setting including any needed remediation and can transfer to a university for the final 2 years without having to change geographical locations. However, Prager (1993: 551–2) argues from her study of transfer within US institutions that offer both 2- and 4-year programmes that the benefits to student transfer of structural alignment can be thwarted by a range of behaviours within institutions:

> To the extent that closely articulated two- to four-year programs are an important factor in student transfer outcomes, survey data suggest that more than a few colleges and universities with two- and four-year programs display some of the same characteristics inhibiting transfer within their institutions more typically described by those writing about transfer between unrelated sets of institutions, namely community and senior colleges. These include elitist judgements degrading two-year students and programs, enrolment caps favouring baccalaureate track students, arbitrary rulings confusing curriculum parallelism and comparability, and archaic notions about program terminality inconsistent with the educational aspirations of occupational-technical students.
>
> The data also indicate that some baccalaureate programs and providers tacitly endorse transfer-inhibiting practices peculiar to articulation issues within four-year institutions. These include the failure of those in authority to enforce articulation policies on the books, where such policies exist. These also include, as well, alienating policies such as those that force subbaccalaureate students wishing to pursue the baccalaureate to reapply for admission as if foreign to the institution or that penalise them for following comparable but not identical curriculum sequences to those in the first two years of a university's four-year track. For those who seriously propose that aligning community colleges structurally to universities can cure the transfer malaise, the evidence presented

here suggests that institutions offering both four-year and two-year education under the same umbrella do not do so *de facto* under prevailing conditions that assure continuity to the baccalaureate.

(Prager 1993: 551–2)

A number of Australian universities have established separate divisions to offer vocational and other sub-baccalaureate programmes, mainly to international students. One of the earliest and most successful of university subsidiaries established to offer sub-bachelor programmes is Insearch, which was established as a wholly owned for profit subsidiary of the University of Technology, Sydney, in 1987. At its Sydney centre, Insearch offers academic pathway programmes to the university, a range of English pathway and language programmes and one of the world's largest testing centres for the International English Language Testing System. In China, Insearch has offered in partnership with Shanghai University since 1994 diplomas in English and business as well as the university's bachelor of business. Insearch established its centre at the University of Essex in 2004 at which it offers IELTS preparation programmes and academic and English pathway programmes that lead to direct access to Essex University.

Monash University established Monash College as a wholly owned for-profit subsidiary in the 1990s and it now offers diplomas at the university's Clayton, Caulfield and Peninsula campuses and also in Singapore, Guangzhou (China), Jakarta, and Colombo. Monash University's English-language centre offers intensive language programmes and the Monash University foundation year is an equivalent Australian year 12 programme offered by Taylors College in Australia and other partners in Laos, Jakarta and Malaysia (Kuala Lumpur and Johor Bahru). The Australian National University has established ANU College as a registered training organization offering a foundation studies programme, an ANU access English programme, English-language instruction for overseas students, extended university English, an advanced secondary studies programme, maths bridging courses and group study tours. Several other universities in other countries have similar arrangements. York College, for example, is an associate college of the University of York and offers a range of sub-bachelor higher education qualifications such as foundation degrees and vocational programmes such as higher national certificates and higher national diplomas.

The sectors are still generally quite distinct in Canada, but Eastern Nova Scotia Institute of Technology amalgamated with Xavier College to form the University College of Cape Breton. Several mergers of vocational and higher education institutions have been proposed in England. The only such amalgamation concluded so far was between Thames Valley University and Reading College. In addition, there are 'mixed economy' institutions in the UK – colleges of further education with sizeable amounts of higher education.

In one of the many attempts to reform German higher education, which many consider to be inflexible, prolonged (the average length of undergraduate studies was 6.4 years) and wasteful, two *Länder* or state governments established *Gesamthochschulen* (comprehensive universities) in the 1970s. *Gesamthochschulen* incorporate in one institution the programmes of universities, technical universities, *pädagogische Hochschulen* (teacher training colleges), *Fachhochschulen* (polytechnics) and *Kunsthochschulen* (art colleges). *Gesamthochschulen* therefore seem similar in scope to Australia's dual-sector universities. They offer programmes that integrate those of *Fachhochschulen* and of traditional universities. However, the experiment does not appear to have been very successful: only six *Gesamthochschulen* were ever established and only one is still in existence.

There are numerous examples of partnerships between vocational and higher education institutions. There is probably no Australian tertiary education institution that does not have some form of collaboration or association with an institution in the other sector and thus is completely separate from the other sector. In the UK, 21 consortia or partnerships of multiple vocational and higher education partners have been formed to offer foundation degrees. For example, the Bedfordshire Federation for Further and Higher Education is a partnership of University of Bedford, Dunstable College, Luton Sixth Form College, Bedford College and Barnfield College for offering year 12 programmes enriched by tertiary studies, foundation degrees and ready transfer to tertiary type A studies. There are also numerous 'franchises' between further and higher education institutions in the UK that allow further education colleges to offer foundation degrees certified and awarded by higher education institutions which involve over half of all higher education institutions and two-thirds of further education institutions (Parry *et al.* 2003: 11).

Likewise there are numerous examples of partnerships between 2- and 4-year colleges in the USA. A survey of the presidents of US 2-year colleges in 1994 found that 78 per cent of 2-year colleges were involved in partnerships or consortia with 4-year institutions (Smith *et al.* 1999: 380). Some partnerships involving public institutions are arranged if not mandated by the state, but numerous other involving both public and private institutions are arranged on the institutions' own initiative to better serve their communities and to support their institution's mission.

A strong example of a multilateral partnership is the university partnership programme launched by Macomb Community College in Michigan in 1991. This allows students enrolled in any one of the Macomb University Center's academic programmes to proceed to some 70 bachelor and masters programmes offered by eight 4-year colleges and universities. Another mulilateral partnership is the University Center established in 1997 by North Harris Montgomery Community College District in Texas and six universities. The centre offers 26 unduplicated bachelor's degrees, 30 master's degrees, two doctoral degrees and two post-baccalaureate teacher certification programmes. The University Center, which has 2000 students, says that it is based on institutional partnerships, seamless articulated programmes, collaborative governance, shared facilities, interactive telecommunications and 'first-stop' student services. An example of a bilateral partnership is that between the University of Texas at Brownsville and Texas Southmost College, which offers certificates, and associate, baccalaureate and graduate degrees in liberal arts, the sciences and professional programmes to over 12,000 students. All 28 public community colleges in Florida have at least one concurrent-use agreement, which might range from an agreement to use some rooms for set times in a semester to a fully shared campus (Windham *et al.* 2001: 41).

8.3.2.2 Campus

One of Australia's earliest associations of vocational and higher education campuses was the location of the South Australian School of Mines and Industries next to the University of Adelaide in 1888. Shoemaker *et al.* (2000) prefer what they call multi-partner campuses – campus partnerships that adopt a new, joint name and logo – since this almost always denotes a higher level of cooperation and integration of sectors than a decision to brand as a branch of an existing institution, which they call multicampus partners. Shoemaker *et al.* (2000: 139–41) propose 12 points for the viability of multi-partner campuses: a central, serviced location; an iconic building; local government support; independent governance; champions; physical co-location; symbolic co-location; the involvement of three educational sectors secondary, vocational and higher education; a strategy to enrich small business; the best of IT infrastructure; a point of difference; and demand.

Shoemaker *et al.* (2000) give as Australian examples of this preferred approach: Coffs Harbour education precinct (which involves Coffs Harbour Senior College, North Coast Institute of TAFE and Southern Cross University); the Esperance Community College (southeast of WA, which involves a senior high school, TAFE, Curtin University, the WA High Schools Hostels Authority and the Shire of Esperance); the Joondalup education precinct (north of Perth, which involves the West Coast Institute of TAFE located adjacent to Edith Cowan University's Joondalup campus and the WA Police Academy); the Rockingham regional campus (45 kilometres south of Perth, which involves the South Metropolitan TAFE co-located with Murdoch's Rockingham campus and Kolbe Catholic College); the central coast campus, Ourimbah (Central Coast Community College, Hunter Institute of TAFE, University of Newcastle); and Nirimba education precinct (Western Sydney Institute of TAFE Nirimba, UWS Hawksbury Blacktown, Terra Sancta Catholic College and Wyndham Senior College).

The experience of at least some of these arrangements has not lived up to their press. The Coffs Harbour education precinct has not developed as strongly as perhaps unrealistically hoped by its partners, probably because of weak student demand. The relationship between the partners of the Rockingham regional campus have become strained, possibly because head office has not always given the satellite campus overriding priority.

Other countries' examples of this stronger form of campus partnership are higher education Almere (an education park 28 kilometres from Amsterdam, which includes business and community premises and involves the University of Amsterdam (UvA), the Institute for Information Engineering established by Hogeschool van Amsterdam (HvA) and Hogeschool Holland, the province of Flevoland and the municipal government of Almere), Universiteit en Hogeschool Amsterdam (UHA) (the University of Amsterdam (UvA) and Hogeschool van Amsterdam (HvA)); Seneca@York (Seneca College of Applied Arts and Technology and York University, Toronto); the Auraria Higher Education Center (Community College of Denver, Metropolitan State College of Denver and the University of Colorado at Denver); Macomb's University Center (Macomb Community College, Michigan and ten higher education institutions); and the University Center (North Harris Montgomery Community College District, Texas and six higher education institutions). In England the University of Kent, Greenwich University and Mid-Kent Further Education College are establishing a joint campus in Chatham called the Universities at Medway.

Examples of the weaker form of campus partnerships – multicampus partners – are the Berwick and Gippsland campuses of Monash University, which are co-located with the locale TAFE institute; Emerald campus of Central Queensland University with Central Queensland Institute of TAFE; the Western Institute of TAFE which is adjacent to Charles Sturt University's Dubbo campus, Orana; several 'concurrent-use' campuses in Florida; and the University of Texas at Brownsville and Texas Southmost College.

8.3.2.3 Division
Australia's Swinburne University of Technology and Victoria University in Melbourne are examples of institutions with type B and A divisions working in partnership and collaboration.

8.3.3 Organizational unit

8.3.3.1 Group
It would be possible to establish levels of association between vocational and higher education within broad supra-faculty groups, although no example has been found.

8.3.3.2 Faculty
Both Australia's RMIT and Charles Darwin University unify vocational and higher education within faculties. Anglia Ruskin University established five regional faculties and a single regional academic council to oversee programmes on its campuses and at 22 partner colleges. The aim is to establish common standards and promote a sense of collegiality between staff teaching the same disciplines across the region.

8.3.3.3 Department
The University of the District of Columbia in Washington functions as both a 2- and a 4-year institution; Washington is the largest city in the United States without a public 2-year college. Its departments apparently unify

vocational and higher education. Thus its Department of Management, Marketing and Information Systems offers certificates, associate degrees, baccalaureates and masters degrees. Another university that integrates vocational and higher education at the department level is Unitec, a dual-sector university in Auckland, New Zealand. Unitec has just over 10,000 equivalent full-time students, 61 per cent of whom are enrolled in higher education programmes. While some of its schools concentrate on vocational or higher education, others have more balanced offerings across sectors. Thus its School of Computing and Information Technology offers certificates, a diploma, bachelor, postgraduate diploma, master and a doctorate.

Thomson Rivers University in the city of Kamloops, south central British Columbia, was founded in 1970 as Cariboo College, it became a university college in 1992 and it attained full university status in 2004. Some 60 per cent of its 10,000 students are enrolled in higher education programmes. The Faculty of Science and the School of Business and Economics seem to have well-integrated vocational and higher education programmes ranging from certificates and diplomas to bachelors and masters degrees. British Columbia's three remaining university colleges offer vocational education programmes and higher education programmes up to the level of bachelor, which are from 20 per cent to 56 per cent of total full-time equivalent enrolments.

London's Thames Valley University is a dual-sector university with about 40 per cent of its student load in higher education. While its history of institutional amalgamations means that its vocational and higher education sectors are distributed unevenly between campuses and faculties, some departments are integrating vocational and higher education programmes. Thus TVU's Business School offers vocational education certificates and diplomas and higher education foundation degrees, bachelors and masters degrees. Nelson Mandela Metropolitan University in Nelson Mandela Metropole (formerly Port Elizabeth) was formed by a merger of three institutions on seven campuses and so its vocational and higher education sectors are also still distributed unevenly between campuses and faculties. However, schools of the Faculty of Business and Economic Sciences offer vocational education certificates and diplomas and higher education bachelor, masters and doctoral degrees. The University of Paisley merged with Bell College in 2007 to become the University of the West of Scotland. The amalgamated university offers vocational education certificate programmes and higher education bachelor programmes and some masters programmes to 18,000 students. The University of the West of Scotland is a dual-sector university but it is too soon to see how closely its sectors will be integrated.

8.3.4 Curriculum

8.3.4.1 Programme

A fully unified vocational and higher education programme would be taught jointly by staff from each sector. Robinson and Misko (2001: 93) call this a blended programme and give as an example staff of the Hunter Institute of TAFE teaching into the University of Newcastle's hospitality programmes at Ourimbah. Charles Darwin University also has some programmes unified in this strong sense, but there seems to be few others. However, there are numerous examples of programmes unified in other ways. Wheelahan (2000: 19–20) describes four types of unified programme: *customized programmes*, which incorporate offerings in each sector within one award; *integrated programmes*, which incorporate two awards normally in the same field within one programme, such as a vocational education laboratory technician's certificate within a higher education bachelor of science; *dual-award programmes*, which are like integrated programmes but involve complementary fields, such as a higher education bachelor of accounting and a vocational education certificate in information technology; and *nested programmes* which integrate programmes in the same field sequentially rather than concurrently.

Wheelahan (2000: 18–19) describes three types of partnership or pathway between programmes: *standardized pathways*, which are formally approved by the educational institution, thus ensuring that all students meeting the specified conditions will be granted the same benefits, usually academic credit in the destination programme; *customized pathways*, which are negotiated for a specified student or group of students and are therefore available only for those students, although they may be a precedent for a standardized pathway; and *guaranteed entry pathways*, which may be based on either standardized or customized pathways but which guarantee entry into the destination programme on completion of the initial programme at a specified standard.

Examples of integrated programmes are Victoria University in Melbourne's certificate, diploma and advanced diploma and bachelor of health science – paramedic and community studies – youth work; RMIT's certificate of engineering production/bachelor of aerospace engineering; and the Joondalup diploma of occupational health and safety/bachelor of health science (safety science). An example of guaranteed entry pathways is Rutgers University's dual-admission programme with each of the 19 public community colleges in New Jersey. Rutgers guarantees students of community colleges accepted in the dual-admission programme transfer with full credit if they complete the required pattern of study with a grade point average of three out of four. Mercer County Community College has dual-admissions agreements with six New Jersey 4-year colleges. Each requires completion of a specified programme and a minimum grade point average, which varies by institution and programme. Ohio also has dual-admission programmes.

Another type of programme partnership is the arrangement in Britain where higher education programmes are offered under franchise in vocational education institutions, known as higher education in further education. Examples are the universities of Bournemouth, Newcastle, Northumbria, Plymouth and Sunderland. Staffordshire University also has a network of colleges in an area where participation in higher education is very low.

Quebec is distinctive among OECD jurisdictions in having unified but end-on vocational and higher education programmes. Its vocational education institutions, *collèges d'enseignement général et professionnel* (colleges of general and vocational education) offer a 2-year *diplôme d'études collégiales* (diploma of collegial studies) for students seeking to transfer to universities and a 3-year terminal vocational track. Quebec students cannot move directly from secondary school to university; university-bound students must first complete a 2-year programme in one of the *collèges d'enseignement général et professionnel.*

Quebec achieved this unusual neatness by a *revolution tranquille* in 1967. The president of the University of Chicago, William Rainey Harper, attempted to establish a similar structure when in 1892 he reconstituted the university into a lower division providing general education and an upper division providing professional education. However, the 4-year colleges retained their lower divisions, which, therefore, overlapped with the programmes offered by the newly established 2-year colleges. Nonetheless, these can be fairly classified as unified programmes in the states, which specify closely the core curriculum requirements of the first 2 years of baccalaureate programmes whether taken in vocational or higher education institutions and thus guarantee full credit transfer between the programmes.

There are, of course, numerous examples of programme collaboration. The Illinois articulation initiative is well-organized and has a good website (Illinois Board of Higher Education *et al.* 1996–2007). An interesting form of programme collaboration is the field of study approach (Wheelahan 2001: 33). This groups vocational and higher education programmes by a combination of discipline and vocational outcome. The fields are used to develop new programmes, particularly dual-award and nested programmes and learning pathways. Field of study groups are also responsible for surveying programmes in their field to ensure appropriate coverage and to anticipate emerging needs for new programmes.

8.3.4.2 Subject

Grubb and colleagues (1991: 15) suggest that vocational and academic education could be integrated by incorporating more academic content in vocational subjects and vice versa, for example by converting some subjects to projects. They also suggest what in this typology would be subject partnerships by what they call horizontal and vertical curricular alignment: modifying and coordinating vocational and academic subjects taken in the same and sequential years. Subject partnerships are established by legislation in Florida, Georgia, Illinois, Massachusetts, Nevada, Rhode Island, South Carolina and Texas, which specify curricula and examinations, including a common subject numbering system and/or core general education curriculum. Another form of subject partnerships is cross-crediting and credit transfer arrangements, which are too familiar to require elaboration here. Grubb and colleagues (1991: 15) suggest a form of collaboration in what they call the academy model, aligning vocational and academic subjects in groups with a common vocational outcome.

8.3.5 Person

8.3.5.1 Manager

In Australia's dual-sector universities responsibility for vocational and higher education programmes is unified in the vice-chancellor, the chief executive officer and in the managers of most central and general services. But in all dual-sector universities most academic responsibility immediately below the vice-chancellor at deputy and pro-vice-chancellor level is split. However, it is combined again at the decanal level at Charles Darwin University and RMIT which have cross-sectoral deans. It splits again – in practice if not in ideal – for heads of department at RMIT and for many at Charles Darwin University.

8.3.5.2 Teacher

The penultimate level of organization – and ultimate level of integration – is to have teachers who teach across all the types of tertiary education. This was achieved briefly by the Western Institute, one of Victoria University in Melbourne's predecessor institutions, when it was first established in 1986. Teaching staff were initially employed on a combined Western Institute award but this was soon disbanded and staff were employed on separate higher education and TAFE awards, apparently due to pressure from the unions. A combined award for teaching staff was also achieved – or imposed – by the Queensland Bjelke-Peterson government at the Hervey Bay College but this, too was dismantled as a result of union pressure with the election of the Goss government.

Wheelahan (2000: 43) reports that of Australia's dual-sector universities, only Charles Darwin has cross-sectoral teaching as part of its industrial agreement. This agreement has four parts. The most substantial part contains conditions that are common to all staff of the university. The other three parts contain provisions specific to each of three groups of staff: vocational education teaching staff; higher education teaching and research staff; and administrative, technical and general staff. Wheelahan (2000: 43) reports that cross-sectoral teaching occurs in reality as well as in the agreement.

Grubb and colleagues (1991: 15) suggest a form of teacher collaboration by associating vocational and higher education teachers in occupational clusters rather than or in addition to conventional departments. The aim would be to align subjects within clusters and to support the development of occupational clusters, 'career paths' and majors which would be coherent sequences of subjects.

8.3.5.3 Student

There is considerable evidence that students overcome various administrative obstacles to combine vocational and higher education studies within one award, sometimes concurrently and sometimes sequentially. This is considered at length in the next chapter, which considers student transfer between vocational and higher education institutions.

9

Student transfer between sectors

This chapter investigates the transfer of students between sectors of tertiary education because it is a key aspect of the differences between sectors and the health of the operation of a tertiary education system as a whole. The chapter describes a technique for comparing student transfer rates in different systems, major differences in data definitions and treatments in each system notwithstanding. The chapter considers what causes different student transfer rates: how sharply the sectors are differentiated, relations between the sectors and the effect of government policies promoting student transfer.

9.1 Salience of student transfer

The most important aspect of education systems is not their institutions and structures but the relations between them – the processes or internal dynamics that make it sensible to talk about a system as a whole. A proper comparison of education systems therefore compares the systems' internal dynamics and not just their institutions and structures. This is, of course, very difficult to do and is usually not attempted in comparisons of educational systems. The transfer of students between vocational and higher education, and between tiers of higher education, is one way of observing a system's internal dynamics. Student transfer is particularly salient because it reflects the nature of a tertiary education system and, depending on that nature, can be an important indicator of the system's success.

In Chapter 1, we noted that there are two broad patterns or tendencies in structuring tertiary education: the tracked systems of Germany and northern continental Europe and the generalist systems of the UK and the USA. Performance in the highly differentiated and tracked systems of tertiary education is optimized when there is a good match of students, sectors and society's needs. In these systems, large numbers of students transferring between vocational and higher education indicate a failure of the system to place students on the appropriate track initially. But in generalist systems, high rates of student transfer indicate their success in providing students with the flexibility to change their education and careers in response to economic and social changes and in response to changes in their life circumstances. This flexibility is said to be more important as people's life expectancy increases and 'lifelong learning' is an important policy goal.

We also noted in Chapter 1 that many jurisdictions accommodate mass higher education by providing broad if not open access to lower funded mass vocational education and the lower tiers of higher education. This preserves the selectivity and funding level of the elite upper tiers of higher education. But in these systems upward student transfer to the elite tier of higher education is important to extend equality of opportunity and provide opportunities for social mobility. High rates of student transfer therefore indicate the success of these systems.

Grubb (1991: 195–6) notes that:

> A strong transfer program is a confirmation of the academic purposes of community colleges and strengthens their claims to being colleges . . . the ability of students to transfer to four year colleges and then compete as equals against students who begin in four year colleges is one test of the acceptability of community colleges within higher education.

Student transfer also has implications for institutional prestige. Institutions and sectors that provide direct access to high-paying and high-status occupations have highest prestige. Institutions and sectors that offer intermediate access through transfer to higher tiers have less prestige. But according to Clark (1983: 63–4) institutions and sectors that do not even offer the possibility of transfer to higher tiers have more sharply defined lower status.

Thus, student transfer is important in six ways:

1. It is one of the mechanisms that regulates students' access to levels of education and with that occupation, prestige, life chances and income.
2. It provides social mobility.
3. It gives students more flexibility to respond to social and economic changes and to changes in their life circumstances.
4. It establishes the lower tier's role as a scholarly institution and its standing in higher education.
5. It raises the standing of lower tiers.
6. It is an important aspect of the relations and interactions between sectors and institutions.

In these systems, a high level of student transfer is therefore an indicator of their success. The rest of this chapter concentrates on student transfer in these systems.

9.2 Upward student transfer

Most studies of student transfer consider the transfer of students from vocational education to higher education or from the lower to the higher tiers of higher education. This is commonly known as upward student transfer.

The extent to which students of each vocational education institution transfer to a higher education institution is often thought to indicate their success in at least one of their important roles or to illuminate important characteristics such as their culture and ideology. But as Gelin (1999: 11) observes: 'Effective transfer is a function of both sending and receiving institutional policies, practices, and culture. Using transfer rates to measure the effectiveness of the sending institution leaves out one half of the equation.'

This section considers upward transfer as an indicator of the structure and performance of the whole system, rather than of the performance of the less noble part or of their students. This approach is advanced by the California Postsecondary Education Commission (2002: 15), which argues that transfer is a function of such an array of elements that it reflects the performance of the whole system. In particular, the section compares the proportion of transfer students admitted by highly selective institutions with the proportion of transfer students admitted by moderately selective institutions.

Selectivity of receiving institution was chosen as the salient factor, rather than, for example, research intensity because as Kerr (1994: 69) argued 'the principle of selectivity is central' to the structuring of tertiary education. Kerr (1994: 69) posited three levels of selectivity:

1. highly selective higher education;
2. selective higher education;
3. non-selective higher education.

The section compares the different rates of transfer of students from, in Kerr's terms, non-selective higher education or vocational education institutions to moderately selective and highly selective higher education institutions. Several US studies compare the rates of transfer from 2- to 4-year institutions between states, but this is misleading unless several factors are controlled for. First, the overall participation rate and the participation rate in each sector must be considered. A state with a very high proportion of the population participating in 4-year colleges is likely to have a lower rate of transfer from 2-year colleges than a state which has high participation in 2-year colleges and a much smaller proportion of students enrolled in 4-year colleges.

Second, a range of inhibitory and facilitative factors needs to be considered: geographic access, socioeconomic factors, flexibility of study mode, school completion rates and type of secondary preparation, curriculum integration and support and encouragement of student transfer. Thus, most 2-year college students study part-time while commuting from home or work and are unlikely to seek to transfer to a college that is beyond convenient commuting distance or to a college that does not support part-time study. Two-year colleges that are distant from 4-year colleges are therefore likely to have lower transfer rates because of their geographic isolation from a receiving institution. States with widely dispersed populations or with 4-year colleges distant from 2-year colleges are likely to have lower rates of upward student transfer because of their geography, not because of the performance of their colleges. In all countries and jurisdictions, participation in higher education is directly related to students' socioeconomic status: many more students from higher socioeconomic backgrounds participate in higher education than those from lower socioeconomic backgrounds, often four times as much. Students from low socioeconomic status backgrounds also have less cultural capital to negotiate complex or technical admission or transfer requirements. A state with a high proportion of its population with low socioeconomic status is therefore likely to have a lower rate of upward student transfer than a state with a high proportion of its population with high socioeconomic status.

Some studies seek to control for this by measuring college preparedness – how adequately students in each state are prepared for education and training beyond high school. This shifts attention on transfer from an indicator of the performance of 2-year institutions to an indicator of the performance of their students. Other studies seek to use as the denominator for transfer rates students who are in transfer programmes or who express an aspiration to transfer on entering higher education, but even the investigators acknowledge that these are inadequate measures or at least that the choice of numerator and denominator depends on the purpose underlying the collection of the information (Gelin 1999: 3). Students change their plans and aspirations as they proceed with their studies – indeed, this transformation is one of the main benefits of education. So many students' eventual transfer intentions are different from their initial intentions, which is indicated by the large number of successful transfers from occupational or terminal programmes.

Third, the selection practices of the receiving institutions are critical to student transfer. Receiving institutions' admissions practices are complemented and are often reinforced by several factors listed by the California Postsecondary Education Commission (2002: 15): 'academic major and general education requirements, course articulation, information dissemination, faculty interaction, program availability, and actual institutional behaviors'.

Correcting for all of these factors makes the comparison of transfer rates very complex. It would be even more complicated attempting to correct for these factors in an international comparison. Instead, I have developed a new measure to compare transfer rates, the student admission ratio.

9.2.1 Student admission ratio

Consider a hypothetical system in which its highly selective universities have an undergraduate intake of 1000 students each year. If 50 of the new students are transfers from vocational education institutes, transfers would be 5 per cent of the intake. If the system's moderately selective universities admitted 1000 transfer students in an intake of 10,000, transfers would be 10 per cent of the intake. In this system the highly selective institutions admit half the proportion of transfer students (5 per cent) as the moderately and less selective institutions (10 per cent). Thus, the transfer student admission ratio is 1:2.

Compare this with a second system where reported transfer is overall much higher. Here, the highly selective institutions admit 66 transfer students out of an intake of 1000, but the moderately selective universities admit 2000 transfers out of a total intake of 10,000. In the second system, the transfer student admission rate at the more selective institutions is 6.6 per cent and the rate at the less selective institutions is 20 per cent. The ratio between the transfer student admissions rates in the second system is 1:3, considerably higher than the ratio of 1:2 in the first system. Thus, the more selective institutions in the second system admit relatively fewer transfer students than the more selective institutions in the first system, notwithstanding that in the second system the more selective institutions admit more transfer students and state-wide transfer is relatively higher than in the first system.

The higher transfer rates reported in the second system may be an artefact of the system's broader definition of transfer. But the student admission ratio is a measure of relative performance within a system and so it treats each institution within a system equally in the system's own terms. Comparing relative performance within a system also makes it unnecessary to account for many of the other differences between jurisdictions and systems. We are thus able to compare the relative performance of quite different systems and jurisdictions. Comparing transfer student admission ratios for formally segmented systems, informally segmented systems and formally undifferentiated systems allows us to test whether segmenting a system into tiers by selectivity of student admissions affects the rate at which transfer students gain entry to the most selective institutions and tiers. One might hypothesize that transfer student admission ratios are higher and that, therefore, transfer admission is relatively harder in the formally segmented systems. However, this study refutes that hypothesis.

This study divides institutions by selectivity of student admissions, but it would be possible to consider other salient characteristics of institutions such as public/private ownership, high/low resources per student, urban/suburban/rural location and high/low proportion of students from a low socioeconomic status background. While this study applies the admission ratio to transfer students, it could equally be applied to other categories of student admission such as race or socioeconomic status. Thus, one could examine whether different state admissions or affirmative action policies affect the rates at which historically black and other institutions admit minority students.

We will start by comparing transfer student admission ratios for three US states. There are problems with the accuracy of US statistics on student transfer. Romano and Wisniewski (2003: 24) demonstrate that US studies have underestimated transfer rates by as much as 25 per cent. The absolute rates found in this study are probably vulnerable to this criticism. Also, differences in data definitions and collection methods may affect the different rates found for each state. But again, this study considers the relative transfer student admission ratios within states rather than absolute transfer levels or even rates and so escapes most of the difficulties with the comparability of data.

9.2.2 *California*

As is elaborated in Chapter 4, California has segmented its higher education system since its master plan for higher education was enshrined in the Donahoe Act of 1960, and Douglass (2004: 11) points out that California had developed three distinct, geographically dispersed and multicampus public segments as early as 1920. The master plan divides California's higher education institutions into three segments: the University of California, whose intake is restricted by legislation to the top 12.5 per cent of high school graduates, the California State University, whose intake is restricted to the top 33.3 per cent of high school graduates and California community colleges, who have open admission.

The California Postsecondary Education Commission (1998; 2000) reports that in 1998–99 a total of 59,906 students transferred from open-entry California community colleges to California universities. Since there were 1,304,554 students in California community colleges in 1996, approximately 4.5 per cent transfer to higher level studies in the same state each year. A total of 10,161 transferred to the highly selective University of California. The University of California enrolled 155,412 students in 1996. So California community college transfer students comprised 6.5 per cent of the University of California's total student population. A total of 44,989 California community college students transferred to moderately selective California State University system. This system enrols 336,803 students, so 13 per cent of its students transferred from California community colleges. These figures can be found in Table 9.1.

Community college transfer students were 6.5 per cent of students at the highly selective University of California but were 13 per cent of students

Table 9.1 Proportion of students at the highly selective University of California and the moderately selective California State University who transferred from a community college, 1998–99

Segment	Number of transfers	Total u/grad. enrolments	% of u/grad. enrolments who are transfers
University of California	10,161	155,412	6.5
California State University	44,989	336,803	13
Total	**59,906**	**492,215**	**12**

Source: California Postsecondary Education Commission (1998)

at the moderately selective California State University, giving a ratio of 1:2 between the two segments.

9.2.3 Colorado

Some 59 per cent of Colorado's higher education students start in 4-year institutions, much higher than the US average (45 per cent) and very much higher than in California (34 per cent), so there are fewer students in 2-year colleges seeking to transfer to 4-year institutions in Colorado. Overall transfer student admission rates are therefore lower in Colorado than in California, which may also be partly due to differences in data definitions and collection methods. Colorado did not formally designate 4-year institutions by selectivity of admissions at the time the data for this study were collected. However, the Colorado Commission on Higher Education (2003: 10) analysed institutions' selectivity to inform its new admissions standards policy from which it was possible to identify Colorado's highly selective 4-year colleges as the Colorado School of Mines, the University of Colorado, Boulder, and Colorado State University. Transfers were 3 per cent of enrolments at the highly selective institutions and 6 per cent of students at the moderately selective institutions. The transfer rates for individual institutions are shown in Chapter 4. Despite Colorado's lower overall transfer student admission rate than California's, the differences in transfer student admission rates between Colorado's highly selective and moderately selective receiving institutions is the same as in California (see Table 9.2).

Transfer students were 3 per cent of students at the highly selective Colorado institutions and 6 per cent of students at the moderately selective Colorado institutions, giving a ratio of 1:2 between the two types of institution.

9.2.4 Texas

Texas has a very strong transfer policy and consequently its 4-year institutions have twice the proportion of transfer students as California. Texas does

Table 9.2 Proportion of students at the highly selective and the moderately selective 4-year public institutions who transferred from a 2-year institution, Colorado, 2001

Institution type	Number of transfers	Total u/grad. enrolments	% of u/grad enrolments who are transfers
Subtotal highly selective institutions	1,192	45,559	3
Subtotal moderately selective institutions	1,399	21,584	6
Total	**2,591**	**67,143**	**4**

Source: Jacobs (2002)

not formally distinguish between its institutions by selectivity of admission. However, for some purposes the state's admissions policies consider the proportion of an institution's commencing students who were ranked in the top 10 per cent of their high school class. Two institutions stood out as being highly selective. In 1999 some 39 per cent of the students at Texas A&M University at College Station were recruited from the top 10 per cent of their high school class and 31 per cent of the students from the University of Texas at Austin were recruited from the top 10 per cent of their high school class. The next selective institutions on this measure were the University of Texas at Dallas (25 per cent) and Texas A&M University-Corpus Christi (21 per cent). This was consistent with the institutions' applicant acceptance rates. Texas A&M University (College Station) had an acceptance rate of 61 per cent and the University of Texas at Austin had an acceptance rate of 64 per cent. The next most selective institutions were Southwest Texas State University (73 per cent) and the University of Texas at Dallas and the University of Texas at El Paso, both of which had acceptance rates of 78 per cent. Some 15 per cent of undergraduate enrolments at the highly selective institutions were transfer students, not much less than the 26 per cent at the moderately selective institutions (see Table 9.3).

Transfer students were 15 per cent of students at the highly selective Texas institutions and were 26 per cent of students at the moderately selective Texas institutions, giving a ratio of 1:1.7 between the two types of institution.

9.2.5 Scotland

Scotland has a formally unified university sector, but universities are informally grouped by age of establishment: ancient universities, which are those founded before the nineteenth century, are the most selective; old universities, which had university status before the Further and Higher Education Act 1992, are the second most selective; new universities, which were redesignated as universities by the Further and Higher Education Act 1992 or which were founded after the Act, are the least selective.

Table 9.3 Proportion of students at the highly selective and the moderately selective 4-year public institutions who transferred from a 2-year institution, Texas, 2000

Institution type	Number of transfers	Total u/grad. enrolments	% of u/grad enrolments who are transfers
Subtotal highly selective institutions	10,594	73,039	15
Subtotal moderately selective institutions	61,968	237,029	26
Total	**72,562**	**310,068**	**23**

Source: Texas Higher Education Coordinating Board (2001b)

McLaurin and Osborne (2002) matched higher education data for 1999–2000 provided by the Scottish Higher Education Funding Council with further education student enrolment data for the years 1994–95, 1995–96, 1996–97, 1997–98 and 1998–99 provided by the Scottish Further Education Funding Council. They matched records by first initial, second initial, surname, date of birth and enrolment number. They found that of the higher education students in 1999–2000 some 18 per cent had studied at a further education college in the previous 5 years. However, the ancient (12 per cent) and old universities (14 per cent) enrolled about half the proportion of further education students as new universities.

The distinctively vocational education and training qualifications are the higher national certificate and the higher national diploma. Some 14 per cent of the former further education students had a higher national certificate or diploma as their highest qualification on entry to the ancient universities compared with 40 per cent at all other higher education institutions. Together 22 per cent of ancient and old former further education students had an HNC/D as their highest qualification, compared with 45 per cent at all other institutions.

Gallacher (2003: 12) reports the numbers and percentages of students entering higher education institutions in Scotland for whom the higher national certificate or diploma or similar further education qualification was the highest on entry. He reports those for ancient universities (3 per cent), 1960s' universities (8 per cent), post-1992 universities (25 per cent) and art/music colleges (13 per cent) Maclennan *et al.* (2000: 12) distinguish between selecting and recruiting universities, observing that: 'Post-1992 HEIs [higher education institutions] often adopt a more promotion-based approach, consistent with a "recruiting" model. In contrast, pre-1992 HEIs have traditionally followed a softer approach, relying more on liaison activities with schools, and in certain cases, with FECs.' Gallacher (2006: 363) observes that the 1960s' universities come somewhere in between the ancient and new universities: 'These universities continue to attract large numbers of well-qualified young applicants in many discipline areas, and in this sense are "selecting" institutions.'

Table 9.4 was calculated by classifying the ancient and the old universities as highly selective universities and the new universities as recruiting universities or moderately selective institutions in this study. It will be noted that 5 per cent of the students entering the ancient and old universities that I categorized as highly selective had a short-cycle further education qualification as their highest qualification on entry, whereas the corresponding proportion for the new universities was 25 per cent. The ratio of transfer student admission rates of highly selective and moderately selective universities is therefore 1:5 for Scotland.

Table 9.4 Number and proportion of entrants to Scottish universities for whom the higher national certificate or diploma (HNC/D) or similar further education qualification was the highest on entry, by university category, 2000

University category	Number of entrants	Number of entrants with HNC/ D as highest qualification	% of all entrants
Ancient universities	10,000	303	3
Old universities	7,000	568	8
New universities	10,500	2,665	25
Art/music colleges	1,300	167	13
Total	**28,800**	**3,703**	**13**

Source: Gallacher (2003: 12)

9.2.6 Australia

Like Scotland, Australia has a formally 'unified national system' (Dawkins 1988) of higher education, in its case since 1988. Nevertheless, Australia's universities differ markedly by selectivity of student admissions. It is convenient to count as the highly selective institutions the group of eight universities that win the biggest share of external research grants and which have formed an association (Group of Eight 2003). Australia also allows a comparison with Prager's (1993) findings on transfer and articulation within US colleges and universities. Prager surveyed 408 chief executive officers of campuses which Peterson's *Directory* identified as sponsors of 2-year tracks within a college, university or system also offering 4-year curricula (Prager 1993: 541). She concluded (1993: 551):

> It appears that students from some two-year programs within four-year contexts may have as much, if not more, difficulty in 'transferring' within their institutions as do students who begin at a community college and seek to transfer to a senior one. Indeed, the findings explored here suggest that problems with internal student transfer and program articulation may be as pervasive within some institutions sharing a common institutional identity as external ones are for some from different sectors, such as community and senior colleges, that do not.

Australia has five so-called 'dual-sector universities', which comprise substantial student load in both bachelor and sub-degree vocational programmes. The average transfer student admission rate for Australian dual-sector universities is shown separately in Table 9.5. It will be noted that while the dual-sector universities had a substantially higher transfer student admission rate than the Group of Eight highly selective Australian universities, they had only a slightly higher rate than the other moderately selective

Table 9.5 Proportion of undergraduate commencing students at the Group of Eight Australian highly selective and other moderately selective universities who were admitted on the basis of a vocational education and training (VET) qualification, 2000

Institution type	Admitted on basis of VET	Total bachelor commencers	% of commencers who are transfers
Group of Eight universities	1,029	45,580	2
Dual-sector universities	1,293	15,184	9
Other universities	9,368	115,741	8
Total	**11,690**	**176,505**	**7**

Source: DEEWR (2001)

institutions. In 2005 the dual-sector universities had doubled their proportion of transfers substantially to 18 per cent, while the Group of Eight universities increased their transfers minimally to 3 percent and the other universities increased their transfers substantially to 12 per cent. This suggests that institutional structure of itself does not affect student transfer: more important are the policies and processes within institutions.

Including the dual-sector universities with the other moderately selective universities shows that the difference in the ratio of transfer student admission rates between the highly selective and moderately selective universities is a high 1:4, although not quite as high as the ratio for Scotland.

9.2.7 Summary of transfer student admission rates

These results are summarized in Table 9.6. They show that the differences in transfer student admission of the highly selective and moderately selective higher education institutions in Australia are twice that for the three US states

Table 9.6 Students transferring from non-baccalaureate programmes to public baccalaureate-granting institutions, Australia, Scotland and three US states, by selectivity of receiving institution

Jurisdiction	Highly selective institutions	Moderately selective institutions	Ratio of highly selective to moderately selective
Texas	15%	26%	1:1.7
California	6.5%	13%	1:2
Colorado	3%	6%	1:2
Australia	2%	8%	1:4
Scotland	5%	24%	1:5

examined, even in Colorado, which has a lower overall transfer rate than Australia. The differences in Scotland are comparable to those in Australia in the figures reported by McLaurin and Osborne (2002) and are even greater in Gallacher's (2003) figures.

This finding is particularly striking when one notes that the difference in transfer student admission rate is lower in California, which formally segments its highly selective and not so selective higher education sectors, than in Australia which has a formally unified national system of higher education and in Scotland which does not formally segment its universities. Clark's (1983: 52) explanation for these highly differentiated transfer student admission rates is that the lack of formal segmentation by tier drives systems to greater internal stratification, which at least in Australia and Scotland is by status, which in turn is strongly related to institutional age.

9.3 Reverse student transfer

This study has followed the literature in considering student transfer first as an upward progression from a lower to a higher level of education. Just as one transfers from primary to secondary to tertiary education, so within tertiary education one transfers from diploma to baccalaureate to masters to doctoral programmes. In most Canadian provinces, in the UK and in the USA, vocational education and training not only prepares students for work, but also prepares them for further study and transfer to baccalaureate programmes. This is such an important role that the dominant understanding of student transfer is from a sub-baccalaureate programme, institution or sector to a baccalaureate programme, institution or sector.

A number of people have argued against considering student transfer as an upward linear process, as progression from 'less noble' to 'noble' (Furth 1973) institutions. Clark (1960) first identified in 1960 the transfer of students from baccalaureate to sub-baccalaureate programmes, what he called 'reverse-flow students' but who are now more commonly known as reverse transfer students. Kajstura and Keim (1992: 39) described two subgroups of reverse transfer students: '1) non-completers, who attended a four-year institution, but did not complete a degree before enrolling at a two-year college; and 2) graduates, who earned at least an undergraduate degree prior to enrolling at a two-year college'.

More recent studies have found that students have multiple enrolments in higher education and vocational education and training – some sequential and others concurrent. Peter and Forrest Cataldi (2005: iii) report from the US National Center for Education Statistics that of the students who had enrolled in postsecondary education for the first time in 1995–96 some 40 per cent had attended more than one institution 6 years later in 2001. Understandably, multiple institutional enrolments were more common for students who first enrolled in a public 2-year college (47.2 per cent) than students who first enrolled in a public 4-year college (38.9 per cent), although the latter rate is still remarkably high. Of the multiple enrolments 32 per cent were students who had transferred from one institution to another and 11 per cent were co-enrolments, by which Peter and Forrest Cataldi mean enrolled in more than one institution for more than 1 month during an academic year. While transfer was predictably much higher for students who first enrolled in a 2-year college (41.5 per cent) than a 4-year college (27 per cent), co-enrolment was slightly lower for students who started in a 2-year college (11.4 per cent) than those who started in a 4-year college (12.4 per cent). The latter included students who took subjects at a 2-year college over summer to count towards their 4-year degree because it was cheaper, closer to their parents' home where they were staying over summer or perhaps because their 4-year institution did not offer an extensive summer programme.

De los Santos and Wright (1990: 32) argue that: 'The movement of students should not be seen as only a straight line; progression for many can better be described as "swirling" between and among community colleges and four year institutions on the way to a baccalaureate.' In their report called 'The community college shuffle', Maxwell and colleagues (2002: 1) argued that: 'Educational enrollment patterns can be likened to a series of playing cards. For many students the path through college is sequential, orderly and similar to a hand that progresses from deuce to ace. Other student patterns are jumbled much like a hand that results from a shuffled deck.'

While swirling is probably the best metaphor to describe transfers between sectors, particularly where lifelong learning is pervasive, vocational education advocates invest considerable rhetorical significance in reverse transfer as an indicator of the limitations of universities and, conversely, of the strengths of vocational education. Some advocates for vocational education see reverse transfer as an opportunity to redress vocational education's low status. But most commentary is based on limited surveys and isolated institutional studies that have little, if any, application to national policy and some make simple statistical mistakes in seeking to compare unlike student populations. This section discusses national data on reverse student transfer in the USA, Canada, Australia and New Zealand.

9.3.1 Reverse transfer in the USA

The most recent US national data on student and transfer is Peter and Forrest Cataldi's (2005) analysis of the US 1996/2001 beginning postsecondary students longitudinal study of students who entered college for the first time during the 1995–96 academic year. Students were surveyed in 1998 and 2001, which was 6 years after they began their postsecondary education. I estimated total numbers of transferring students by applying the percentage transfer rates found by Peter and Forrest Cataldi to the US Department of Education National Center for Education Statistics' (1998: table 181) table of total first-time freshmen enrolled in institutions of higher education and degree granting institutions in fall 1995. This shows that while almost 282,000 of commencing students' first transfer was upward, only 132,000 or less than half commencing students' first transfer was downward. Of course students' subsequent transfers may have been in the opposite direction, but 81 per cent of transfer students transferred only once, so the direction of subsequent transfers would not change the broad trend for the volume of upward transfers to be about twice than of downward transfers.

9.3.2 Reverse transfer in Canada

Canada's national graduates survey interviews a large structured sample of graduates from programmes offered by Canadian public universities, community colleges and trade-vocational colleges 2 and 5 years after graduation. The survey found that 23 per cent of the graduates in 1990 had completed a second qualification by 1995. A relatively high proportion of graduates who complete a second qualification complete one at the same or at a lower level than their initial qualification. Thus, of the 24 per cent of bachelor graduates in 1990 who completed a second qualification by 1995, some 44 per cent completed another bachelor and 18 per cent completed a diploma. I took Statistics Canada's estimates of the underlying national population of the graduates from whom it constructed its survey and applied the percentages found in the national graduates survey to estimate the number of graduates who completed another qualification at each level. They show that approximately 4600 bachelor graduates in 1990 completed a diploma by 1995, while approximately 5200 diploma graduates subsequently completed a bachelor degree. That is, while Canadian graduates' reverse transfer is sizeable, it is still not as large as upward transfer.

9.3.3 Reverse transfer in Australia

Enrolment figures for vocational and higher education in Australia are collected by different agencies using different data definitions. There are therefore not directly comparable and there are doubts about the accuracy of the data. However, if one examines enrolments or stocks of students and considers students enrolled in one sector who had previously completed a qualification in the other sector, reverse transfer is about 40 per cent less than upward transfer (Moodie 2004; 2005). Most results from the enrolment data are consistent with the results of student and population surveys which find that reverse transfer is about half upward transfer.

The Australian Bureau of Statistics' survey of education, training and information technology was conducted over 14 weeks from the end of April to the start of August 2001. Information was collected by personal interviews conducted by trained interviewers. The initial sample size for the survey was approximately 18,000 dwellings, from which approximately 13,200 households were selected and 12,100 (92 per cent) were fully responding. In total, 24,377 people responded fully to the survey (Australian Bureau of Statistics 2002: 2). The survey collected respondents' enrolment in a tertiary programme in the current year, whether they were enrolled in a different programme in the previous year and whether they completed their previous year's programme.

The survey found that of the students enrolled in university in 2001 a total of 32,700 had enrolled in a different vocational education qualification in 2000. Two-thirds of these students had completed their previous vocational education. Of the students enrolled in vocational education in 2001 only 13,200 had enrolled in university in the previous year: that is, that direct reverse transfer is less than half that of direct upward transfer. Interestingly, almost 80 per cent of reverse transfer students had not completed their university programme (Australian Bureau of Statistics 2004). The bureau's survey of education and work conducted in May 2003 found that direct reverse transfer was 62 per cent of direct upward transfer (Australian Bureau of Statistics 2003). Curtis (2006: 1) found from the longitudinal surveys of Australian youth that upward transfer from vocational to higher education is approximately 50 per cent greater than reverse transfer from higher to vocational education.

9.3.4 Reverse transfer in New Zealand

Scott's (2004) detailed *Pathways in Tertiary Education 1998–2002* tracked the enrolment of tertiary education students who commenced study in 1998 over the 4 subsequent years. He used a sophisticated matching algorithm to track students who changed institutions and therefore sectors. He checked his matching algorithm with a unique student identifier introduced in 2003 and found that it identified students correctly in 93.6 per cent of the cases. Scott (2005) found that: 'Upward transfers of 4.7% are a little higher than reverse transfers 3.6%, and there is slightly higher transfer from university to the non-university sector than vice-versa.'

One may thus conclude that intersectoral transfer is not high in New Zealand, and further that reverse transfer is about the same size as upward transfer. There are three possible explanations. Until recently the government offered loans for tuition fees to as many students an institution enrolled, so any quota or enrolment limit was imposed by institutions rather than by government and all institutions including universities had a financial incentive to enrol as many students as had a reasonable prospect of success. Second, there is considerable overlap between the sectors in New Zealand: both university and non-university providers offer both degrees and sub-degree programmes. Students may be more likely to gain admission to their preferred institution and programme on their initial entry to higher education, reducing the need to transfer later to another institution or programme. Scott (2005) adds that:

Around 40–50% of starters dropout, and so this large group in the denominator acts to lower transfer rates. For those subgroups with less attrition (eg degree and above, or in unis), transfer rates are quite a bit higher (eg between 10% and 30%). 'Progression rate' data also show higher transfer rates if you complete (16% upward and 6% reverse).

9.3.5 Reverse transfer summed up

The first finding of this study is that the relative size of upward and reverse transfer depends on the concept or measure of transfer used. Intersectoral transfer is not high in New Zealand, but reverse transfer is about the same size as upward transfer. The national data for Canada suggest that reverse transfer is about the same size or probably smaller than upward transfer. The most recent US national data on student and transfer show that reverse transfer is a little less than half upward transfer. At most the national enrolment counts for Australia suggest that reverse transfer is about the same size as upward transfer, but most data suggest that reverse transfer is about half that of upward transfer.

Second, as other writers have observed, the metaphors of both upward and reverse transfer posit a linear progression from one programme, institution or sector to another. However, institutional studies show that at least some students have studied in multiple programmes, institutions or sectors, usually not following a 'pathway' defined by institutions and sometimes with multiple enrolments concurrently. This suggests that the better metaphor is of 'swirling' (de los Santos and Wright 1990: 32) or 'shuffling' the deck of study options (Maxwell *et al.* 2002: 1).

The third finding is that the national data on tertiary education student transfer in all of the jurisdictions studied are not good enough to support many conclusions about the direction or even prevalence of student transfer. The same conclusion is reached by most studies of student transfer. For example, Osborne (2002a: 2) concluded for Scotland that the present quantitative data on progression from higher education offered by further education colleges to higher education offered by higher education institutions were limited, due to the lack of a unique identifier for students across the sector. The UK's Dearing report (1997: para. 7.44) proposed a unique student record number to follow students' progress from school to further education and higher education. Following a recommendation of the New Zealand Ministry of Education Te Tāhuhu o te Mātauranga (2001: 8), in 2003 the government introduced the national student index, a system that assigns a unique lifetime identifier to each tertiary student that will be used to collect and combine data for policy and analysis (Ministry of Education 2002).

Some 33 US states collect data on student transfers and many of these require institutions to report students' social security number. This not only helps to protect the integrity of the student support and reporting systems, but also allows the state to calculate accurate retention and transfer rates taking into account all transfers between institutions and sectors. It also allows the state to collect other longitudinal data on student flows more useful for planning and policy analysis than the snapshot data commonly available. The US Spellings Commission (US Department of Education 2006: 22) supported the development of a privacy protected higher education information system that collects, analyses and uses student level data for various purposes including tracking student transfer. The commission said that a privacy-protected system would not include in federal records individually identifiable information such as student names or social security numbers.

9.4 Student transfer policies

Kintzer (1973) categorized measures to support student transfer in a descending order of formalization and specificity, from detailed legislated prescriptions, to state policies not imposed by legislation and then to voluntary agreements between institutions or segments. In a study of transfer rates of 97 rural 2-year colleges Higgins and Katsinas (1999) found that colleges subject to detailed requirements specified in legislation or the state constitution had an average transfer rate of 23 per cent whereas colleges participating in just non-binding agreements between institutions or segments had a transfer rate of 14 per cent. Higgins and Katsinas note that while their sample comprised 13 per cent of 736 publicly controlled rural 2-year colleges, a stratified random sample could not be developed from their dataset since participants were self-selecting. Furthermore, they did not study any of the 330 publicly controlled suburban and urban 2-year institutions which enrol 68 per cent of all community college students. While Higgins and Katsinas' conclusion that 'state policy clearly does matter, and states serious about implementing "seamless" K-16 education systems should seriously re-examine their transfer policies to promote better interinstitutional articulation and transfer' perhaps goes beyond their data, it provides at least some support for the thesis that different transfer rates are associated with the existence and strength of formal student transfer policies and mechanisms.

Ignash and Townsend (2000: 2–3) evaluated state articulation policies on four measures: transfer directions, the types of institution covered, whether policies provided for the transfer of parts rather than whole qualifications and the involvement of academic staff. Ignash and Townsend evaluated policies as strong on the first measure if they covered transfer in all directions – horizontal and reverse as well as the traditional vertical transfer. Articulation policies are strong on the second measure if they include private as well as public institutions. Ignash and Townsend evaluated articulation agreements as strong on the third measure if they accommodate not only students who have completed an associate's degree but also students who complete a significant block of coursework such as the general education requirements. Articulation policies are strong on the fourth measure if academic staff of both 2- and 4-year colleges are very involved in developing them. Ignash and Townsend added that in time articulation policies should be assessed on whether they are evaluated systematically.

Ignash and Townsend found that by 1999 some 34 states or 79 per cent of the 43 states that responded to their questionnaire reported that they had developed a state-wide articulation agreement. They classified 44 per cent of states' articulation agreements strong in covering horizontal and reverse transfer as well as vertical transfer. Only 4 per cent of articulation agreements were strong in covering at least half of undergraduates at private institutions. Some 21 per cent of states had 'fairly strong' articulation agreements because they included not only degrees and general education but also the transfer of individual subjects with through state-wide common subject numbering. Some 12 per cent were strong on this measure by providing for the articulation of various programme majors. Some 63 per cent of states reported that academic staff were 'very involved' in developing their articulation agreements. Ignash and Townsend (2000: 16) concluded that five states or 12 per cent of the 43 responding states had strong statewide articulation agreements overall because they were 'strong' on at least three out of four measures and no weaker than 'moderate' in one remaining measure, or 'strong' in two measures and 'fairly strong' in the other two.

Anderson *et al.* (2006) examined the effect on upward student transfer of mandated state-wide articulation policies that stipulate that the completion of a defined programme or set of subjects would be transferable to a public 4-year institution within the state. Anderson *et al.* examined data from the National Center of Education Statistics' survey BPS89 of students who first entered postsecondary education in the 1989–90 academic year. They examined whether students who initially enrolled at a public 2-year college in states which had a mandated state-wide articulation policy in 1991 were more likely to transfer to a 4-year institution in the state by 1994. Anderson *et al.* (2006: 276) found that after holding constant students' demographic, educational, socioeconomic status and enrolment characteristics, students in states that had a mandated state-wide articulation policy had the same probability of transferring from a community college to any 4-year college or university as students who enrol in a state without such an articulation agreement. This was true of all community college students in the sample and it was also true of a restricted sample of community college students who aspired to a bachelor's degree.

While Anderson and colleagues' finding suggest that mandated state-wide articulation policies do not increase upward student transfer, there are at least two qualifications to their study. First, as they discuss, mandated state-wide articulation policies were introduced relatively recently before students were surveyed; arguably the policies need longer to have their full effect. Second, Anderson *et al.* defined mandated state-wide articulation policies as those that stipulate the transfer of credit, but they assessed their effectiveness by the number of students who transferred. To have a symmetrical study

Anderson and colleagues should have considered states with policies that stipulate the transfer of students rather than the transfer of credit. Alternatively, they should have evaluated policies that stipulate the transfer of credit by the proportion of credit that was granted to transferring students rather than whether students transferred or not.

Wellman (2002) studied six US states that rely heavily on transfer from 2-year colleges to give low-income students access to the baccalaureate degree. She selected three states that received high grades and three states that received low grades on retention and degree completion in *Measuring up 2000*, the state report card for higher education released by the National Center for Public Policy and Higher Education (2000). Wellman characterized state policies influencing transfer from community to baccalaureate colleges as structural or academic. Structural polices are those that affect the overall approach to postsecondary education: governance, institutional and sector mission and differentiation, state-wide information system capacity, funding, planning capacities and accountability mechanisms. Wellman argues that the preconditions of student transfer are determined by these structural policies and by demography, economic conditions and institutional histories. Wellman understands academic policies to be those specific to transfer from 2- to 4-year institutions. They are designed to influence the internal alignment of students, programmes and subjects within and across institutions. Academic policies concern admissions standards, curriculum requirements, articulation and transfer of credit.

Wellman found that the key difference between the three high-performing states and the others in her study seems to lie in the state-wide governance structure for higher education. The low-performing states construct transfer as mainly an academic and institutional matter and grant institutions considerable autonomy while the high-performing states of Florida, New York and North Carolina have a comprehensive, integrated approach to transfer implemented by stronger state governance or coordinating mechanisms. For example, the 16 public baccalaureate-granting institutions of North Carolina are part of the University of North Carolina and the state's 58 public community colleges form the North Carolina Community College system governed by the State Board of Community Colleges. In New York public community colleges are part of either the State University of New York or the City University of New York and thus report to the same governing board as the 4-year institutions, which Wellman says may facilitate transfer within those sectors. However, Prager (1993: 551) found in her study that transfer within such institutions can be as difficult as transfer between segmented institutions.

Wellman also found that all three of the high-performing states also use data better to improve transfer performance, including reporting to campuses about their performance relative to others. This echoes Rifkin's (1998: 6) finding that: 'Effective transfer programs benefit from a well developed technical infrastructure that includes statewide student information and tracking systems, articulation databases and research on transfer. The most effective programs have all three and often are found in states where higher education is closely coordinated at the state agency level.' However, Wellman (2002: vii) notes that states' 'accountability structures typically focus on two-year college transfer performance instead of also looking at the responsibilities of the four-year institutions'.

In contrast to the large differences in structures between the states, Wellman (2002: 39) found that: 'There is a good deal of commonality between the states on the academic policy side of the equation, as they have all adopted similar approaches to core curriculum, transfer of credit, remediation and testing, and statewide articulation agreements and course catalogues.' However, she concluded that academic policy alone is not sufficient to achieve strong transfer. Grubb (2006: 36) argues that:

> Active transfer works particularly well in geographic areas where a community college becomes a 'feeder school' for a nearby four-year college – with transfer relatively routine, many students expecting to transfer, all instructors knowledgeable about transfer requirements, and various bridging activities to smooth the transition. This may happen in urban areas with a dominant local university, or in rural areas with one nearby state college.

We now examine in more detail the student transfer provisions of the jurisdictions considered in this study and will observe that while there are differences, all three US states have strong government provisions. This contrasts with the other jurisdictions that have much weaker government provisions supporting student transfer.

9.4.1 USA

Student transfer has long been problematized in the USA and has thus been the subject of government policy which has been distinctive of the USA. Transfer has also been studied extensively. For example, the California Post-secondary Education Commission (2002: 25–7) and its predecessor published 28 papers on student transfer since 1979. In 2001 the Education Commission of the States (2001) found that of the 50 US states, 30 had legislation supporting transfer, 40 had state-wide cooperative transfer agreements, 33 states regularly collected and reported transfer data, 18 states offered incentives and rewards to either transfer students or sending or receiving institutions and 26 states maintained a state-wide guide to transfer.

Russell (2005) reports that at least 30 states identify a general education core that, when completed at one institution, counts toward the general education requirements of other institutions; and at least 14 states have common subject numbering to remove ambiguity in which subjects are transferable. Institutions in California, Ohio, New Jersey and other states have adopted dual-admissions programmes, which are specialized transfer agreements that guarantee students who initially enrol in 2-year colleges admission and transfer of credits to participating 4-year colleges and universities. Mercer County Community College, for example, has dual-admissions agreements with six New Jersey colleges. Each requires completion of a specified programme and a minimum grade point average, which varies by institution and programme (Rifkin 1998).

Pappas Consulting Group (2006: 19) argue that:

> Few, if any, states can match Florida for its transfer friendly policies and practices or its scope of collaborations between community colleges and colleges and universities (both public and private). From 2 + 2 articulation to common course numbering, to common prerequisites, to concurrent use/joint use (facilities and programs), Florida has often blazed a trail.

However, much of US states' policies seem to be exhortatory. Of the 30 states with legislation supporting transfer, only six states specified minimum conditions for the transfer of students and only seven other states specified even minimal conditions for the transfer of credit. Ten states required a transfer agreement without specifying what it might contain, seven states exhorted cooperation in transfer and two states legislated broad support for transfer. The Spellings Commission (US Department of Education 2006: 15) claimed that:

> Barriers to the recognition of transfer credits between different types of institutions pose challenges to students and prevent institutions from increasing capacity. Students too often receive conflicting information about credit-transfer policies between institutions, leading to an unknown amount of lost time and money (and additional federal financial aid) in needlessly repeated course work. Underlying the information confusion are institutional policies and practice on student transfers that are too often inconsistently applied, even within the same institution.

9.4.2 California

Chapter 9.2 of the California education code states the legislature's intention 'that the transfer function shall be a central institutional priority of all segments of higher education in California, and that the segments shall have as a fundamental policy and practice the maintenance of an effective transfer system' (California Legislative Counsel 2001).

The California education code makes the governing board of each public postsecondary education segment accountable for the development and implementation of formal system-wide articulation agreements and transfer programmes and other procedures to support and enhance the transfer function; it provides for the development of new programmes of outreach, recruitment and cooperation between and among the three segments of public higher education to facilitate the successful transfer of students between the community colleges and the universities; it requires the development, maintenance and dissemination of a common core curriculum in general education subjects for the purposes of transfer; it specifies that students who complete the common core curriculum be exempted from all lower division general education requirements; and it requires each university department, school and major which has lower division prerequisites to develop discipline specific articulation agreements and transfer programme agreements in conjunction with community college faculty (California Legislative Counsel 2001).

The California Legislature has mandated a core transfer curriculum at least since 1991 (California Postsecondary Education Commission 2002: 10). In 1996 the California Postsecondary Education Commission reported that all of the then 106 community colleges offered 'an approved list of courses [subjects] from which students may select to meet general education curricular requirements at either the State University or University [of California] campuses of their choice'. In 1999 the University of California established a partnership with the state to increase community college transfer enrolments by 50 per cent, or 15,300 transfers annually by 2005. The university is seeking to expand its transfers by (1) improving subject articulation procedures; (2) increasing its participation at local community college transfer centres; (3) expanding outreach programme activities; (4) providing training to community college counsellors who advise transfer students; and (5) expanding part-time options at the university for transfer students (California Postsecondary Education Commission 2003: 9). While the university did not achieve its ambitious target of a 50 per cent increase in transfers, it increased transfers by 17 per cent to 11,984 transfers in 2005. The Commission believes that a promising state-wide initiative is the dual-admission programme, which was adopted by the University of California Board of Regents in 2001 and funded by the state legislature in 2002. The programme offers admission to high school seniors who are placed within the top 4 and top 12.5 per cent of their local graduating class provided they fulfil their freshman and sophomore requirements at a community college (California Postsecondary Education Commission 2003: 9).

Hayward and colleagues (2004: 35) observed that the California community colleges with strong reputations for transfer to 4-year colleges and universities seem to have close relations with the California State University and the University of California. They have transfer guarantees (extensive lists of California articulation numbered subjects that are assured acceptance of credit transfer) and working partnerships with staff at selected senior campuses. Transfer seems to be encouraged by community colleges being sizeable and relatively close to the 4-year college or university campus where they transfers their students. Hayward *et al.* (2004: 35) report that: 'These and other factors have resulted in a small number of community colleges in the State accounting for more than 60% of the state's transfer students.' Hayward and colleagues' informants said that an on line database of articulation agreements among the higher education institutions in California was valuable in providing accurate and accessible articulation information. Most community college campuses have transfer centres which host regular visits from university representatives, schedule visits to colleges and hold 'transfer days' (Hayward *et al.* 2004: 36).

9.4.3 Colorado

The Colorado Commission on Higher Education says that Colorado statute C.R.S. 23-1-108(7) guarantees that all acceptable course work be transferred from one Colorado public college to another. In particular, 4-year colleges are obliged to accept the core curriculum completed in a 2-year college as a fulfilment of lower division general education requirements. Students may qualify for transfer in three ways: finishing 30 semester units or 1 year's full-time load of transferable college credit with a passing grade point average of 2.0, finishing 12 semester hours of transferable college credits with a credit grade point average of 2.5 or completing an associate's degree with an average higher than credit. This last option guarantees students junior class status in a 4-year college. Colorado also has policies for 4- to 4-year transfer including a change of major within a college. Each 4-year college's admissions office has a 4-year transfer plan for each major (Colorado Department of Higher Education 2007).

In 2001 the Colorado Legislature observed that each public college and university had adopted different general education core curriculum for its undergraduates that differ in scope, number of subjects and design, ranging from 33 to 49 required general education credits. It concluded that differences in general education requirements create transfer barriers. The legislature therefore passed HB 01-1263 and HB 01-1298, which mandate the development of common general education requirements for public higher education institutions and common subject numbering for general education subjects. The legislature seeks to ensure that Colorado undergraduate students receive a general education experience of consistent and high quality regardless of their major or area of study; to protect 'students' rights regarding the transfer of general education courses'; and to facilitate transfer from 2- to 4-year institutions, among 4-year institutions, from 4- to 2-year institutions and within institutions.

9.4.4 Texas

The Texas Legislative Council (2002) has adopted a strong prescription of core curriculum, which it defines as 'the curriculum in liberal arts, humanities, and sciences and political, social, and cultural history that all undergraduate students of an institution of higher education are required to complete before receiving an academic undergraduate degree'. It requires all public higher education institutions to adopt a common core curriculum of a minimum of at least 42 semester credit hours which is just under 1.5 of a full-time student load. The legislature provides for common numbering of the subjects in the common core and requires institutions to give students who complete the common core full credit for the common core.

Section 61.823 of the Texas Education Code directs the coordinating board to develop field of study curricula for various academic programmes. The statute defines a field of study curriculum as a 'set of courses [subjects] that will satisfy the lower division requirements for a bachelor's degree in a specific academic area at a general academic teaching institution.' All public 4-year institutions of higher education are required to accept field-of-study subjects approved by the coordinating board in fulfilment of lower division requirements for bachelor's degrees. Receiving institutions may not require incoming transfer students to repeat subjects with the same content as field of study subjects. The board has approved field of study curricula for child development/early childhood education (April 1999), middle grade education and business (July 2000) and music (October 2000). The board is further required to evaluate the transfer practices of each higher education institution. The Texas Higher Education Coordinating Board (2001a: 16, 32) reports that in 2000 Texas community college students presented with an average of 1.7 years' equivalent full-time study and were granted credit for 1.2 years equivalent full-time study or 70 per cent of the study they had completed.

9.4.5 *Scotland*

Maclennan and colleagues (2000: 2) noted in their review of credit transfer from further education to higher education in Scotland several recent developments that recognized and increased the importance of further education in widening access to higher education, but no government policy that supported student transfer explicitly. Gallacher (2002: 12) observed that while further education colleges had considerable success in widening access, routes to progress to higher education are limited. He observed that the introduction of the Scottish credit accumulation and transfer system has not made a major change and that the Scottish credit and qualifications framework is unlikely meet the expectations put on it to facilitate transfer with credit between sectors.

The Scottish Higher Education Review (2002: 18) reported that the number of formal articulation agreements between higher education institutions and further education colleges remains relatively small. Osborne (2002b: 69) concluded from both the literature and his statistical analysis that incentives to support student transfer are not at present sufficient for many older and ancient universities. Osborne concluded that the imposition of a requirement to accept transfers and respect credit tariffs would be unlikely to improve transfer because of the different traditions of institutions, their autonomy in selecting students and the differential demand for places across the sector. Instead, Osborne suggested incentives in the form of a collaboration incentive grant and strengthening existing regional fora. The Scottish Executive (2002: 34) proposed that prospective and current students be given better information, advice and guidance; it encouraged institutions to collaborate in developing qualifications; and it expected to receive proposals for programme mapping and student tracking. Thus Scotland is still at an early stage of developing student transfer policies and programmes.

9.4.6 Australia

Since the Australian 'unified national system of higher education' is not formally segmented its internal stratification is tacit and therefore until recently no problem has been articulated that requires a response from government. However, in May 2005 the state, territory, Australian government and New Zealand ministers responsible for education, employment, training and youth affairs adopted good practice principles for credit transfer and articulation. As the council itself says, these 'are broad in nature and do not compromise academic or institutional autonomy in assessing and awarding credit' (MCEETYA 2005). The council commissioned a national study of the practices in credit transfer and articulation from vocational to higher education, changed data collection to collect better data on the transfer of students and credit and it asked the Australian Universities Quality Agency and the National Quality Council for vocational education to audit more actively credit transfer and articulation practice against the national good practice principles.

While the ministerial council has been active recently, the measures it has adopted so far are weak in comparison with the measures adopted by many US state governments. Australian governments' attention tends to be directed to the transfer of credit which diverts attention from the transfer of students from vocational to higher education. But the transfer of credit arises only for students who have been admitted to higher education and arguably the transfer of students currently needs to be improved more than the transfer of credit. Unfortunately, the amount of credit granted is reported as a proportion of the programme the student is beginning, not of the studies that the student has completed. So it is not possible to estimate how much study may be repeated by students transferring within the same or similar field. This limitation is not fixed by the new data collection requirements.

Keating and colleagues (2002: 169) suggest additional measures that might be adopted by Australian governments such as introducing short-cycle tertiary courses and dual qualifications and building links between training awards and apprenticeships and degrees, but imply that an obstacle to governments' action may be that such arrangements would require them to re-examine their funding arrangements.

9.5 Conclusion

This chapter has shown that significant numbers of students transfer between vocational and higher education institutions in the USA, Canada, Scotland and Australia. This may be considered a strength or a weakness of the system, depending on one's perspective. Since at least the 1960s the USA has constructed vocational education or community college sector as both a screen and a route to access the upper levels (Clark 1983: 51). Significant upward transfer may therefore be interpreted as a success for the US system since it demonstrates that it does indeed provide the upward academic and social mobility that it promises. In contrast, since 1992 Australia has constructed the vocational education sector as training for work and therefore distinctively different from the higher education sector, which includes cultural transmission and education for life among its core roles. At least in theory, prospective Australian tertiary students are expected to choose the vocational education sector for a direct vocational outcome and the higher education sector for more general education. In this system, significant transfer is thus evidence not of the strength of the system, but of its failure to differentiate the roles of its parts sufficiently clearly, at least to prospective students. High student transfer is also evidence of the failure of the system's sorting–selecting mechanism to direct students to the part that best suits them. But whether upward student transfer is considered a strength or a weakness of a division of roles or functions within a system, it constitutes considerable interaction between its parts.

While this chapter has found that reverse student transfer has been overstated, it is nonetheless significant. Most reverse student transfer seems to be 'drop down' – students who do not complete their baccalaureate transferring to a sub-baccalaureate programme. This can be fitted readily into tertiary education's sorting role. However, reverse transfer augmenters – students who enrol in a sub-baccalaureate programme after completing a baccalaureate – cannot be fitted into the traditional understanding of a segmented higher education system. This phenomenon is most commonly explained – and lauded – as an aspect of lifelong learning (Faure 1972; Delors 1996). The chapter found that neither upward nor reverse transfer is adequate to explain students' enrolment practices, which are not confined to a linear progression from one sector to another. Students have multiple enrolments in vocational and higher education – some sequential and others concurrent. 'Swirling' (de los Santos and Wright 1990: 32) is a better metaphor to explain this practice, which is also understood to exemplify lifelong learning. It isn't possible to determine the extent of swirling from the national data currently available. However, an Australian national survey found that about half of university graduates and almost one-third of vocational education graduates had multiple qualifications, but only about 10 per cent had qualifications from both sectors.

Many students seem to transfer between sectors despite rather than because of their system's policy and processes. Furthermore, student transfer is at least evidence of an informal and tacit structuring of some systems. Thus, the chapter found that Australia's formally unified national system of higher education and Scotland's undifferentiated higher education system had greater differences in transfer student acceptance ratios than California's formally segmented system. Even on the best interpretation of the data, the informal segmentation within Australian and Scottish higher education is greater than the formal segmentation of California. Student transfer thus minimally reveals a structure not established by explicit policy. But, arguably, it does more. Student selection is a significant marker of institutional differentiation, as is evident from the attention given to application and rejection rates and mean entry and cut-off scores. It is influenced by and influences students' applications. So arguably student transfer constructs as well as reflects a system's tacit structuring.

10

Summary and conclusion

10.1 Defining vocational education

For a work with the title *From Vocational to Higher Education: An International Perspective*, the first problem is to define 'vocational education'. It seems that many identify vocational education by what is generally accepted as vocational education in their jurisdiction. This understanding may be programmatic (vocational education is an identified group of programmes understood to be vocational) or it may be institutional (vocational education is what the institutions identified as vocational education institutes do). While such a pragmatic understanding of vocational education is appropriate for many purposes, it is unsatisfactory for some historical studies because what is considered vocational education can change over time even within the same jurisdiction. It is particularly unsatisfactory for an international study because of the variety of terms used to identify 'vocational education' in different countries and because of the substantial differences in countries' arrangement of vocational education and its relations with other educational sectors and employment.

Chapter 3 therefore considers three main types of definition of vocational education. Epistemological definitions posit that vocational education is based on a distinctive way of knowing or, possibly, a distinctive way of learning. Teleological definitions base vocational education's identity on a distinctive purpose such as preparing students for a vocation. Hierarchical definitions locate vocational education within a classification of occupational, educational or cognitive levels. None of these types of definition identifies vocational education uniquely. I therefore sought to establish vocational education's identity not on a unique characteristic, but on a unique combination of characteristics. I defined vocational education by the four general characteristics considered: epistemological, teleological, hierarchical and pragmatic. I defined vocational education as the development and application of knowledge and skills for middle level occupations needed by society from time to time. This was contrasted with higher education, which with vocational education make up tertiary education, the domain of this study.

10.2 Comparative education

The study sought to understand vocational and higher education by comparing them with each other and by comparing vocational and higher education in different countries. It therefore used a method of comparative education, which was developed in Chapter 2. Of the several comparative methods available the study followed Przeworski and Teune's (1970) most similar systems design. This method compares systems that are as similar as possible except in the issue of interest, in this case the effect of the segmentation of higher education into sectors or tiers on the transfer of students from vocational education to the most selective higher education institutions. By comparing systems that are as similar in many respects as possible one eliminates all the factors that the systems share as possible causes for the different upward student transfer rates. One is thereby able to examine the remaining differences between the systems for factors that might cause their different rates.

10.3 Countries compared

The similarity and differences between the countries studied was explored in Chapter 4. Three US states were chosen for comparison because they differ in the formality of their segmentation of higher education institutions. California has long formally segmented its public universities into the highly selective University of California system and the moderately selective California State University system. Colorado distinguishes its public universities by admissions selectivity, but less formally and more recently than California. Texas doesn't formally segment its higher education institutions, although there are clear differences in admission selectivity. These were compared with Australia and Scotland, which both have formally unified university sectors, although there are evident differences between universities' status and admissions selectivity.

10.4 Tracked and generalist systems

In Chapter 1, we noted that there are two broad patterns or tendencies for structuring the relations between vocational and higher education. The tracked systems of Germany and other northern continental European countries direct students to either a vocational or academic track from the post-compulsory years and often earlier from the middle to upper years of compulsory secondary education. The separate upper secondary tracks lead to separate tertiary education sectors and thence to an occupation specific to their vocational or higher education track. The more generalist systems of the UK and the USA still separate vocational and academic education, but the sectors merge and overlap. Students can generally defer their choice between vocational and academic routes until later and they often have more opportunity to transfer between vocational and academic routes without a considerable loss of progress.

We noted further that these patterns in tertiary education provision coincide with two patterns for structuring economies described by Hall and Soskice (2001). The tracked systems are commonly associated with coordinated market economies in which the social partners seek to align educational provision with occupational training and thence employment. In contrast the generalist systems are commonly associated with liberal market economies which rely more on the market to sort and match graduates and employment. In the unpredictable liberal market economies students need more general tertiary education and greater mobility between vocational and higher education to match their education with employment opportunities.

10.4.1 Implications of tracked and generalist systems

In Chapter 5, we noted that qualifications frameworks have been developed by countries with liberal market economies. This reflected one of the roles of qualifications frameworks in sorting and matching graduates and employment in liberal market economies. Qualifications frameworks are useful in establishing a 'common currency' or medium of exchange between qualifications and between qualifications and employment opportunities. In contrast, in coordinated market economies, this sorting and matching is done by the education systems and employer groups cooperatively.

We noted in Chapter 6 that vocational education is much more closely engaged with national economies and industries than higher education. Therefore the European Union's attempts to enhance cooperation in European vocational education and training are likely to encounter obstacles as there remain marked differences in member countries' economies and industrial structures. It seems particularly difficult to find common approaches in vocational education between countries with liberal market economies and those with coordinated market economies.

We noted in Chapter 9 that performance in the tracked systems of tertiary education is optimized when there is a good match of students, sectors and society's needs. In these systems, large numbers of students transferring between vocational and higher education indicate a failure of the system to place students on the appropriate track initially. In contrast, high levels of student transfer in the generalist systems of tertiary education indicate that these systems are succeeding in opening opportunities to students to proceed to more desirable destinations and also indicate that the system is responding flexibly to the changing needs of the economy.

10.5 Four tiers of tertiary education

In Chapter 7, I posited four tiers, segments or sectors of tertiary education: world research universities, selecting universities and colleges, recruiting universities and colleges and vocational education institutes. While the distinguishing characteristics of these tiers are variously research strength, strength of student demand and predominance of vocational programmes, Hirsch's (1976) concept of positional value provides an organizing principle for the whole classification. The tiers are organized in order of their positional value from world research universities, which have the highest positional value, in descending order to vocational institutes, which generally have the lowest positional value in tertiary education, although they still have markedly more positional value than secondary education.

10.6 Student transfer between the sectors

The study's central question was whether the formal segmentation of higher education into sectors or tiers is an obstacle to student transfer from vocational education, which is vital to preserve the equity of tertiary education that uses vocational education as both a screen and a route to the upper tiers of higher education. Since the most similar systems design was used the study compared student transfer rates of systems that were as similar as possible except in how formally they segmented sectors of higher education. Nonetheless, there remained substantial differences between the jurisdictions compared that would have confounded a simple comparison of crude transfer rates in each the jurisdiction.

For example, rates of student transfer from vocational to higher education are affected significantly by the relative size and relations between vocational and higher education in each jurisdiction. Thus, while over half of California's public tertiary education students are enrolled in community colleges over half of Colorado's students are enrolled in 4-year colleges. There is therefore much greater demand to transfer from 2- to 4-year colleges in California than in Colorado. A simple comparison of states' crude student transfer rates is also confounded by a range of other differences between US states that affect student transfer rates such as their overall tertiary education participation rates, definitions of student transfer, levels of affluence, school completion rates and type of secondary preparation, etc. Such comparisons are even more problematic between countries that have different methods for collecting and counting student enrolments and different notions of student transfer.

The study therefore developed a new measure to compare upward student transfer in different jurisdictions, the student admission ratio. This method starts by calculating the transfer student admission rate at the most selective higher education institutions in a jurisdiction. It compares that rate with the transfer student admission rate at the moderately and less selective higher education institutions in the jurisdiction. The ratio between those two transfer student admissions rates indicates the relative barrier to vocational education students transferring to the most selective tier of higher education. In the highly segmented Californian system, the ratio is 1:2 – for every one vocational education student who transfers to the most selective University of California system another two transfer to the moderately selective State University of California system. In contrast, the ratios are 1:4 and 1:5 in the formally unified higher education systems of Australia and Scotland.

This result is counterintuitive. One might have expected that the systems that have formal organizational divisions between their tiers of higher education establish greater barriers for students to transfer from vocational to the top tier of higher education than formally unified systems of higher education. But the results reported in Chapter 9 demonstrate quite the opposite. Furthermore, the student transfer admission ratio of 1:2 in the formally segmented system in California is similar to the ratios found in Colorado's less formally but still segmented system and unsegmented system found in Texas. From this I concluded that the formal segmentation of higher education into tiers is not necessarily less equitable than the formally unified systems if they are complemented by strong student transfer policies and practices.

The study also considered reverse transfer, students' transfer from higher education to vocational education. The relative size of upward and reverse transfer depends on the concept or measure of transfer used, but a review of transfer rates in Australia, Canada, New Zealand and the USA suggest that at most reverse transfer is about the same size as upward transfer, but most data in Australia and the USA suggest that reverse transfer is about half that of upward transfer. This is rather less than the exaggerated claims of the relative size of reverse transfer advanced by some vocational education's champions. Nonetheless, reverse transfer is significant, as is concurrent enrolment in vocational and higher education and multiple swapping between vocational and higher education. So the linear progression from one programme, institution or sector to another along a pathway defined by institutions that is posited by the metaphors of both upward and reverse transfer is inaccurate. A more accurate metaphor proposed by de los Santos and Wright (1990: 32) is of students 'swirling' between vocational and higher education.

10.7 Mechanisms for bridging the sectoral divide

The book noted that there have been several attempts to bridge the divide between vocational and higher education. These are reviewed systematically in Chapter 8. Two dimensions of collaboration between the sectors were considered: level of organization and level of association. One can imagine that a jurisdiction with a small population might have just one system of tertiary education that combined vocational and higher education. Or one can imagine that while a jurisdiction may establish separate specialized sectors and institutions in areas of high population density it may establish combined institutions in sparsely populated regions. We may further imagine that in fields with low enrolments there might be combined vocational and higher education departments or programmes. There are examples of managers and teachers combining vocational and higher education in their responsibilities and we have seen that many students enrol concurrently in vocational and higher education. At each organizational level, vocational and higher education may be unified, they may be formally associated in a partnership, there may be collaboration or the two types may be quite separate.

Chapter 8 gives several examples of many of these mechanisms for bridging the divide between vocational and higher education, in many jurisdictions. The number and variety of these mechanisms suggests that the divide between vocational and higher education is often considered a problem, but that there is no single mechanism for bridging it which is effective in all contexts.

10.8 Options for structuring vocational and higher education

The distinctions between vocational and higher education are deeply entrenched in most jurisdictions and are likely to continue for the foreseeable future, notwithstanding the numerous attempts at bridging the sectoral divide described in Chapter 8 and despite the lack of a universal rational for the distinction between vocational and higher education found in Chapter 3. This final section draws from the description of countries' structuring of vocational and higher education in Chapter 4 and from the survey of the relations between the sectors in Chapter 8. It posits six options for structuring the relations between the sectors: segregation, duplication, integration, systematizing a transfer role, establishing an intermediate sector and 'wise and masterly inactivity' (Mackintosh 2006 [1791]: 45). Each is discussed in turn.

10.8.1 Segregation

One option is to separate vocational and higher education completely, but build opportunities for arm's length exchange between them. Institutions are quite separate in most jurisdictions and qualifications are segregated between community colleges and 4-year institutions in many tightly regulated Canadian provinces and US states. Segregating the sectors has several advantages. Institutions and their staff are able to specialize in their distinctive functions. The roles of the sectors are clearly delineated not only in the minds of experts who are daily involved in tertiary education, but also in the minds of employers who mostly engage with tertiary education episodically and in the minds of prospective students and their parents who might encounter tertiary education twice in their lifetime: once as a student and then as a parent.

Segregating vocational and higher education is also mostly simpler for legislators to determine and managers to implement. Just three sets of policies and principles need to be determined, implemented and monitored: one for higher education, one for vocational education and one for the exchange between them. However, this policy simplicity comes at the expense of a sophisticated response to the complexities of life. Not all tertiary education needs arise and are predefined as exclusively vocational or higher education. Some needs are at the boundary between the sectors. This raises difficult and to some extent arbitrary decisions about the location of an activity in a sector. Other needs emerge as being most appropriately met by one sector but develop aspects more appropriately handled by the other sector. None of these difficulties is necessarily fatal to the segregation of the sectors. However, as a rule one may expect that the stricter the segregation of vocational and higher education the more difficult the boundary problems.

10.8.2 Duplication

At the other extreme is to allow vocational and higher education to duplicate their programmes, but with different orientations and approaches. Arguably as Germany's *Fachhochschulen* have developed from polytechnics to being permitted to call themselves in English universities of applied sciences they have developed similarities with universities. From the 1990s New Zealand's polytechnics and universities developed considerable overlap and at least some duplication of awards. The government believed this became excessive and from 2007 has been shaping different profiles for institutions. There is increasing overlap of vocational and higher education programmes in Australia and less but still some overlap between colleges of further education and universities in England. This is the result of the complementary academic drift of vocational education institutions and the vocational drift of higher education institutions.

Allowing vocational and higher education institutions to duplicate their programmes completely is unproblematic and indeed is the appropriate policy if one believes, as many do, that the sectors are converging and that sectoral distinctions will in time fade away. However, this study has found that the divide between vocational and higher education is widespread among otherwise quite dissimilar countries and has been remarkably persistent over time, significant changes to tertiary education notwithstanding. If one therefore concluded that different vocational and higher education provision was likely to be needed for some time into the future one would be very wary of allowing vocational and higher education to duplicate their activities. For there would be a risk of all tertiary institutions converging to the most popular and best funded activities, leaving some functions under-served, most likely the less popular or less glamorous activities of vocational education. These activities could be preserved by specific regulation, but if there are many activities requiring specific provision policymakers may eventually have to recreate a vocational education sector that had been allowed to drift to higher education.

10.8.3 Integration

Another option would be to harmonize the financing, curriculum, coordination and other arrangements for vocational and higher education so that there is a 'seamless' interface between the sectors. This is argued by many writers who have observed the differences between the sectors to be barriers to the ready transfer of students between the sectors. There are three difficulties with this option. First, there are multifarious differences between the sectors that would require considerable effort and disruption to harmonize. Second, the sectors operate with different dynamics. As was observed in Chapter 6, vocational education is closely engaged with industry and the economy and changes as industries change. Higher education is engaged more closely with academic disciplines and changes as the disciplines change. These different dynamics mean that the sectors are changing continuously, but in different ways. As a consequence, the work that is required to harmonize the sectors is not only an initial investment, but requires a continuing investment as each sector follows its own different dynamic. It is not clear that these major investments would be justified by the increased convenience or even increased volume of student transfer.

There is, however, a more substantial objection. The differences between the sectors are inconvenient for many transferring students and seem to discourage some students from transferring. There are no doubt some vocational education students who never even contemplate transferring to higher education because it seems too different and thus remote. However, a different perspective is given by the higher education equity literature which investigates why some students complete secondary education and proceed to higher education while large numbers, in many countries the majority, either do not complete secondary education or do not proceed to higher education. The literature has concluded that the most significant reasons for students not completing secondary education and proceeding to higher education are not financial, curriculum or other barriers to further study. Rather, the literature has found that students who do not proceed to higher education have different aspirations and expectations from those who do proceed to higher education, and that these are formed in the early and middle years of school. If this is right investing substantial effort in harmonizing vocational and higher education is misplaced: more students would proceed to higher education, and perhaps more students would transfer from vocational education, if there were a greater investment in raising aspirations and expectations among junior and middle year secondary students.

10.8.4 Systematizing a transfer role

A fourth option would be to follow many US states and Scotland in systematizing a role for vocational education in preparing students to transfer to higher education. A jurisdiction could learn much from the USA in adopting such an approach: as is evident from Chapter 9, the USA has extensive and longstanding experience of student transfer, a variety of approaches has been trialled as states have sought to improve transfer in their circumstances and there is an extensive scholarly and policy literature on student transfer.

While student transfer is fundamental to US tertiary education, it has limitations and may not be appropriate for other circumstances. As was developed in Chapter 1, the USA's liberal market economy encourages general vocational education which is more compatible with preparing students for further study. Even so, the balance between occupational preparation and preparing students for transfer seems to be perennially debated in the USA and there is much critical commentary about the incompatibility of these roles. Vocational education in other jurisdictions that is more concerned with preparing students for employment in specific occupations may be less compatible with adopting a strong transfer role and role conflict or at least fragmentation may be more of a concern in these jurisdictions.

10.8.5 Establishing an intermediate sector: higher vocational education

A fifth option would be to remove the overlap in the sectors' responsibilities for short-cycle higher education by transferring this responsibility to a newly established sector of higher vocational education. This is rarely if ever done in Anglophone jurisdictions. But it has been achieved in bilingual Quebec, which neatly places its general and vocational colleges (*collèges d'enseignement général et professionnel*) distinctively between secondary and higher education. As was described in Chapter 8, in Quebec it is not possible for students to proceed from school to university without first completing the CEGEP's diploma of collegial studies (*diplôme d'études collégiales*), which normally takes 2 years full-time after completing the secondary school diploma.

This option has the attraction of neatness and indeed would return vocational education institutions to the vision of the originators of US community colleges in the mid- to late nineteenth century as substitutes for lower level undergraduate preparation which would be discarded by universities. Transferring responsibility for all lower level higher education to an intermediate sector of higher vocational education also has the potential for considerable savings of resources since lower level higher education would be conducted by institutions without the expensive research role and higher cost structure of universities. Quebec describes its introduction of this system in 1967 as revolutionary, albeit a quiet one (*revolution tranquille*) and the biggest obstacle to adopting this option may be the attendant disruption to the organization, funding, staffing and curriculum of established vocational and higher education institutions.

10.8.6 'Wise and masterly inactivity'

In discussing the response of the Third Estate of commoners to a constitutional position adopted by the Second Estate of nobles in the early history of the French Revolution the Scottish jurist, politician and historian James Mackintosh (2006 [1791]: 45) wrote that: 'The commons, faithful to their system, remained in a wise and masterly inactivity.' This would be a final option for dealing with the relations between vocational and higher education: do nothing or, more likely, continue fiddling at the margins. This would be a sensible option since arguably vocational and higher education's most important engagements are not with each other, but with their own dynamics: vocational education with industry and higher education with the academic disciplines.

10.9 Conclusion and future work

This study has helped us understand how vocational and higher education are structured as tertiary education systems in developed countries and possibilities for alternative structures. The book did so by comparing arrangements in different countries and to do this it developed an analytical framework for international educational comparisons. The book found that there are two broad patterns for structuring the relations between vocational and higher education and that these are related to countries' economic systems. This suggests that there is a limit in the extent to which a jurisdiction may change its relations between vocational and higher education without also changing its economic system.

However, the study found that the structure of vocational and higher education sectors seem less important than the relations between the sectors and that these may be influenced by strong government policy and mechanisms for monitoring its implementation. There is therefore considerable scope for action by interested governments and various options were canvassed. However, the field is by no means settled and considerable further work remains to be done.

The book considered the transfer of students within tertiary education to illuminate at least part of the operation of the system. It could be extended to consider other aspects of tertiary education's internal dynamics.

An interesting comparison with the present study would be the movement of staff between institutions and types of institution. One might categorize academic staff by the sector of their first tertiary qualification – vocational education, recruiting higher education, selecting higher education and world research universities – and examine how many are teaching in a different sector. One would expect there to be a general downward drift – that more graduates of world research universities would be working in selecting and recruiting universities than there would be vocational education graduates working in world research universities – but again the ratios in different jurisdictions would be most informative.

A more adventurous study would venture beyond the internal dynamics of tertiary education to study the system's interactions with other sectors. The closest is secondary education. Chapter 4 noted that 80 per cent of vocational education students in Canada study full-time. At the other extreme, only 9 per cent of Australian vocational education students are full-time. This suggest a far higher transition from school to vocational education institutions in Canada than in Australia. Two-year colleges also seem to be promoted as an acceptable destination for high school graduates in the USA. The greater plurality of destinations of high school graduates in North America might explain why higher education institutions seem to have far less control over the senior secondary curriculum in North America than in Australia and the UK.

Moving beyond education, one may consider the interaction between tertiary education and the labour market. This is not just a direct transfer on graduation from full-time study to full-time work. Work experience is incorporated within the formal curriculum in higher education programmes such as education, medicine and nursing and presumably there is considerable interaction between higher education and employment in these fields. While there are internships in liberal arts and sciences programmes, a lower proportion of students in these programmes incorporate work experience within their formal education than in the explicitly vocational programmes. One might expect these patterns to be broadly consistent across the jurisdictions we have been considering. But such consistency may not extend to vocational education programmes.

First, counterintuitively, some vocational education programmes in some jurisdictions may not incorporate much more work experience than higher education programmes. Apprenticeships are the archetypal vocational education programmes, but they are a small and shrinking proportion of vocational education enrolments in many Anglo countries. Second, the very different rates of part- and full-time study in vocational education programmes across jurisdictions suggest different proportions of students studying to transfer, to enter the skilled work force and to upgrade skills. Systemwide data on this are collected in Australia and by several US states and so offer the prospect of some interesting comparisons. One could also investigate the extent of ostensibly full-time students' engagement in part-time work not directly related to their studies. Although data are not collected routinely on this, there are probably enough studies of the phenomenon to support sensible comparisons between jurisdictions.

Readers will have their own questions and lines of inquiry about the relations between vocational and higher education. The sectors may expect further changes from governments directly in their own right, indirectly through changes to occupational and industrial regulation and planned changes to the economy and through supra-national agreements such as the European Union and free trade agreements. In addition, vocational and higher education will continue to be changed by broader and more general forces: globalization, new technology and economic change. The field is therefore likely to be the subject of continuing lively study and debate.

References

Allais, S. M. (2007) Why the South African NQF failed: lessons for countries wanting to introduce national qualifications frameworks. *European Journal of Education*, 42(4): 523–47.

Anderson, C. A. (1961) Methodology of comparative education. *International Review of Education*, VII(1): 1–22.

Anderson, D. (1998) Chameleon or phoenix: the metamorphosis of TAFE. *Australia and New Zealand Journal of Vocational Education Research*, 6(2): 1–43.

Anderson, G. M., Sun, J. C. and Alfonso, M. (2006) Effectiveness of statewide articulation agreements on the probability of transfer: a preliminary policy analysis. *The Review of Higher Education*, 29(3): 261–91.

Aristotle, *Metaphysics*, book A, ch. 1, 981b; book A, ch. 1, 993b. W. D. Ross (1928) (trns), 2nd edn. Oxford: Clarendon Press.

Aristotle, *Nichomachean Ethics*, book VI, 3. The qualities by which truth is obtained, 1139b–1141a. M. Ostwald (1962) (trns). Indianapolis: The Bobbs-Merrill Company.

Aristotle, *The Politics*, book VIII. T. A. Sinclair (trns), T. J. Saunders (revised) (1992). London: Penguin Books.

Ashby, E. (1974) *Adapting Universities to a Technological Society*. San Francisco: Jossey-Bass.

Australian Bureau of Statistics (2002) 2001 education and training experience (cat. no. 6278.0) (http://www.abs.gov.au/AUSSTATS/abs@.nsf/ProductsbyCatalogue/252D868F10B905F3CA2568A9001393AF?OpenDocument). Accessed 23 December 2007.

Australian Bureau of Statistics (2003) Education and work, Australia, May 2003 (cat. no. 6227.0) (http://www.abs.gov.au/AUSSTATS/abs@.nsf/ProductsbyCatalogue/556A439CD3D7E8A8CA257242007B3F32?OpenDocument). Accessed 23 December 2007.

Australian Bureau of Statistics (2004) Survey of education and training, 2001, table provided by Ms L. Edmunds, National Centre for Education & Training Statistics, Australian Bureau of Statistics, personal communication 21 September 2004.

Barlow, M. L. (1965) The challenge to vocational education, in M. L. Barlow (ed.) *64th Yearbook of the National Society for the Study of Vocational Education*. Chicago: University of Chicago Press.

Batrouney, T. J. (1985) The national co-ordination of technical and further education. Unpublished PhD thesis, Monash University.

Bennett, C. A. (1926) *History of Manual and Industrial Education up to 1870.* Peoira, IL: Chas A. Bennett Co.

Bennett, C. A. (1937) *History of Manual and Industrial Education 1870 to 1917.* Peoira, IL: Chas A. Bennett Co.

Bereday, G. Z. F. (1964) *Comparative Method in Education.* New York: Holt, Rinehart & Winston.

Berg, M. (1993) Small producer capitalism in eighteenth-century England. *Business History*, 35(1): 17–40.

Bhaskar, R. (1998) [1979] *The Possibility of Naturalism: A Philosophical Critique of the Contemporary Human Sciences*, 3rd edn. London and New York: Routledge.

Bliss, I. and Garbett, J. (1990) Learning lessons from abroad, in P. Summerfield and E. Evans (eds) *Technical Education and the State since 1850: Historical and Contemporary Perspectives.* Manchester: Manchester University Press.

Blunden, R. (1995) Practical intelligence and the metaphysics of competence. *Australian and New Zealand Journal of Vocational Education Research*, 3(2): 1–20.

Bourdieu, P. (1988) [1984] *Homo Academicus.* Oxford: Basil Blackwell.

Brockmann, M., Clarke, L. and Winch, C. (2007) Knowledge, skills, competence: European divergences in vocational education and training (VET) – the English, German and Dutch cases. *Oxford Review of Education*, 1–21.

Burgess, T. (1986) *New Technology and Skills in British Industry*, MSC Skills series no. 1. Sheffield: Manpower Services Commission, quoted in P. Ainley (1993) *Class and Skill: Changing Divisions of Knowledge and Labour.* London: Cassell Educational Ltd.

California Legislative Counsel (2001) California education code, title 3 post secondary education division, ch. 9.2 student transfer (http://www.leginfo.ca.gov/cgi-bin/calawquery?codesection=edc&codebody=&hits=20). Accessed 23 December 2007.

California Postsecondary Education Commission (1998) Factsheet 98–1, composition of higher education in California (http://www.cpec.ca.gov/FactSheets/FactSheet1998/fs98–01.pdf). Accessed 23 December 2007.

California Postsecondary Education Commission (2000) Performance indicators of California higher education, 2000, Commission report 01–3 (http://www.cpec.ca.gov/completereports/2001reports/01–03.pdf). Accessed 23 December 2007.

California Postsecondary Education Commission (2002) Student transfer in California postsecondary education, Commission report 02–3 (http://www.cpec.ca.gov/completereports/2002reports/02–03.pdf). Accessed 26 March 2008.

California Postsecondary Education Commission (2003) A regional study of undergraduate enrollment demand and capacity for the University of California, Commission report 03–06 (http://www.cpec.ca.gov/CompleteReports/2003Reports/03–06.pdf). Accessed 23 December 2007.

Carmichael, L. (1992) *The Australian Vocational Certificate Training System* (Carmichael report). Canberra: Employment and Skills Formation Council, National Board of Employment, Education and Training.

Clark, B. R. (1960) *The Open Door College: A Case Study.* New York: McGraw-Hill.

Clark, B. (1973) Some comments on the Grenoble meeting, in OECD, *Short-cycle Higher Education: A Search for Identity.* Paris: OECD.

Clark, B. R. (1983) *The Higher Education System: Academic Organization in Cross-national Perspective.* Berkeley, CA: University of California Press.

Clarke, L. and Winch, C. (2006) A European skills framework? – but what are skills?

Anglo-Saxon versus German concepts. *Journal of Education and Work*, 19(3): 255–69.

Cobban, A. B. (1975) *The Medieval Universities: Their Development and Organisation.* London: Methuen.

Coles, M. and Oates, T. (2005) European reference levels for education and training: promoting credit transfer and mutual trust. Study commissioned to the Qualifications and Curriculum Authority, England. Luxembourg: Office for Official Publications of the European Communities (http://www2.trainingvillage.gr/etv/publication/download/panorama/5146_en.pdf). Accessed 23 December 2007.

Coles, M. and Werquin, P. (2007) Qualifications systems: bridges to lifelong learning (http://www.oecdbookshop.org/oecd/display.asp?sf1=identifiers&lang=EN&st1=912007031p1). Accessed 23 December 2007.

Colorado Commission on Higher Education (2003) *Admissions Standards.* Denver, CO: Colorado Department of Higher Education.

Colorado Department of Higher Education (2007) Statewide transfer policy (http://highered.colorado.gov/Publications/Policies/Current/i-partl.pdf). Accessed 23 December 2007.

Commission of the European Communities (2006) European credit system for Vocational Education and Training (ECVET). A system for the transfer, accumulation and recognition of learning outcomes in Europe. Commission staff working document. Brussels, 31.10.2006. SEC(2006) 1431 (http://ec.europa.eu/education/ecvt/work_en.pdf). Accessed 23 December 2007.

Comte, A. (1975) [1830–1842] *Cours de philosophie positive*, in G. Lenzer (ed.) *Auguste Comte and Positivism: The Essential Writings.* New York: Harper & Row.

Cotgrove, S. F. (1958) *Technical Education and Social Change.* London: Allen & Unwin.

Council of Europe (2004) [1997] Convention on the recognition of qualifications concerning higher education in the European region (Lisbon convention) (http://conventions.coe.int/Treaty/EN/Treaties/Html/165.htm). Accessed 23 December 2007.

Cowen, R. (2006) Acting comparatively upon the educational world: puzzles and possibilities. *Oxford Review of Education*, 32(5): 561–73.

Crosier, D., Purser, L. and Smidt, H. (2007) Trends V: universities shaping the European higher education area, an European University Association report (http://www.ond.vlaanderen.be/hogeronderwijs/bologna/documents/EUA_Trends_Reports.htm). Accessed 23 December 2007.

Cunningham, S. and Hartley, J. (2001) Creative industries – from Blue Poles to fat pipes. Paper presented to the National Humanities and Social Sciences Summit, Canberra, 2001 (http://www.dest.gov.au/NR/rdonlyres/C785B22C-E7EC-47D0-9781-C5AA68546FCD/1426/summit701.pdf). Accessed 26 March 2008.

Curtis, D. D. (2006) Inter-sectoral transfers: sense, status, prevalence and purpose. Paper presented at the 15th national vocational education and training research conference, 12–14 July, Mooloolaba, Australia (http://www.voced.edu.au/docs/confs/ncver/vetconf15/tr15curtis.pdf). Accessed 23 December 2007.

Dawkins, The Hon J. S., MP (1988) *Higher Education: A Policy Statement* ('the White Paper'). Canberra: Australian Government Publishing Service.

Dawson, J. (2005) A history of vocation: tracing a keyword of work, meaning and moral purpose. *Adult Education Quarterly*, 55(3): 220–31.

Dearing, R. (chair) (1997) Higher education in the learning society, report of the National Committee of Inquiry into Higher Education (http://www.leeds.ac.uk/educol/ncihe/). Accessed 23 December 2007.

DEEWR (Department of Education, Training and Youth Affairs) (2001) *Higher Education Student Statistics, 2000.* Canberra: DEEWR

Delors, J. (chair) (1996) Learning: the treasure within, report to UNESCO of the International Commission on Education for the Twenty-first Century (http://www.unesco.org/delors/delors_e.pdf). Accessed 23 December 2007.

De los Santos, A. G. Jr and Wright, I. (1990) Maricopa's swirling students: earning one third of Arizona state's bachelor's degrees. *AACJC Journal,* June/July: 32–4.

Department of Consumer Affairs (2001) Licensee information (http://www.dca.ca.gov/about_dca/profession.shtml). Accessed 23 December 2007.

Department of Regulatory Agencies (DORA) (2001) Occupational/ industry licensing database (http://www.dora.state.co.us). Accessed 23 December 2007.

Dewey, John (1916) *Democracy and Education: An Introduction to the Philosophy of Education.* New York: Free Press.

Douglass, J. A. (2000) Institutional differentiation and coordination: a case study of California. Mimeo, Centre for Studies in Higher Education, University of California, Berkeley.

Douglass, J. A. (2004) The dynamics of massification and differentiation: a comparative look at higher education systems in the United Kingdom and California. *Higher Education Management and Policy,* 16(3): 9–33.

Durkheim, E. (1938) [1895] *The Rules of Sociological Method.* S. H. Solovay and J. H. Mueller (trns), 8th edn. New York: Free Press.

Durkheim, E. (1977) [1938] *The Evolution of Educational Thought.* P. Collins (trns). London: Routledge & Kegan Paul.

Education Commission of the States (2001) Transfer and articulation policies (http://www.ecs.org/clearinghouse/23/75/2375.htm). Accessed 23 December 2007.

Engeström, Y. (1994) *Training for Change.* Geneva: Labour Office.

European Commission (2003) Stocktaking report of the Copenhagen coordinating group (http://ec.europa.eu/education/policies/2010/doc/ccg_report_october_2003_final_en.pdf). Accessed 23 December 2007.

European Communities (2002a) [1957] Consolidated version of the Treaty Establishing the European Community (Treaty of Rome) Official Journal of the European Communities, C325, 24.12.2002 (http://eur-lex.europa.eu/en/treaties/dat/12002E/pdf/12002E_EN.pdf). Accessed 23 December 2007.

European Communities (2002b) [1992] Consolidated version of the Treaty on European Union (Maastricht Treaty), Official Journal of the European Communities, C325, 24.12.2002 (http://eur-lex.europa.eu/en/treaties/dat/12002M/pdf/12002M_EN.pdf). Accessed 23 December 2007.

European Communities (2007) europass. Opening doors to learning and working in Europe (http://europass.cedefop.europa.eu/europass/preview.action?locale_id=1). Accessed 23 December 2007.

European Council (2000) Presidency conclusions, Lisbon European Council 23 and 24 March 2000 (http://ue.eu.int/ueDocs/cms_Data/docs/pressData/en/ec/00100-r1.en0.htm). Accessed 23 December 2007.

European Ministers of Education (2003) [1999] The Bologna declaration of 19 June 1999, Brussels: European University Association (http://www.ond.vlaanderen.be/hogeronderwijs/bologna/documents/MDC/BOLOGNA_DECLARATION1.pdf). Accessed 2 December 2007.

European Ministers of Education (2004) [1998] Sorbonne joint declaration, Brussels: European University Association (http://www.eua.be/eua/jsp/en/

upload/OFFDOC_BP_bologna_declaration.1068714825768.pdf). Accessed 23 December 2007.

European Ministers of Vocational Education and Training and the European Commission (2002) The Copenhagen Declaration. Declaration of the European Ministers of Vocational Education and Training, and the European Commission, convened in Copenhagen on 29 and 30 November 2002, on enhanced European cooperation in vocational education and training (http://ec.europa.eu/education/copenhagen/copenahagen_declaration_en.pdf). Accessed 23 December 2007.

European Parliament (2007) Qualifications framework for lifelong learning, texts adopted by Parliament, Wednesday, 24 October 2007 – Strasbourg (http://www.europarl.europa.eu/sides/getDoc.do?pubRef=-//EP//TEXT+TA+P6-TA-2007-0463+0+DOC+XML+V0//EN#title2). Accessed 23 December 2007.

Faure, E. (chair) (1972) *Learning to Be: The World of Education Today and Tomorrow.* Report of the international commission on the future of education. Paris: UNESCO.

Feinberg, W. (1983) *Understanding Education: Towards a Reconstruction of Educational Inquiry.* Cambridge: Cambridge University Press.

Furth, D. (1973) Short-cycle higher education: some basic considerations, in D. Furth (ed.) *Short-cycle Higher Education: A Search for Identity.* Paris: OECD.

Furth, D. (1992) Short-cycle higher education: Europe, in B. R. Clark and G. R. Neave (eds) *The Encyclopedia of Higher Education,* vol. 2. Oxford: Permagon.

Gallacher, J. (2002) Articulation links between further education colleges and higher education institutions in Scotland, in M. Osborne, J. Gallacher and M. Murphy (eds) A research review of FE/HE links – a report to the Scottish Executive Enterprise and Lifelong Learning Department (http://www.scotland.gov.uk/about/ELLD/HESP/00016640/annexe2p1.pdf). Accessed 23 December 2007.

Gallacher, J. (2003) *Higher Education in Further Education Colleges: The Scottish Experience.* London: The Council for Industry and Higher Education (http://www.ciheuk.com/docs/PUBS/0303HEinFECScottish.pdf). Accessed 23 December 2007.

Gallacher, J. (2006) Widening access or differentiation and stratification in higher education in Scotland. *Higher Education Quarterly,* 60(4): 349–69.

Gautherin, J. (1993) Marc-Antoine Jullien ('Jullien de Paris') (1775–1848) Prospects: the quarterly review of comparative education, XXIII(3/4): 757–73 (http://www.ibe.unesco.org/publications/ThinkersPdf/julliene.pdf). Accessed 23 December 2007.

Geiger, R. L. (1992) Introduction, the institutional fabric of the higher education system, in B. R. Clark and G. R. Neave (eds) *The Encyclopedia of Higher Education.* Oxford: Pergamon.

Gelin, F. (1999) Transfer rates: how to measure and for what purpose? A discussion paper, Vancouver: British Columbia Council on Admissions and Transfer (http://www.bccat.bc.ca/pubs/transrates.pdf). Accessed 23 December 2007.

Gibbons, M., Limoges, C., Nowotny, H., Schwartzman, S., Scott, P. and Trow, M. (1994) *The New Production of Knowledge: The Dynamics of Science and Research in Contemporary Societies.* London: Sage.

Goedegebuure, L. and van Vught, F. (1994) Intellectual context and methodological framework, in L. Geodegebuure and F. Vught (eds) *Comparative Higher Education Policy Studies.* Utrecht: Centre for Higher Education Policy Studies.

Goozee, G. (2001) [1993] *The Development of TAFE in Australia. An Historical Perspective,*

3rd edn. Adelaide: NCVER (http://www.ncver.edu.au/publications/574.html). Accessed 23 December 2007.

Grendler, P. F. (2002) *The Universities of the Italian Renaissance*. Baltimore, MA: The Johns Hopkins University Press.

Group of Eight (2003) About the Group of Eight (http://www.go8.edu.au/about/go8.htm). Accessed 23 December 2007.

Grubb, N. (1991) The decline of community college transfer rates: evidence from national longitudinal surveys. *Journal of Higher Education*, 62(2): 194–222.

Grubb, N. (2005) Alternatives to universities revisited, in R. Sweet and D. Hirsch (eds) *Education Policy Analysis 2004*. Paris: OECD.

Grubb, N. (2006) Vocationalism and the differentiation of tertiary education: lessons from US community colleges. *Journal of Further and Higher Education*, 30(1): 27–42.

Grubb, N. W., Davis, G., Lum, J., Plihal, J. and Morgaine, C. (1991) *'The Cunning Hand, the Cultured Mind': Models for Integrating Vocational and Academic Education*. Berkeley, CA: National Center for Research in Vocational Education, University of California at Berkeley.

Hall, P. A. and Soskice, D. (2001) An introduction to varieties of capitalism, in P. A. Hall and D. Soskice (eds) *Varieties of Capitalism: The Institutional Foundations of Comparative Advantage*. Oxford: Oxford University Press.

Hans, Nicholas (1964) Functionalism in comparative education. *International Review of Education*, 10(1): 94–7.

Harvey, L. (1996) The nature and role of quality in the federal omniversity. Conference paper: Dilemmas in mass higher education, 10–12 April, Staffordshire University.

Hayward, G. C., Jones, D. P., McGuinness, A. C. Jr and Timar, A. (2004) Ensuring access with quality to California's community colleges, report #04–3, San José, California: National Center for Public Policy and Higher Education (http://www.highereducation.org/reports/hewlett/Hewlett3.pdf). Accessed 23 December 2007.

Henninger, G. R. (1959) *The Technical Institute in America*. New York: MacGraw-Hill.

Higgins, C. S. and Katsinas, S. G. (1999) The relationship between environmental conditions and transfer rates of selected rural community colleges: a pilot study, *Community College Review*, 27(2): 1–25.

Hirsch, F. (1976) *Social Limits to Growth*. London: Routledge & Kegan Paul.

Huisman, J., Kaiser, F. and Vossensteyen, H. (2003) The relations between access, diversity and participation: searching for the weakest link, in M. Tight (ed.) *Access and Exclusion*. Oxford: Elsevier Science Ltd.

Hume, D. (1964) [1738] *A Treatise of Human Nature*, vol. 1. London: Dent & Sons.

Huxley, T. H. (1877) Technical education, in T. H. Huxley, *Collected Essays III*. London: Macmillan.

Hyland, T. (1999) *Vocational Studies, Lifelong Learning and Social Values. Investigating Education, Training and NVQs under the New Deal*. Aldershot: Ashgate.

Ignash, J. M. and Townsend, B. (2000) Evaluating state-level articulation agreement according to good practice. *Community College Review*, 28(3): 1–19.

Illinois Board of Higher Education, Illinois Community College Board, and Transfer Coordinators of Illinois Colleges and Universities (1996–2007) Illinois articulation initiative (http://www.itransfer.org/). Accessed 23 December 2007.

Jacobs, J. (2002) Colorado Commission on Higher Education, transfer data, personal communication 26 November (data file available from author).

James, R. (2007) Social equity in a mass, globalised higher education environment:

the unresolved issue of widening access to university. Faculty of Education Dean's lecture series 2007, 18 September (http://www.edfac.unimelb.edu.au/news/lectures/pdf/richardjamestranscript.pdf). Accessed 23 December 2007.

Jochimsen, R. (1978) Aims and objectives of German vocational and professional education in the present European context. *Comparative Education*, 14(3): 199–209.

Jullien, M. (1817) *Esquisse et vues préliminaires d'un ouvrage sur l'éducation comparée* [Outline and preliminary views of a work on comparative education]. Paris: L. Colas.

Kajstura, A. and Keim, M. C. (1992) Reverse transfer students in Illinois community colleges. *Community College Review*, 20(2): 39–44.

Kandel, I. L. (1933) *Studies in Comparative Education*. London: Harrap & Co.

Kangan, M. (chair) (1974) Australian Committee on Technical and Further Education *TAFE in Australia. Report on Needs in Technical and Further Education*. Canberra: Australian Government Publishing Service.

Keating, J., Medrich, E., Volkoff, V. and Perry, J. (2002) Review of research: comparative study of VET systems – national vocational education and training systems across three regions under pressure of change (http://www.ncver.edu.au/research/proj/nr9009.pdf). Accessed 23 December 2007.

Kerr, C. (1963) The idea of a multiversity, in C. Kerr (ed.) *The Uses of the University*. Cambridge: Harvard University Press.

Kerr, C. (1994) *Higher Education cannot Escape History: Issues for the Twenty-first Century*. Albany, NY: State University of New York Press.

King, E. (1967) Comparative studies and policy decisions. *Comparative Education*, 4(1): 51–63.

Kintzer, F. C. (1973) *Middleman in Higher Education*. San Francisco: Jossey-Bass.

Koehl, R. (1977) The comparative study of education: prescription and practice. *Comparative Education Review*, 21(2/3): 177–94.

Labaree, D. F. (2006) Markets, politics, and American higher education: an institutional success story (http://www.stanford.edu/%7Edlabaree/). Accessed 23 December 2007.

Lachenmann, G. (1988) Vocational and general education in England, in H. Rohrs (ed.) *Vocational and General Education in Western Industrial Societies*. London: Symposium Books.

Legal Information Institute (2002) US code collection, title 20, ch. 44, section 2302, subsection 29 (http://www4.law.cornell.edu/uscode/20/2302.html). Accessed 23 December 2007.

Lipinska, P., Schmid, E. and Tessaring, M. (2007) Zooming in on 2010. Reassessing vocational education and training, Cedefop European Centre for the Development of Vocational Training. Luxembourg: Office for Official Publications of the European Communities (http://www.trainingvillage.gr/etv/Information_resources/Bookshop/publication_details.asp?pub_id=474). Accessed 23 December 2007.

Lisbon European Council (2000) Presidency conclusions, 24/3/2000 (http://www.consilium.europa.eu/ueDocs/cms_Data/docs/pressData/en/ec/00100-r1.en0.htm). Accessed 23 December 2007.

Mackintosh, J. (2006) [1791] *Vindiciae Gallicae: Defence of the French Revolution and its Admirers against the Accusations of the Right Hon. Edmund Burke, Including some Strictures on the Late Production of M. de Calonne*, in D. Winch *Vindiciae Gallicae and Other Writings on the French Revolution*. Indianapolis, IN: Liberty Fund (http://oll.libertyfund.org/title/1665/62366). Accessed 26 December 2007.

Maclennan, A., Musselbrook, K. and Dundas, M. (2000) *Credit Transfer at the FE/HE Interface – Research Report for the Scottish Further Education Funding Council.* Edinburgh: Scottish Further Education Funding Council.

Magnus, P. (1888) *Industrial Education.* London: Kegan, Paul, Trench & Co.

Marginson, S. (1997) *Markets in Education.* St Leonards: Allen & Unwin.

Martorana, S. V. (1973) Community-junior colleges in the United States, in OECD, *Short-cycle Higher Education: A Search for Identity.* Paris: OECD.

Marx, K. (1990) [1867] *Capital,* vol. 1. London: Penguin.

Maxwell, W., Hagedorn, L. S., Brocato, P., Moon, H. S. and Perrakis, A. (2002) The community college shuffle: student patterns of multiple enrolments. Presented at annual meetings of the American Educational Research Association.

McLaurin, I. and Osborne, M. (2002) Data on transfer from FECs in Scotland to HEIs in Scotland, in M. Osborne, J. Gallacher and Murphy, M. (eds) *A Research Review of FE/HE Links – A Report to the Scottish Executive Enterprise and Lifelong Learning Department* (http://www.scotland.gov.uk/about/ELLD/HESP/00016640/annexe2p1.pdf). Accessed 23 December 2007.

Mechi, L. (2004) Vocational training from the birth of the ECSC to the early years of the EEC, in A. Varsori (ed.) *Towards a History of Vocational Education and Training (VET) in Europe in a Comparative Perspective.* Proceedings of the 1st international conference, October 2002, Florence. Volume II The development of VET in the context of the construction of the EC/EU and the role of Cedefop, Cedefop Panorama series; 101. Luxembourg: Office for Official Publications of the European Communities, pp. 12–23 (http://www.trainingvillage.gr/etv/Information_resources/Bookshop/publication_details.asp?pub_id=373). Accessed 23 December 2007.

Medsker, L. L. (1960) *The Junior College: Progress and Prospect.* New York: McGraw-Hill.

Medsker, L. L. and Tillery, D. (1971) *Breaking the Access Barriers: A Profile of Two-Year Colleges.* New York: McGraw-Hill.

Mill, J. S. (1925) [1843] *A System of Logic, Ratiocinative and Inductive.* London: Longmans, Green & Co.

Ministerial Council on Education, Employment, Training and Youth Affairs (MCEETYA) (2005) Good practice principles for credit transfer and articulation (http://www.mceetya.edu.au/mceetya/report_of_the_national_study_on_credit_transfer,11910.html). Accessed 23 December 2007.

Ministry of Education Te Tāhuhu o te Mātauranga (2001) Interim statement of tertiary education priorities (STEP) 2002–3 (http://www.minedu.govt.nz/index.cfm?layout=document&documentid=7366&indexid=1216&indexparentid=1028). Accessed 23 December 2007.

Ministry of Education Te Tāhuhu o te Mātauranga (2002) National student index (http://www.minedu.govt.nz/index.cfm?layout=document&documentid=5724&indexid=1200&indexparentid=1028#P86_6553). Accessed 23 December 2007.

Mitter, W. (1988) Problems of the interrelationship between general and vocational education in Europe: a historical and conceptual approach, in H. Rohrs (ed.) *Vocational and General Education in Western Industrial Societies.* London: Symposium Books.

Moodie, G. (2004) Reverse transfer in Australia. *International Journal of Training Research,* 2(2): 24–48.

Moodie, G. (2005) *Student Transfers.* Adelaide: National Centre for Vocational Education Research.

Murray-Smith, S. (1965) Technical education in Australia: a historical sketch, in E. L. Wheelwright (ed.) *Higher Education in Australia*. Melbourne: F. W. Cheshire.

National Board of Employment, Education and Training (NBEET) (1994) *Cross-sectoral Collaboration in Postsecondary Education and Training*. Canberra: Australian Government Publishing Service.

National Center for Public Policy and Higher Education (2000) Measuring up 2000: the state by state report card for higher education (http://measuringup2000.highereducation.org/stateprofilenet.cfm). Accessed 23 December 2007.

Newman, J. H. (1959) [1853] *The Idea of a University*. New York: Image Books.

Northwest Education Research Center (NORED) (2000) Steady progress: higher education governance in Colorado at the dawn of the 21st century (http://www.nored.us/Colorado%20Report.pdf). Accessed 23 December 2007.

Oklahoma State Regents for Higher Education (1970) *The Role and Scope of Oklahoma Higher Education*. Oklahoma City: Oklahoma State Regents for Higher Education.

Organisation for Economic Co-operation and Development (OECD) (1971) *Towards New Structures of Postsecondary Education: A Preliminary Statement of Issues*. Paris: OECD.

Osborne, M. (2002a) Introduction, in M. Osborne, J. Gallacher and M. Murphy (eds) *A Research Review of FE/HE Links – A Report to the Scottish Executive Enterprise and Lifelong Learning Department* (http://www.scotland.gov.uk/about/ELLD/HESP/00016640/annexe2p1.pdf). Accessed 23 December 2007.

Osborne, M. (2002b) Implications, in M. Osborne, J. Gallacher and M. Murphy (eds) A Research Review of FE/HE Links – A Report to the Scottish Executive Enterprise and Lifelong Learning Department (http://www.scotland.gov.uk/about/ELLD/HESP/00016640/annexe2p2.pdf). Accessed 23 December 2007.

Palmer, J. (1990) Is vocationalism to blame? *AACJC Journal*, June/July: 21–5.

Pappas Consulting Group Inc. (2006) Proposing a blueprint for higher education in Florida: outlining the way to a long-term master plan for higher education in Florida (http://www.flbog.org/ForwardByDesign/). Accessed 23 December 2007.

Parry, G. and Thompson, A. (2002) *Closer by Degrees: The Past, Present and Future of Higher Education in Further Education Colleges*. London: Learning and Skills Development Agency (http://www.lsneducation.org.uk/pubs/Pages/021164.aspx). Accessed 23 December 2007.

Parry, G., Davies, P. and Williams, J. (2003) *Dimensions of Difference: Higher Education in the Learning and Skills Sector*. London: Learning and Skills Development Agency (http://www.lsneducation.org.uk/pubs/Pages/031536.aspx). Accessed 23 December 2007.

Paulston, R. (2000) Imagining comparative education: past, present, future. *Compare*, 30(3): 353–67.

Peter, K. and Forrest Cataldi, E. (2005) *The Road Less Traveled? Students who Enroll in Multiple Institutions* (NCES 2005–157). US Department of Education, National Center for Education Statistics. Washington, DC: US Government Printing Office (http://nces.ed.gov/pubs2005/2005157.pdf). Accessed 23 December 2007.

Popper, K. (1972) *The Logic of Scientific Discovery* [first published as *Logik der Forschung* in 1934]. London: Hutchinson.

Prager, C. (1993) Transfer and articulation within colleges and universities. *Journal of Higher Education*, 64(5): 539–54.

Pratt, J. (1970) *Policy and Practice: The Colleges of Advanced Technology.* London: Allen Lane/Penguin.

Przeworski, A. and Teune, H. (1970) *The Logic of Comparative Social Inquiry.* New York: Wiley-Interscience.

Raffe, D. (2003) 'Simplicity itself': the creation of the Scottish Credit and Qualifications Framework. *Journal of Education and Work,* 16(3): 239–57.

Raffe, D. (2005) National qualifications frameworks as integrated qualifications frameworks. Towards an NQF research agenda. Proceedings of the NQF colloquium, 13–14 June. Pretoria: South African Qualifications. *SAQA Bulletin.* 8(1): 21–31 (www.saqa.org.za). Accessed 23 December 2007.

Raffe, D., Howieson, C., Spours, K. and Young, M. (1998) The unification of post-compulsory education: towards a conceptual framework. *British Journal of Educational Studies,* 46(2): 169–87.

Ragin, C. (1987) *The Comparative Method: Moving beyond Qualitative and Quantitative Strategies.* Berkeley, CA: University of California Press.

Rainbird, H. (1996) Negotiating a research agenda for comparisons of vocational training, in L. Hantrais and S. Mangen (eds) *Cross-national Research Methods in the Social Sciences.* London: Cassell.

Raivola, R. (1985) What is comparison? Methodological and philosophical considerations. *Comparative Education Review,* 29(3): 362–74.

Rifkin, T. (1998) Improving articulation policy to increase transfer, *ECS Policy Paper,* Education Commission of the States, in R. J. Coley (2000) *The American Community College Turns 100: A Look at its Students, Programs, and Prospects.* Princeton, NJ: Educational Testing Service (www.ets.org/research/pic). Accessed 26 March 2008.

Robinson, C. and Misko, J. (2001) *Extending Learning Opportunities. A Study of Co-operation Between TAFE Institutes and Schools and Universities in Queensland.* Leabrook: National Centre for Vocational Education Research.

Romano, R. M. and Wisniewski, M. (2003) Tracking community college transfers using national student clearinghouse data, paper presented at the 45 annual conference of the Council for the Study of Community Colleges, 4–5 April, Dallas, TX (http://www.studentclearinghouse.org/colleges/Tracker/pdfs/SUNY_casestudy.pdf). Accessed 23 December 2007.

Rushbrook, P. (1997) Tradition, pathways and the renegotiation of TAFE identity in Victoria. *Discourse: Studies in the Cultural Politics of Education,* 18(1): 103–12.

Russell, A. (2005) Developing transfer and articulation policies that make a difference. *American Association of State Colleges and Universities,* 2(7): 1–4 (http://www.aascu.org/policy_matters/pdf/v2n7.pdf). Accessed 23 December 2007.

Ryle, G. (1975) [1949] *The Concept of Mind.* London: Hutchinson.

Sadler, Sir Michael E. (1964) [1900] How far can we learn anything of practical value from the study of foreign systems of education?, in G. Z. F. Bereday (ed.) Notes of an address given at the Guilford educational conference, on 20 October, Guildford. *Comparative Education Review,* 7(3): 307–314.

Sanderson, M. (1999) *Education and Economic Decline in Britain, 1870 to the 1990s.* Cambridge: Cambridge University Press.

Schriewer, J. (2006) Comparative social science: characteristic problems and changing problem solutions. *Comparative Education,* 42(3): 299–336.

Schuman, R. (1950) *Declaration of 9 May 1950* (http://europa.eu/abc/symbols/9-may/decl_en.htm). Accessed 23 December 2007.

Scott, P. (2000) A tale of three revolutions? Science, society and the university, in P. Scott (ed.) *Higher Education Re-formed*. London: Falmer Press.

Scott, D. (2004) Pathways in tertiary education 1998–2002, Ministry of Education Te Tāhuhu o te Mātauranga (http://educationcounts.edcentre.govt.nz/publications/tertiary_education/pathways_in_tertiary_education_1998–2002). Accessed 23 December 2007.

Scott, D. (2005) Personal communication, 2 May 2005.

Scottish Executive (2002) A framework for higher education in Scotland, higher education review: phase 2 (http://www.scotland.gov.uk/library5/lifelong/herp2.pdf). Accessed 23 December 2007.

Scottish Higher Education Review (2002) Second consultation paper: shaping our future (http://www.scotland.gov.uk/consultations/lifelonglearning/sher2.pdf). Accessed 23 December 2007.

Shapin, S. and Barnes, B. (1976) Head and hand: rhetorical resources in British pedagogical writing, 1770–1850. *Oxford Review of Education*, 2(3): 231–53.

Shoemaker, A., Allison, J., Gum, K, *et al.* (2000) Multi-partner campuses. The future of Australian higher education? Evaluations and investigations programme 00/13, Department of Education, Training and Youth Affairs (http://www.dest.gov.au/archive/highered/ eippubs/eip00_13/00_13.pdf). Accessed 23 December 2007.

Shulock, N. (2004) The impact of recent budget reductions and enrollment pressures on access and quality, in G. C. Hayward, D. P. Jones, A. C. Jr. McGuinness and A. Timar (eds) *Ensuring Access with Quality to California's Community Colleges*, report #04–3. San José, CA: National Center for Public Policy and Higher Education (http://www.highereducation.org/reports/hewlett/Hewlett3.pdf). Accessed 23 December 2007.

Skilbeck, M., Connell, H., Lowe, N. and Tait, K. (1994) *The Vocational Quest: New Directions in Education and Training*. London: Routledge.

Skilbeck, M., Wagner, A. and Esnault, E. (1998) *Redefining Tertiary Education*. Paris: Organisation for Economic Co-operation and Development (http://www.oecdbookshop.org/oecd/display.asp?sf1=identifiers&st1=911998021P1). Accessed 23 December 2007.

Smith, A. B., Opp, R. D., Armstrong, R. L., Stewart, G. A. and Isaacson, R. J. (1999) Community college consortia: an overview. *Community College Journal of Research & Practice*, 23(4): 371–85.

Sommerlad, E., Duke, C. and McDonald, R. (1998) Universities and TAFE collaboration in the emerging world of 'universal higher education', Higher Education Council (http://www.dest.gov.au/NR/rdonlyres/6692C59F-18F6–471C-B95F-30710BA4F87E/3956/98_10.pdf). Accessed 23 December 2007.

Stevenson, J. (1992) Australian vocational education: learning from past mistakes. *Vocational Aspects of Education*, 44(2): 236–7.

Stevenson, J. (1995) The political colonisation of the cognitive construction of competence. *Vocational Aspect of Education*, 47(4): 353–64.

Stevenson, J. (1996) The metamorphosis of the construction of competence. *Studies in Continuing Education*, 18(1): 24–42.

Stevenson, J. (1997) Legitimate learning. *Australia and New Zealand Journal of Vocational Education Research*, 5(2): 1–43.

Stevenson, J. C. (1998a) Finding a basis for reconciling perspectives on vocational education and training. *Australia and New Zealand Journal of Vocational Education Research*, 6(2): 134–65.

Stevenson, J. C. (1998b) Dismantling the barricades: the interface between TAFE and higher education, in P. C. Candy (ed.) *TAFE at the Crossroads: Relationships with Government, Secondary and Higher Education.* Armidale: Department of Administrative and Higher Education Studies, University of New England.

Stevenson, J. (2003) The implications of learning theory for the idea of general knowledge. Paper presented to the Journal of Vocational Education and Training's fifth international conference, 16–18 July, University of Greenwich, London.

Strathdee, R. (2003) The qualifications framework in New Zealand: reproducing existing inequalities or disrupting the positional conflict for credentials. *Journal of Education and Work,* 16(2): 147–64.

Summerfield, P. and Evans, E. (1990) Introduction: technical education, the state and the labour market, in P. Summerfield and E. Evans (eds) *Technical Education and the State since 1850: Historical and Contemporary Perspectives.* Manchester: Manchester University Press.

Teichler, U. (1988) *Changing Patterns of the Higher Education System.* London: Jessica Kingsley.

Teichler, U. (1997) Reforms as a response to the massification of higher education: a comparative view, in A. Arimoto (ed.) *Academic Reforms in the World: Situation and Perspective in the Massification Stage of Higher Education.* Hiroshima: Hiroshima University Press.

Texas Higher Education Coordinating Board (2000) Community and Technical Colleges Division, 2000 College Profiles, Public Community and Technical Colleges of Texas (http://www.thecb.state.tx.us/reports/pdf/0328.pdf). Accessed 23 December 2007.

Texas Higher Education Coordinating Board (2001a) 2001 Statewide Annual Licensure Report (http://www.thecb.state.tx.us/reports/pdf/0431.pdf). Accessed 23 December 2007.

Texas Higher Education Coordinating Board (2001b) Report on the performance of Texas public universities (http://www.eric.ed.gov/ERICDocs/data/ericdocs2sql/content_storage_01/0000019b/80/1a/5e/92.pdf). Accessed 23 December 2007.

Texas Higher Education Coordinating Board (2002) About us (http://www.thecb.state.tx.us/about/). Accessed 12 January 2002.

Texas Higher Education Coordinating Board (2005) Texas charter for public higher education (http://www.thecb.state.tx.us/reports/PDF/0081.pdf). Accessed 23 December 2007.

Texas Legislative Council (2001) Texas statutes, Education Code, subtitle B. State coordination of higher education, ch. 61. Texas Higher Education Coordinating Board. Subchapter C. Powers and duties of board, section 61.051. Coordination of institutions of public higher education (http://tlo2.tlc.state.tx.us/statutes/ed.toc.htm). Accessed 23 December 2007.

Thompson, J. F. (1973) *Foundations of Vocational Education.* Englewood Cliffs, NJ: Prentice-Hall Inc.

Thompson, E. P. (1980) [1963] *The Making of the English Working Class.* London: Penguin.

Times Higher Education Supplement (*THES*) (1973) Wearing of the green, 2 February.

Tribe, K. (2004) Educational economies. *Economy and Society,* 33(4): 605–20.

Trow, M. (1974) Problems in the transition from elite to mass higher education, in OECD, *Policies for Higher Education*. Paris: OECD.

Tuck, R. (2007) *An Introductory Guide to National Qualifications Frameworks: Conceptual and Practical Issues for Policy Makers*. Geneva: International Labour Organization (http://www.ilo.org/public/english/employment/skills/download/nqf-frame.pdf). Accessed 23 December 2007.

Turnage, R. and Yatooma, C. (2006) *California Community Colleges 2007–08 System Budget Proposal*. Sacramento, CA: California Community Colleges (http://www.cccco.edu/Portals/4/CFFP/budget_news/2007–08SystemBudgetProposal.pdf). Accessed 23 December 2007.

United Nations Educational, Scientific and Cultural Organisation (UNESCO) (1986) *The Integration of General and Technical and Vocational Education*. Paris: UNESCO.

United Nations Educational, Scientific and Cultural Organisation (UNESCO) (1997) International Standard Classification of Education. (http://www.unesco.org/education/docs/isced_1997.htm). Accessed 23 December 2007.

US Department of Education, National Center for Education Statistics (1998) Fall enrollment in higher education, various years. Fall enrollment in colleges and universities survey; Integrated Postsecondary Education Data System (IPEDS): Fall enrollment surveys [table prepared May 1998] (http://nces.ed.gov/programs/digest/d98/d98t181.asp). Accessed 23 December 2007.

US Department of Education, National Center for Education Statistics (2000) Higher Education General Information Survey (HEGIS): Fall enrollment in colleges and universities surveys; Integrated Postsecondary Education Data System (IPEDS): Fall enrollment surveys (http://nces.ed.gov/pubs2001/digest/dt201.html). Accessed 13 January 2002.

US Department of Education (2006) *A Test of Leadership. Charting the Future of U.S. Higher Education. A Report of the Commission appointed by Secretary of Education Margaret Spellings*. Jessup, MD: US Department of Education (http://www.ed.gov/about/bdscomm/list/hiedfuture/index.html). Accessed 23 December 2007.

Venables, P. (1978) *Higher Education Developments: The Technological Universities 1956–1976*. London: Faber & Faber.

Vlaeminke, M. (1990) The subordination of technical education in secondary schooling, 1870–1914, in P. Summerfield and E. Evans (eds) *Technical Education and the State Since 1850: Historical and Contemporary Perspectives*. Manchester: Manchester University Press.

Waterhouse, R. (1998) A university for life, in P. Mitchell (ed.) *Beyond the Universities: The New Higher Education*. Aldershot: Ashgate.

Waterhouse, R. (2000) The distributed university, in P. Scott (ed.) *Higher Education Re-formed*. London: Falmer Press.

Watson, K. (1997) Potentials and pitfalls. *Light & Salt*, 9(1), cited in B. Dahl (2004: 1) Development of a democratic Europe: the use of education policy. Paper presented at the 48th annual conference of the Comparative and International Education Society, 9–12 March, Salt Lake City, Utah, USA (http://www.geocities.com/hyllebusk/DahlBettinaS-CIES48.pdf). Accessed 23 December 2007.

Wellman, J. V. (2002) State policy and community college-baccalaureate transfer, National Center Report #02–6, The National centre for Public Policy and Higher Education (http://www.highereducation.org/reports/transfer/transfer.shtml). Accessed 23 December 2007.

Wheelahan, L. (2000) *Bridging the Divide: Developing the Institutional Structures that most effectively Deliver Cross-sectoral Education and Training*. Adelaide: National Centre for Vocational Education Research (http://www.ncver.edu.au/publications/509.html). Accessed 23 December 2007.

Wheelahan, L. (2001) *The 'Best Fit' or 'Screening Out': An Evaluation of Learning Pathways at Victoria University*. Melbourne: Victoria University of Technology – a DETYA Higher Education Innovation Programme-funded project.

Wheelahan, L. and Moodie, G. (2005) Separate post-compulsory education sectors within a liberal market economy: interesting models generated by the Australian anomaly, in M. Osborne and J. Gallacher (eds) *A Contested Landscape. International Perspectives on Diversity in Mass Higher Education*. Leicester: National Institute of Adult Continuing Education.

White, T. (2001) *Investing in People: Higher Education in Ireland from 1960 to 2000*. Dublin: Institute of Public Administration. Wikipedia (2008) Money (http://en.wikipedia.org/wiki(Money). Accessed 23 May 2008.

Williams, H. S. (1961) Technical education – state or national? *The Australian Journal of Higher Education* (formerly *The Educand*), 1(1): 98–103.

Williams, H. S. (1963) Tertiary technical in Australia. *The Australian University*, 1(1): 89–119.

Williams, H. S. (1965) The technical colleges, in J. Wilkes (ed.) *Tertiary Education in Australia*. Sydney: Angus & Robertson.

Williams, B. (1970) A functional differentiation? *Vestes*, 13(2): 121–5.

Williams, B. R. (1979) *Education, Training and Employment, Report of the Committee of Inquiry into Education and Training*. Canberra: Australian Government Publishing Service.

Windham, P., Perkins, G. R. and Rogers, J. (2001) Concurrent-use campuses: part of the new definition of access. *Community College Review*, 29(3): 39–55.

Wittgenstein, L. (1968) *Philosophical Investigations*, G. E. M. Anscombe (trns). Oxford: Basil Blackwell.

Young, M. (2002) Contrasting approaches to the role of qualifications in the promotion of lifelong learning, in K. Evans, P. Hodkinson and L. Unwin (eds) *Working to Learn: Transforming Learning in the Workplace*. London: Kogan Page.

Young, M. (2003) Comparing approaches to the role of qualifications in the promotion of lifelong learning. *European Journal of Education*, 38(2): 199–211.

Young, M. (2005) National qualifications frameworks: their feasibility for effective implementation in developing countries. Skills Working Paper #22. *InFocus Programme on Skills, Knowledge and Employability*. Geneva: International Labour Office (http://www.ilo.org/public/english/employment/skills/download/wp22young.pdf). Accessed 23 December 2007.

Young, M., Howieson, C., Raffe, D. and Spours, K. (1997) Unifying academic and vocational learning and the idea of a learning society. *Journal of Education Policy*, 12(6): 527–37.

Zgaga, P. (2004) The Bologna process. Between Prague 2001 and Berlin 2003: contributions to higher education policy (http://www.see-educoop.net/education_in/pdf/report-min-educ-signatory-countr-oth-enl-t02.pdf). Accessed 23 December 2007.

Index